Innovation and Experiential Learning in Academic Libraries

INNOVATIONS IN INFORMATION LITERACY

About the Series

This series for librarians and information literacy instructors provides information on the newest ideas and findings emerging from the field of information literacy, from teaching methods to emerging technologies to promising collaborations.

Books in the series engage in dialogues surrounding matters that are both conceptual and practical to librarians and instructors who are interested in teaching information literacy with local, cross-cultural, and international appeal.

The books are aimed at librarians at all types of institutions, from academic to public libraries, and also to non-library faculty members and teachers who are interested and invested in the conversations and advancements in information literacy.

About the Series Editor

The **Innovations in Information Literacy** series was conceived by and is edited by Trudi Jacobson, MLS, MA, distinguished librarian and head of the Information Literacy Department, University at Albany Libraries.

Trudi Jacobson co-chaired the ACRL Information Literacy Competency Standards for Higher Education Task Force that created the ACRL Information Literacy Framework for Higher Education. She received the Miriam Dudley Instruction Librarian of the Year award in 2009.

Titles in the Series

Innovation and Experiential Learning in Academic Libraries

Meeting the Needs of Today's Students

Edited by Sarah Nagle and Elías Tzoc

ROWMAN & LITTLEFIELD
Lanham • Boulder • New York • London

Published by Rowman & Littlefield
An imprint of The Rowman & Littlefield Publishing Group, Inc.
4501 Forbes Boulevard, Suite 200, Lanham, Maryland 20706
www.rowman.com

86-90 Paul Street, London EC2A 4NE

British Library Cataloguing in Publication Information Available

Library of Congress Cataloging-in-Publication Data

Names: Nagle, Sarah, 1985– editor. | Tzoc, Elías, 1976– editor.
Title: Innovation and experiential learning in academic libraries : meeting the needs of today's students / edited by Sarah Nagle and Elías Tzoc.
Description: Lanham : Rowman & Littlefield, [2022] | Series: Innovations in information literacy | Includes bibliographical references and index. | Summary: "Innovation and Experiential Learning in Academic Libraries addresses the multitude of ways that academic librarians are collaborating with faculty and helping students develop these enduring skills by developing and integrating active and experiential learning approaches into teaching activities"— Provided by publisher.
Identifiers: LCCN 2021052266 (print) | LCCN 2021052267 (ebook) | ISBN 9781538151846 (paperback) | ISBN 9781538151853 (epub)
Subjects: LCSH: Academic libraries—Relations with faculty and curriculum—United States. | Information literacy—Study and teaching (Higher)—United States—Case studies. | Experiential learning—United States.
Classification: LCC Z675.U5 I5753 2022 (print) | LCC Z675.U5 (ebook) | DDC 027.7—dc23/eng/20211203
LC record available at https://lccn.loc.gov/2021052266
LC ebook record available at https://lccn.loc.gov/2021052267

♾™ The paper used in this publication meets the minimum requirements of American National Standard for Information Sciences—Permanence of Paper for Printed Library Materials, ANSI/NISO Z39.48-1992.

Contents

Series Editor's Foreword

Trudi Jacobson

Innovation, creation, experience, transformation, creativity, and partnerships: these are the focus of this remarkable collection of inspiring ideas in the form of chapters. You may crave innovative approaches to effective teaching and library services that meet the needs of students and other patrons. You may have heard or read about remarkable programs instituted elsewhere that you would like to explore for your institution. You may be a library administrator planning to advocate for innovation. You may fit in multiple categories. And, chances are, you work in a library experiencing a range of impacts wrought by COVID-19 and the pandemic. Whatever your reason for opening this book, you will find it filled with innovative ideas.

Many of the chapters provide concrete information that will help to formulate a similar initiative. The chapters might also spark ideas for a program, a class, or a service that meets the needs of your institution and your students. These sparked ideas may have little to do with that chapter's topic—the author(s) may have written something that generates an idea that takes you in a whole new direction.

I will keep this foreword short because I have several things that I would like to ask you to move on to:

First, look through the table of contents, find a handful of chapters that jump out at you, and read them. I warn you—you may have a difficult time selecting just a few to start with.

Second, invite your colleagues to read one or more of these chapters as well. Next, form a group to discuss them. What was most inspiring? What would you like to try to implement? What lessons will you need to keep in mind? But do not stop at discussion: start drafting a plan to move the ideas you think to be the most promising from concept to fruition. And perhaps you might involve students and other stakeholders in your planning. This step will take time and effort, but it will be an exciting endeavor.

The following two steps come later. Once you have built your own library's innovative [fill in the blank], please write to the chapter author(s) to let them know what their chapter brought about. Then, start thinking about sharing what you have done with others to keep the process going!

Trudi E. Jacobson
Series Editor
Innovations in Information Literacy
September 10, 2021

Introduction

Jerome Conley

Nearly two decades ago, I wrote an article with some library colleagues that examined the framework of the Kano Model when compared against library services. The model was developed by Dr. Noriaki Kano in 1984 during his time as a professor of quality management at the Tokyo University of Science. Our article discussed the various categories (Basic, Excitement, and Performance) of the model as applied to the customer expectation, experience, and satisfaction. An organization had to meet the basic level of a customer's expectation or the customer would be dissatisfied and seek out other opportunities elsewhere. Ultimately, the entity needed to develop the "Excites" that would provide the customer with a heightened and possibly an unexpected experience. Although the "Excite" phase provides the customer with a new experience, this experience becomes ubiquitous over time and becomes a basic expectation of the customer. Therefore, entities must continue to evolve and offer new "Excites."

In many ways the experiential learning experience is a prime example of what Dr. Kano envisioned nearly four decades ago. I remember a colleague discussing the need for us to secure a 3D, full-color printer nearly a decade ago. I had no idea what he was talking about, but he articulated with passion for us to partner with our mechanical engineering and nursing college on a state-led grant in order to provide this service to our community. I couldn't say no. We got the grant, and our offerings in this space have grown immensely over the years. Things definitely have evolved since that first 3D printer. This book highlights some of the great ways in which innovative academic library services have evolved over the years, and it offers glimpses of what the future may hold for libraries, maker/creative industries, and for our users. Libraries must continue to push the envelope on ways to deliver this exciting technology or the user will become dissatisfied, and you know what happens when the basic expectation isn't met: they take their business elsewhere. As I examined the topics in this book, I am sure that Sarah, Elias, and all the authors have positioned us well so that won't happen. The maker and creative world is constantly evolving, challenging, and expensive, but it is so rewarding and vital for the future workforce. It is serving as a "halo" effect by bringing individuals into our spaces who normally wouldn't step foot into our libraries. It is an equalizer for individuals to discover and create, whether in a public, community, or academic library. This ethos is what makes librarianship so incredibly special—providing the resources "to empower discovery, creation, and success." This book contains twelve chapters, which are organized into three Sections: "Innovation and Leadership," "Examples and Case Studies," and "Future Literacy Developments." As you read the content, I also invite you to check this book's companion website, which continues the conversation around innovation and experiential learning in academic libraries.

Jerome Conley
Dean and University Librarian
Miami University Libraries
September 15, 2021

Section 1

INNOVATION AND LEADERSHIP

1

Planning, Advocating, and Fostering Creativity and Innovation

Elías Tzoc

In times of unprecedented change and transformation, library leaders must continue to plan, advocate, and foster creativity and innovation efforts at their libraries, especially those efforts and initiatives that support effective, emerging, and multidisciplinary learning and teaching environments. Creativity and innovation have always been integral elements of personal and institutional success. For academic libraries, it is imperative to constantly assess how their services align with their institutional goals and priorities—especially during times of quick changes and uncertainty. I think it is fair to say that every crisis or challenge can also be an opportunity to rethink how we do things. COVID-19 is definitely a good example of a crisis that forced us to change how we work, how we live, how we interact, and even how we have fun. In March 2020, in a matter of days, millions of students had to leave their campus homes and needed to engage with alternative forms of learning away from classrooms, labs, and libraries. During those days in early March 2020, many of us found ourselves in meetings where the common denominator was uncertainty and a growing tension and need for quick solutions to new problems, which is exactly what creativity is supposed to do; creativity is often defined as the ability to perceive the world in new ways and to generate new and innovative solutions. Examples of innovative library services that we, and many other libraries, implemented in 2020 include: access to virtual labs, custom modules embedded in learning management systems, online software checkout, curbside pickup, home and office delivery, virtual webinars and conferences, and so on.

In this chapter, we will have four main sections. First, I will start with a brief overview of the transformation of learning—from reflective to active—and its impact in the evolution of library services. Second, I will discuss the role of leadership in advocating and implementing innovative services in order to further support emerging learning needs in higher education. Third, I will share my leadership journey, from professional development opportunities to the ongoing work of identifying and building networks of allies on campus and in the profession. Fourth, I will talk about specific examples of creative and innovative services that we have implemented at Miami University in the recent past. Finally, I will conclude this chapter with some final reflections on the future roles of academic libraries in a post-COVID learning environment. Welcome aboard, and we look forward to continuing this conversation with you through the companion website that we have built for this book!

EVOLUTION OF LEARNING AND SERVICES

Academic libraries have always played an important role in providing diverse, safe, and equitable access to content (books, databases, digitized collections) as well as access to physical spaces (study rooms, computer labs, printing stations, instruction rooms). However, as we think about the demands for the future workforce and the way teaching and learning have changed in the last twenty to thirty years, mainly because of the internet, it is clear that new technologies can effectively support teaching and learning that require hands-on experience. The literature confirms that students learn more when they actively participate in the process of learning.[1] We also know that the future workforce will require a more active and ongoing approach to training in which employees learn through practical experience. Many believe that this is where colleges and universities can play an important role in preparing students to have the proper training and competencies when they join the workforce. In many ways, the new technologies along with the new ways/levels of learning are also changing or expanding the definitions and teaching practices of literacy.

As the learning activities change from reflective (memorizing and thinking concepts) to more active forms (processing and creating new forms of scholarship), academic libraries are creating spaces such as learning commons and makerspaces, which provide safe spaces that encourage creative and innovative thinking. In *Innovations in Learning and Teaching in Academic Libraries*, Llewellyn reviewed ninety-five articles to identify themes in relation to innovations in learning and teaching in academic libraries in Europe, the United States, and Australia. She concluded that "the changing context of higher education as well as far-reaching societal changes provide opportunities not only for innovations in the learning, teaching and research functions of the library, but also create a potent context for the reconceptualization of the academic library."[2] As universities continue to work on more welcoming and inclusive initiatives at their campuses, academic libraries will continue to play an important role as the central and neutral locations where students, regardless of their majors or discipline of study, can access services and spaces that will facilitate and empower different learning styles.

We all have different learning styles and, in most cases, we use a mix of visual, auditory, and kinesthetic learning, depending on the activity we are engaged in. For hands-on learning, the learner actively participates and interacts with the learning process, as opposed to passively listening or taking in the information from the instructor. Part of the challenge in academic libraries has to do with the need to reconfigure or create new spaces that can facilitate different types of learning. In 2017, Bieraugel and Neill conducted a literature review on learning spaces in academic libraries. They collected comprehensive data at eight selected locations at a large, predominantly undergraduate university, on the West Coast. Then, they analyzed data and compared how different spaces support two approaches to creativity and innovation: exploiting and exploring. One of their conclusions was, "it is important that academic libraries use their spaces to foster the highest level of Bloom's taxonomy, that of creativity and innovation."[3]

In response to the new opportunities and challenges in how we access, create, and share information; in the last twenty years, academic libraries have worked and developed competency standards that can help teach information literacy. The six core concepts in the "ACRL Framework for Information Literacy for Higher Education" have elements that support active and hands-on learning; in particular, information creation as a process, research as inquiry, and scholarship as conversation.[4] The new opportunities to create and share information online also require a new set of skills, which can be organized and taught as new literacies. In *Reframing Information Literacy as a Metaliteracy*, Mackey and Jacobsen review several literacy frameworks that have emerged in response to the new ways of teaching information creation in the digital age. They recognize both the need for blended learning models as well as the strong relationships between core information literacy competencies and other emergent literacies. In their conclusion, they state: "while information literacy prepares individuals to access, evaluate, and analyze information, metaliteracy prepares individuals to actively produce and share content through social media and online communities."[5]

While frameworks and models can guide us in developing clear and specific learning outcomes, the other reality is that the exponential amount of information we all access these days comes in different formats such as web pages, PDFs, data sets, image galleries, interactive maps and timelines, 3D models, and so on. Thus, it is clear that in order to fully and ethically participate in the creation of new information/knowledge, it is imperative to constantly adapt and provide the resources that students need to create works in new formats. Many students continue to create and submit assignments in text format (thesis, capstone reports, etc.), but we are also seeing a new trend where students are creating content in other forms such as audio, video, 3D models, maps, and timelines—all of which provide a whole new level of interactivity and understanding of their work. And for many, those new forms of deliverables can also be key elements of student digital portfolios or living transcripts, which can help explain/showcase their work experience when they apply for graduate school or internships. To this end, we understand that the role of spaces that can facilitate and cultivate experiential learning must also encourage learning or behavior activities such as: observing, questioning, experimenting, brainstorming, reflecting, and networking. Thus, the question becomes: How can academic libraries further support learning activities that empower creation, curiosity, and innovation? In the next section, we will talk about the role of library leaders in planning and advocating for creative and innovative library services.

LEADERSHIP AND INNOVATION

Successful and effective leaders and innovators are often associated with actions that demonstrate a proactive and entrepreneurial mindset. Those individuals are also champions of starting or implementing new initiatives that drive growth, reduce cost, differentiate experience, and increase efficiency. For leaders and innovators, a key question is: How does one remain proactive and entrepreneurial during difficult times and with limited resources? With the changing landscape of higher education, along with the effects of the recent pandemic, leaders and innovators now, more than ever, must continue to find effective strategies to motivate their teams and meet the new/demanding needs of learning in a post-pandemic environment. The book *The 7 Habits of Highly Effective People* starts with a definition of proactivity and a reminder that being "proactive is about taking responsibility for one's life."[6] In times of crisis and uncertainty, leaders are often faced with two choices: "freeze to the point of inaction . . . or transform fear into engagement."[7] Many will agree that the latter choice is what makes individuals and organizations not only survive but thrive during difficult times.

The challenging trends for higher education are also inspiring institutional investments in innovation strategies. Given the number of change pressures, such as financial, demographic, technological, political, and so forth, many institutions have started innovative plans that leverage change in order to move higher education in new and promising directions. In 2018, the Learning House, Inc. and the Online Learning Consortium (OLC) published a report: *The State of Innovation in Higher Education.*[8] The report includes topics such as: the results of a survey and interviews with academic administrators, the drivers and barriers of innovation at institutions across the country, the development and support for a culture of innovation, as well as how colleges and universities can prioritize innovation for student success. In another 2018 publication, *The Rise of the Chief Innovation Officer in Higher Education*, Selingo highlights the importance of managing change on campuses. He talks about the need for institutions to consider creating a high-level leadership position that oversees innovation, "someone who can coordinate disparate projects from across campus and build a systems approach to change management."[9] Some of the key responsibilities suggested for such positions include: generate and build momentum for ideas and develop an innovative mindset within the campus community, develop processes for innovation, connect with partners and funders outside of the institution, administer seed funding and release time for promising projects, to name a few. In response to this trend, in fall 2020, Miami University hired its first vice president for research and innovation.

Based on the number of publications on leadership and innovation in academic libraries, we are seeing an increase in interest and research on these topics in the last decade. Some indicate that, in the twenty-first century, innovation is no longer an option but a necessity; in this regard, the next question is: What type of resources do academic libraries need to provide so that innovation can flourish even in times of uncertainty and constant change? Perhaps one of the most comprehensive studies available on the topic of innovation in academic libraries is the work by Ronald Jantz. He has researched and published extensively on topics such as technological and cultural innovation, managing creativity, and leadership. In his 2012 article "Innovation in Academic Libraries: An Analysis of University Librarians' Perspectives," he conducts a comprehensive literature review of innovation in academic libraries; then, he interviews six university librarians from ARL libraries. One of his conclusions is: "more flattened structures and transformational styles that empower organization members will undoubtedly create a more innovative environment in the library and increase the flow of new ideas."[10] In a similar 2016 publication, "The Future of Academic Libraries: Conversations with Today's Leaders about Tomorrow," John Meier interviews forty-four university librarians and deans from institution members of the Association of American Universities (AAU).[11] Meier's key findings include the value of collaborative decision making, strategic planning processes, support for digital projects, and innovative ways for instruction and research assistance; moreover, he identifies that professional development programs for the next generation of library leaders is also essential for the profession. In "Innovations in Learning and Teaching in Academic Libraries," Llewellyn featured seventeen case studies from a variety of higher ed and international institutions; the studies exemplify a clear commitment to excellence through innovation in teaching and learning.[12]

A more efficient and innovative structure was a key element of an organizational change that we started at Miami University Libraries. In 2018, we created six forward-looking departments that emerged from a 2017 libraries master planning process that examined services, organization, and facilities. This collective and strategic work has allowed us to envision the future "from encompassing the technologies students need to master to offering the spaces where they will toil into the night, this vision for a reinvigorated King Library captures the vibrancy of Miami's academic culture and the dedication of its student body."[13] In the fifth section of this chapter, I will describe specific examples that my department has implemented and supported in the last few years, including creating a program for open educational resources, supporting digital scholarship/humanities projects, establishing a makerspace and a virtual reality lab with eye-tracking technology.

THE LEADERSHIP JOURNEY

The journey to leadership is definitely a mix of personal and collective experiences, and while some start their journey better prepared than others, there is no question that as organizations change, leaders also go through their own transformation. The field of academic librarianship has a number of programs and opportunities for leadership development. A list of more than twenty leadership development training opportunities, specifically for library professionals at all levels and specialties, is available on the "Library Leadership Training Resources page," which is maintained by the ALA Training, Orientation, and Leadership Development Committee.[14] For those of us working in academic libraries, the UCLA Library Senior Fellows Program is one of the longest and highly prestigious programs that has identified and developed a number of academic library leaders.[15] The Association of Research Libraries (ARL) offers two programs: the ARL Leadership Fellows Program and the ARL Leadership and Career Development Program.[16] The Association of College and Research Libraries (ACRL), in collaboration with Harvard's Graduate School of Education (GSE), offers the Leadership Institute for Academic Librarians.[17] *Additionally*, Harvard's GSE also offers the program Contemporary Challenges in Library Leadership: Building Community, Leading Change, formerly titled Library Leadership in a Digital Age.[18]

For me, the journey started in 2010 when I attended the Minnesota Institute for Early Career Librarians from Traditionally Underrepresented Groups.[19] The institute is a week-long program and is held at the University of Minnesota every two years. The institute was instrumental in my professional journey; in 2010, I was in my second year of the tenure clock at Miami University. Coming from Guatemala where the system of tenure is not well known, I felt both overwhelmed and a bit lost with the work that I needed to do in order to create a strong and successful dossier at the end of the fifth year. One of the activities we did during our days in Minnesota was to create a personal/professional plan with some specific goals, which later became the foundation for a personal plan for the next seven years. Between 2010 and 2017, I worked with other librarians and several faculty members on projects, including two that were funded by federal agencies: the Institute of Museum and Library Services and the National Endowment for the Humanities. I also worked on a number of publications that allowed me/us to share our work and successes with the library community. Perhaps the most important leadership lesson from the institute was about understanding the need and value of a strong network of allies on campus and in the profession, because, ultimately, teamwork is essential for organizational success.

In 2018, as I was promoted to principal librarian, I also became the head of the Create and Innovate Department. I quickly realized that my day-to-day activities had changed significantly and that I need to adapt to my new responsibilities. My time of writing and testing code was gone; instead, I was writing job descriptions. I also found myself in meetings where the main topics were strategic planning and budget. Later that year, I decided to apply for the Harvard Institute on Library Leadership in a Digital Age, and, in March 2019, I found myself in Cambridge for an inspiring three-day program. One of the initial reminders at the start of the program was that successful leaders see the opportunities in every difficulty rather than the difficulties in every opportunity. For one of the group activities, we were asked to discuss an innovative project that might have challenges with implementation; I talked about the makerspace project that my team was working on. The discussion with the fellow participants, their questions and feedback proved to be helpful as we finalized the plans for the makerspace in the fall of 2019. Some of the key takeaways from the institute were: balance between a culture of perfection and a culture of experimentation; aligning and adding value to institutional goals and priorities; tech projects must be implemented faster; value of qualitative data when communicating success; and cultivating a culture of innovation is an ongoing agenda.

In the spring of 2019, I also applied to the Institute for Miami Leadership Development (IMLD), which is sponsored by the Office of the Provost.[20] The goal of the institute is to improve leadership potential among both Miami faculty and staff. The IMLD is an eighteen-month program; it starts with a one-day retreat, followed by monthly meetings with university leaders, and it ends with an applied experience project. The conversations throughout the duration of the institute—with fellow participants, steering committee members, and guest speakers—allowed me to broaden my perspective of higher education as an enterprise and enhanced my ability to think beyond my immediate circle in the University Libraries. The applied experience project is a personal/professional project where participants choose a topic that is important for their units or divisions. In my case, and in consultation with my assistant dean and dean, we decided to find answers to the question: How can/should the library further support innovation and experiential learning on campus? I conducted informational interviews with two groups of participants: eight national library leaders and ten Miami faculty members. Interestingly enough, there were similarities in their answers; for instance, establishing a diverse/inclusive group of faculty to re-envision library collaboration, revisiting the infrastructure to support campus research activities, creating custom library portals for just-on-time content, rethinking spaces for experiential learning activities, and considering fellowship or residency programs for faculty and students. The IMLD has been instrumental in my leadership journey—it allowed me to further develop and improve my leadership capacity and it has opened the doors to more conversations with other university leaders on campus as well as across the nation.

More recently, and as part of the lessons learned during the interviews with other library leaders, I decided to apply for the EDUCAUSE Mentoring Program.[21] This unique mentoring system is quite robust, it starts with the mentee in creating a profile and providing answers to questions about past experiences, current responsibilities, and skills/competencies for further development; once the profile is completed, the system matches the mentee with a list of potential mentors. After I created a full profile, I saw a list of potential mentors with a percentage indicating how well they match with the skills and competencies I selected for further development; it is quite impressive! Needless to say, that same day, I contacted the person who I thought would be the *right* mentor. And, two days later, I received a confirmation indicating that we both were paired to work for this mentoring program. Thus, in the next few months, I will be working and learning along with my new mentor. One of the key features of the EDUCAUSE program is that it has all the mentoring activities built into the system—from setting up the first get-to-know meeting to the assessment and implementation of mentoring activities. I am definitely excited about this new opportunity to learn from a national leader, which will help me further understand how to best navigate and advocate for the right emerging technology decisions in higher education.

I will end this section with a quote that I often read, especially in those tough moments we experience on certain days: "The challenge of leadership is to be strong, but not rude; be kind, but not weak; be bold, but not bully; be thoughtful, but not lazy; be humble, but not timid; be proud, but not arrogant."[22]

EXAMPLES OF INNOVATIVE SERVICES

As mentioned in section three of this chapter, in 2018, we created six new and forward-looking departments as part of a library master planning process that we started to examine and re-envision services, organization and facilities. The team of the Create and Innovate (C+I) Department is a group of creative librarians and technologists. Our C+I vision statement is: "Become an entrepreneurial library department supporting innovative services and spaces that will help teach creativity and support experiential learning and research across disciplines."[23] Our C+I services include: full-service 3D printing and scanning, open educational resources, maker scholarship, digital scholarship/humanities, and copyright. In this section, I will describe services that support innovation and creativity as well as experiential learning.

DIGITAL SCHOLARSHIP AND DIGITAL HUMANITIES

Digital scholarship or digital humanities are often interdisciplinary and collaborative projects that make extensive use of one or more of the new possibilities for teaching, learning, and research opened up by the unique affordances of digital tools and methods. Since 2013, we have supported a number of digital scholarship/humanities projects with faculty and students. We provide support for course-based project development, including the planning and integration of scaffolded assignments, rubrics, and instruction. We can help identify resources such as appropriate platforms, an existing corpus of texts, images, data sets, and other materials that meet faculty research or pedagogical needs. We also assist with the identification, development, and application of tools for a variety of tasks such as data visualization, mapping, text mining, and transcription. A key partner for our work in this area is the Humanities Center, two important and ongoing collaborations are: digital research fellowships, each year, up to two faculty are awarded financial support for a one-year project, we provide the technical support that often translates into a website using platforms such as Omeka or WordPress; and Geoffrion Public Projects, up to six students are selected annually and we work closely with them to produce and publish a collaborative public humanities project.

MAKERSPACE

Maker-centered learning is increasingly being adopted in higher education as an engaging, multidisciplinary, and experiential way of learning. One of the great benefits of makerspaces, especially in the neutral space of the campus library, is the opportunity for transdisciplinary collaboration. Students of all majors and backgrounds can ignite the spark of learning through making and learning activities in ways that they may not get to in their normal courses. The makerspace is designed to give students the skills and experience in design, prototyping, and fabrication, the lab provides access to hardware and software that students can use to turn a concept into a reality. The equipment and machinery in the makerspace include high-end and teaching 3D printers, CNC desktop machines, a laser cutter, digital cutting machines, embroidery and sewing machines, and sublimation printers. In the same space, we also have a soundproofed multimedia lab that can be used for video and video production. We launched the makerspace in the fall of 2019; during that first semester, we made significant connections with a number of faculty from different disciplines, and we also hosted a number of maker/fun events with students.

DATA VISUALIZATION AND VIRTUAL REALITY LAB

Visualizations in 2D or 3D formats are important methods for understanding and visualizing microscopic objects or complex ecosystems. The visualization and virtual reality lab allows students to visualize their work or related content in an immersive and interactive experience. Our goal is to provide an entry-level access to visualization and XR technologies. We do this by working with faculty and students and identifying applications that can enhance engagement and add value and interactivity to their teaching and learning activities. Some of the most popular VR applications we have used with faculty and students include: Nanome, Wander, Google Earth, Traveling While Black, CalcFlow, 3D Organon, Tiltbrush, Gravity Sketch, and BeatSaber. It is also encouraging to know that there is a growing number of content providers for XR applications for higher education. The lab features equipment and resources that include a ninety-inch touch display for data visualization, two additional eighty-inch displays, two HTC Vive headsets with eye-tracking technology, iMotions software for VR analytics, six Oculus Quest headsets, and access to a number of applications that we have identified for different disciplines. A key partnership we had in 2019 was hosting collaborative learning and discussion sessions with the Student VR Club on campus.

MODULES FOR EXPERIENTIAL LEARNING

In mid-March 2020, as the COVID-19 pandemic spread across the United States, most universities decided to switch to online/virtual learning. The move was necessary, but it came with a number of challenges for active and experiential learning activities such as specialized computer and science labs, makerspaces, and special collections. For making activities, we hosted virtual sessions and modified assignment deliverables; instead of printing a 3D model, students only uploaded a 3D design of their project. During the summer of 2020, as we continued to anticipate and plan for new ways of supporting classes in the fall semester, we decided to expand and package our content into Canvas modules. One of the best benefits in publishing modules in Canvas Commons is that faculty can integrate those modules (with any type of Canvas resources such as readings, videos, quizzes, assignments, etc.) into their Canvas courses in a matter of minutes. In support of online/virtual classes, the C+I team created Canvas modules for topics such as: maker learning, 3D printing, 360-degree videos, podcasting, virtual reality, digital scholarship, and more. Since the content in Canvas Commons is primarily for faculty, we are also repackaging most of the content from Canvas Modules into LibGuide pages, which will allow students to find the same content, even if they are not enrolled in those classes, using the new modules. For spring 2021, a few faculty members have asked us to customize modules for their specific classes, which is also a great way to embed library resources into the new hyflex learning experience.

AFFORDABLE LEARNING AND
OPEN EDUCATIONAL RESOURCES

Affordable learning (AL) initiatives involve reducing or eliminating the cost of instructional materials for students by using libraries, learning management systems, and existing open educational resources (OER). In 2014, two librarians led a Faculty Learning Community that researched best practices and strategies to implement an OER program at Miami University. The OER initiative was officially launched by the University Libraries and the Office of the Provost in 2016, and it currently offers two programs. OER Explore is a two-hour workshop where faculty learn about OER and then find and review an existing OER for their discipline. OER Adopt is an option for faculty to select and adopt an existing OER that will replace a commercial textbook for one of their courses. As the conversations around affordability became a major topic in higher education, we also added other affordable learning options that help reduce or eliminate the cost of instructional materials. AL programs include: Course Pack Consultation Service, which helps eliminate the course pack costs by taking advantage of best practices and exceptions found in US copyright law; Alternative Textbook is an option for faculty who cannot find an OER for their courses, they work with library staff to develop a reading list comprised of resources pulled from Miami University Libraries' purchased electronic collections, legal online resources, and reading selections made in compliance with US copyright law. Since 2017, and thanks to the dedication and commitment of a strong group of colleagues in the library and on campus, the OER/AL initiatives have meant more than $1 million in student savings.

CONCLUSION

In 2020, leaders were forced into decision-making situations that leadership programs had not prepared them for. Discussions were filled with more questions than answers and with so many uncertainties facing leaders—concerns over services, staffing, health and wellness, and growing budgetary issues. As we prepare for a post-pandemic reality, it will remain important to balance our actions and priorities for both immediate and long-term strategic planning. I think a key question for library leaders will be: What type of library services will be more effective, impactful, and equitable for physical and virtual environments? Those services will have to meet the needs and expectations of twenty-first-century students. In the age of data-driven decisions, immersive technologies, and machine learning, academic libraries will have to continue to adapt and respond to emerging services. Regardless of all the challenges ahead of us, most academic libraries continue to be well-positioned to help, due to their central role on campus, longer operating hours, important roles in providing safe and collaborative spaces, 24/7 access to digital scholarly content, and ongoing initiatives with other campus units. Library leaders will have to become more proactive and innovative about advocating for library services that align and contribute to institutional goals and priorities.

Finally, because library leaders will also need to work on strategic and transformational changes that will allow their libraries to implement and support learning environments that meet the expectations of twenty-first-century students, I think it is important to conclude this chapter by taking a look at two recent publications and how their findings relate to leadership and innovation. The *2021 Environmental Scan*, provided by the ACRL Research Planning and Review Committee, includes topics such as: diversity, equity, and inclusion; expanding literacies, open science and research data services, evolving library systems, and immersive (XR/VR/AR) technologies.[24] Also, the "Key Technologies and Practices" section of the *2021 EDUCAUSE Horizon Report* includes technologies such as: artificial intelligence, learning analytics, microcredentialing, and open educational resources.[25] We all know that there are already a number of initiatives that address many of the trends mentioned above; for example, a number of library initiatives are related to open educational resources, data services, makerspaces, microcredentials, virtual reality, and so forth. As for library services related to learning analytics, artificial intelligence and machine learning are areas where more academic libraries still need to research and figure out how to best use them to further customize the library experience.

Potential new emerging and data-driven services could include the following: collaboration with admission offices to create custom library orientation sessions for first-year students; working with IT, eLearning and faculty to better understand students' progress throughout the semester and providing just-on-time assistance with scholarly resources; working with career offices and offer custom badging programs based on students' professional milestones, such as summer internships, graduate school applications, or first employments. We look forward to transforming fear into engagement and use this challenging time to become more efficient and resourceful!

NOTES

1. Judith Grunert O'Brien, Barbara J. Millis, and Margaret W. Cohen, *The Course Syllabus: A Learning-Centered Approach*, vol. 135 (Hoboken, NJ: John Wiley & Sons, 2009).

2. Anne Llewellyn, "Innovations in Learning and Teaching in Academic Libraries: A Literature Review," *New Review of Academic Librarianship* 25, nos. 2–4 (2019): 143–44.

3. Mark Bieraugel and Stern Neill, "Ascending Bloom's Pyramid: Fostering Student Creativity and Innovation in Academic Library Spaces," *College & Research Libraries* 78, no. 1 (2017): 35.

4. Association of College and Research Libraries (ACRL), "Framework for Information Literacy for Higher Education," 2016, http://www.ala.org/acrl/standards/ilframework.

5. Thomas P. Mackey and Trudi E. Jacobson, "Reframing Information Literacy as a Metaliteracy," *College & Research Libraries* 72, no. 1 (2011): 62–76.

6. Stephen R. Covey, *The 7 Habits of Highly Effective People* (New York, NY: Simon & Schuster, 1997): 78.

7. "Achieving Results in Unpredictable Times," FranklinCovey, accessed June 26, 2021, https://www.franklincovey.com/usaidlearning/.

8. "The State of Innovation in Higher Education: A Survey of Academic Administrators," Online Learning Consortium, accessed June 26, 2021, https://onlinelearningconsortium.org/read/state-of-innovation-in-higher-education/.

9. Jeffrey J. Selingo, "The Rise of the Chief Innovation Officer in Higher Education," Entangled Solutions, February 7, 2018, accessed June 26, 2021, https://www.entangled.solutions/portfolio/the-rise-of-the-chief-innovation-officer-in-higher-education/.

10. Ronald C. Jantz, "Innovation in Academic Libraries: An Analysis of University Librarians' Perspectives," *Library & Information Science Research* 34, no. 1 (2012): 3–21.

11. John J. Meier, "The Future of Academic Libraries: Conversations With Today's Leaders About Tomorrow," *portal: Libraries and the Academy* 16, no. 2 (2016): 263–88.

12. Llewellyn, "Innovations in Learning and Teaching in Academic Libraries."

13. "Miami University Libraries Strategic Planning," Miami University Libraries, accessed June 26, 2021, https://www.lib.miamioh.edu/strategic/.

14. "Library Leadership Training Resources," American Library Association, accessed June 26, 2021, https://www.ala.org/aboutala/offices/hrdr/abouthrdr/hrdrliaisoncomm/otld/leadershiptraining.

15. "UCLA Library Senior Fellows," The UCLA Library, accessed June 26, 2021, https://seniorfellows.library.ucla.edu/.

16. "ARL Leadership Fellows Program," Association of Research Libraries, accessed June 26, 2021, https://www.arl.org/category/arl-academy/arl-leadership-fellows-program/.

17. "Leadership Institute for Academic Librarians," Harvard Graduate School of Education, accessed June 26, 2021, https://www.gse.harvard.edu/ppe/program/leadership-institute-academic-librarians.

18. "Contemporary Challenges in Library Leadership: Building Community, Leading Change," Harvard Graduate School of Education, accessed June 26, 2021, https://www.gse.harvard.edu/ppe/program/contemporary-challenges-in-library-leadership.

19. "The Minnesota Institute for Early Career Librarians from Traditionally Underrepresented Groups," University of Minnesota Libraries, accessed June 26, 2021, https://www.lib.umn.edu/about/institute.

20. "Institute for Miami Leadership Development," Miami University Office of the Provost, accessed June 26, 2021, https://www.miamioh.edu/academic-affairs/admin-affairs/imld/.

21. "EDUCAUSE Mentoring Program" EDUCAUSE, accessed June 26, 2021, https://mentoring.educause.edu.

22. Jim Rohn, "Motivational Quote by Jim Rohn about Leadership," 99MotivationalQuotes, accessed June 26, 2021, https://99motivationalquotes.com/the-challenge-of-leadership-is-to.

23. "Create and Innovate Department," Miami University Libraries, accessed June 26, 2021, https://create.lib.miamioh.edu.

24. *2021 ACRL Environmental Scan*, Association of College and Research Libraries, accessed June 26, 2021, https://acrl.ala.org/acrlinsider/2021-acrl-environmental-scan/.

25. *2021 EDUCAUSE Horizon Report® Teaching and Learning Edition*, EDUCAUSE, accessed June 26, 2021, https://library.educause.edu/-/media/files/library/2021/4/2021hrteachinglearning.pdf.

BIBLIOGRAPHY

American Library Association. "Library Leadership Training Resources Page." Accessed June 26, 2021. https://www.ala.org/aboutala/offices/hrdr/abouthrdr/hrdrliaisoncomm/otld/leadershiptraining.

Association of College and Research Libraries. *2021 Environmental Scan*. May 13, 2021. Accessed June 26, 2021. https://acrl.ala.org/acrlinsider/2021-acrl-environmental-scan/.

———. "ACRL Framework for Information Literacy for Higher Education." January 11, 2016. http://www.ala.org/acrl/standards/ilframework 2016.

Association of Research Libraries. "ARL Leadership Fellows Programs." Accessed June 26, 2021. https://www.arl.org/category/arl-academy/arl-leadership-fellows-program/.

Bieraugel, Mark, and Stern Neill. "Ascending Bloom's Pyramid: Fostering Student Creativity and Innovation in Academic Library Spaces." *College & Research Libraries* 78, no. 1 (2017): 35.

Covey, Stephen R. *The 7 Habits of Highly Effective People*. New York, NY: Simon & Schuster, 1997.

EDUCAUSE. *2021 EDUCAUSE Horizon Report*. April 27, 2021. https://library.educause.edu/-/media/files/library/2021/4/2021hrteachinglearning.pdf.

FranklinCovey. "Achieving Results in Unpredictable Times." Accessed June 26, 2021. https://www.franklincovey.com/usaidlearning.

Harvard Graduate School of Education. "Contemporary Challenges in Library Leadership: Building Community, Leading Change." Accessed June 26, 2021. https://www.gse.harvard .edu/ppe/program/leadership-institute-academic-librarians

———. "Leadership Institute for Academic Librarians." Accessed June 26, 2021. https:// www.gse.harvard.edu/ppe/program/leadership-institute-academic-librarians.

Jantz, Ronald C. "Innovation in Academic Libraries: An Analysis Of University Librarians' Perspectives." *Library and Information Science Research* 34, no. 1 (2012): 3–12.

Llewellyn, Anne. "Innovations in Learning and Teaching in Academic Libraries: A Literature Review." *New Review of Academic Librarianship* 25, nos. 2–4 (2019): 129–49.

Mackey, Thomas P., and Trudi E. Jacobson. "Reframing Information Literacy as a Metaliteracy." *College & Research Libraries* 72, no. 1 (2011): 62–78.

Meier, John J. "The Future of Academic Libraries: Conversations with Today's Leaders About Tomorrow." *portal: Libraries and the Academy* 16, no. 2 (2016): 263–288.

Miami University Libraries. "Create and Innovate Department." Accessed June 26, 2021. https://create.lib.miamioh.edu.

———. "Miami University Libraries Strategic Planning." Accessed June 26, 2021.https:// www.lib.miamioh.edu/strategic/.

Miami University Office of the Provost. "Institute for Miami Leadership Development." Accessed June 26, 2021. https://www.miamioh.edu/academic-affairs/admin-affairs/imld/.

O'Brien, Judith Grunert, Barbara J. Millis, and Margaret W. Cohen. *The Course Syllabus: A Learning-Centered Approach*. Volume 135. Hoboken, NJ: John Wiley & Sons, 2009.

Online Learning Consortium. "The State of Innovation in Higher Education." Accessed June 26, 2021. https://onlinelearningconsortium.org/read/state-of-innovation-in-higher -education/.

Rohn, Jim. "Motivational Quote by Jim Rohn about Leadership." 99MotivationalQuotes. Accessed June 26, 2021. https://99motivationalquotes.com/the-challenge-of-leadership-is-to.

Selingo, Jeffrey J. "The Rise of the Chief Innovation Officer in Higher Education." Entangled Solutions, February 7, 2018, accessed June 26, 2021. https://www.entangled.solutions /portfolio/the-rise-of-the-chief-innovation-officer-in-higher-education/.

UCLA Libraries. "UCLA Library Senior Fellows." Accessed June 26, 2021. https://seniorfel lows.library.ucla.edu.

University of Minnesota Libraries. "Minnesota Institute for Early Career Librarians from Traditionally Underrepresented Groups." Accessed June 26, 2021. https://www.lib.umn .edu/about/institute.

2

Leadership for Innovation

Strategies and Considerations

Bohyun Kim

This chapter will discuss how library workers in various roles and positions can advance and sustain innovation with their leadership skills. What is leadership and what counts as innovation? Although these terms are widely used, their meanings are not always clear. Leadership is not a concept easily defined or agreed upon among scholars. We also seem to use this term to mean many things, some of which appear to even contradict each other. For example, we often refer to those in a position of formal authority—such as a manager or a director—as leaders. But leadership is not something conferred by a job title. Rather, it is a set of skills and qualities that *should* be successfully exercised by those in a position of formal authority. When we call certain people "leaders," we mean that they possess a set of qualities and abilities that enable them to lead people effectively and successfully. Those include forming a group endeavor by presenting a goal, inspiring others to join and contribute, and motivating people to work together to achieve a shared goal. The term, "leadership," is used in other ways, too. For example, leadership can be attributed to a group instead of an individual. A team can be seen as exercising leadership when they successfully persuade people and create a positive change in an organization. Similarly, even organizations themselves can be considered as leaders if they continuously pioneer appropriate new endeavors, thereby setting up a model for other organizations of the same type to follow.

Leadership does not always entail innovation. The bulk of everyday library work has to do with managing and executing routine processes that enable a library's services and operations. Libraries go through many projects related to such work on a regular basis. Common examples include redesigning a library website, renovating a particular service area such as a reference desk, or implementing a new space-booking system with a more efficient workflow. Leadership is required to carry through those projects and bring positive outcomes. But those changes are gradual and predictable improvements, which most of us do not consider to be particularly innovative.

So why is innovation regarded as such an important indicator of leadership, as if successful leadership must always lead an organization to innovation? This is because almost all organizations—including libraries—have been facing rapid and profound changes in recent years. Those changes stem from the digital revolution, which has brought us a series of new technologies such as the internet, the Internet of Things, and artificial intelligence. Those changes have often been fundamentally disruptive to established industries and their traditional business models. As a result, many organizations came to face a crisis, and it is to this type of change and crisis that the combination of leadership and innovation became a sought-after solution. Leaders are now expected to lead their organizations to overcome the crisis by making radical changes and turn the crisis into a new opportunity by producing innovation.[1]

This common narrative about innovation and leadership appears to also be accepted in libraries. A 2013 report from the Association of Research Libraries states that research libraries increasingly prize innovation as a key to sustaining a competitive edge in a rapidly changing landscape of library services and content.[2] In the literature, it has been noted that libraries are facing times of unprecedented challenge and unparalleled change and innovation has moved from a consideration to a necessity.[3] Library administrators and managers are urged to employ leadership practices that effectively support rapid change and integrate innovation into organizational culture in the face of the changes in library users' needs due to technological advancement.[4] And academic library leaders have been recommended to innovate with effective communication and social skills to encourage a collaborative and agile culture in academic institutions in order to meet the fundamental challenge of rapid change due to technological advances.[5]

WHAT INNOVATION IS AND IS NOT

If we consider leadership in its most basic sense, the elements of successful leadership—such as a vision, strategic thinking, communication, trustworthiness, reliability, and facilitating collaboration—are not difficult to identify. But as noted above, leadership is exercised when the nature of the work is not necessarily innovative as much as when it is. What qualifies certain work as innovative? Leonard-Barton and Swap define innovation as "the embodiment, combination, and/or synthesis of knowledge in novel, relevant, valued new products, processes, or services."[6] To better understand the relationship between leadership and innovation, let us take a closer look at what innovation is, its types, characteristics, and other related attributes.

A helpful list of classifications and characterizations of innovation is found in Jantz's study of organizational innovation at research libraries.[7] In his article, Jantz summarizes the classifications of innovation from the middle-range theories of organizational innovation, which are: administrative, technical, radical, and incremental.[8] According to those structural theories of organizational innovation, administrative and technical are two types of innovation.[9] The administrative innovation relates to the inner workings of an organization and the staff, such as administrative processes, budget, and human resources. On the other hand, technical innovation relates to the use of technology that generates new services or products for the client. In its character, an innovation can also be incremental or radical. A radical innovation involves new knowledge that is used to make fundamental changes in a product or process technology. It is also disruptive of the status quo and involves changes in the organization's subsystems, values, incentives, and power. By contrast, an incremental innovation uses existing knowledge and creates improvements in a product or process technology.

To discuss innovation at academic libraries, Lewis adopts Clayton Christensen's classification of three types of innovation: sustaining, disruptive/market-growing, and efficiency.[10] Sustaining innovations make existing products or services better but do not change the existing market share. In sustaining innovations, the business model and the required resources for the improved products or services remain the same. By contrast, disruptive/market-growing innovations introduce a product, which almost always deploys a new technology in combination with a new business model. Unlike sustaining innovations, disruptive innovations increase the market share, create dramatic change, and restructure industries. They are also less common and carry more risks. The third type, efficiency innovations, lower the cost of existing products or services through technological, process, or organizational changes.

These various types and attributes of innovation show that innovation spans a broader range of activities than what many of us think. Lewis observes that sustaining and efficiency innovations are both common at libraries and identified several examples in a library setting: a better workflow, a different pedagogical approach, better wayfinding in the building, approval plans, and patron-driven acquisition.[11] Nevertheless, non-radical, less disruptive, less technological innovations rarely receive the same kind of attention given to radical, disruptive, and technological innovations at libraries. Innovation is commonly associated with radical change, dramatic disruption, and leading-edge technologies.

I believe that this phenomenon originates from common misconceptions about what innovation in academic libraries is and should look like. First, introducing new technology does not make something automatically innovative. A new technology often serves as an important element in turning an innovative idea into a concrete solution, but it is not an essential component of innovation. What makes something innovative is a creative idea that reveals and fulfills people's unmet needs.[12] When such an idea requires a significant shift from conventional thinking, we call that "innovative." For example, patron-driven acquisition is innovative because of its creative approach of linking library patrons' demand directly with the library's purchasing decision. What makes the wireless hotspot lending service innovative is the idea that a library can provide library patrons with reliable Wi-Fi access at their homes, thereby directly addressing the digital divide in a new way. Although it may sound obvious, the point that not all innovations are technological in nature and the use of new technology does not automatically generate an innovation needs to be fully understood because technology is frequently and mistakenly equated with innovation.[13]

Second, novelty is not equivalent to innovation. No matter how novel a new product or service may be, it does not create or add value if it is not relevant to people's real needs or is a poor solution to the problem that it aims to solve. Suppose that a library purchases a holography system and displays a hologram of a rare book in its lobby. This new hologram will clearly attract people's attention. But does this count as innovation? Simply purchasing a new product and procuring a new service—a holography system and the creation of the custom hologram of the rare book in this case—does not qualify as innovation because it does not address or solve any existing problem or reveal and fulfill library patrons' unmet needs in new ways.

Third, that something is disruptive does not mean that it is therefore innovative. Some people believe that all innovations are disruptive and regard disruption as a sign of innovation. This is a misunderstanding. "Disruptive" can mean many things depending on what or whom it affects. If a new product, service, or workflow is disruptive to target users, that is likely to indicate a flaw. What radical innovations disrupt is an industry and its traditional business model, not the quality of user experience or customer service. Airbnb disrupted the hotel industry and Uber the taxi industry. But in user experience, both Airbnb and Uber created lodging and transportation services with less friction for their customers. It is worth remembering that innovations do not have to be severely disruptive. An incremental innovation, for example, uses existing knowledge and creates improvements in a product or process technology. Similarly, sustaining innovations that make existing products or services better do not change the existing market share nor disrupt an organization or an industry. Innovation can cause a varying degree of disruption, but part of a leader's role in managing innovation is to lower its level of disruption to her organization while maximizing its positive impact. As Deiss points out, innovations are things that *change* the way we can do what we want to do, thereby adding *value* to our daily lives.[14] Understanding what innovation is and is not helps us discern what is truly innovative from what only appears so on the surface. Chasing after one innovation after another without such an understanding will only result in innovation theater, which creates no real value for library patrons.

ENABLING INNOVATION AND AVOIDING INNOVATION FATIGUE

If simply buying new and disruptive technology products and services can make a library innovative, innovation would be relatively easy to achieve, but that is not the case. This takes us to the question of why innovation is so difficult to create and realize in the real world. The two necessary conditions for innovation are (1) generating creative ideas and (2) achieving buy-in from both staff and users. Innovation requires a creative idea that fulfills people's unmet needs in new ways. Buy-in is crucial for the successful implementation and adoption of any innovative solution. The fact that innovative projects tend to carry more risks increases the importance of buy-in. No innovation can succeed if it fails to obtain staff buy-in at the implementation stage or if it is not adopted by users after the release.

Library staff are the biggest source of creative ideas for innovation at libraries. Even when innovation is touted as an important goal for a library, however, a concrete connection between one's daily work and innovation is not always made explicit to staff by the library leadership. When that happens, it becomes hard for staff to see the value of the library's innovative efforts and their role in them. For this reason, library leadership must ensure that every staff person understands what innovation means in relation to their daily work. Libraries should also provide library staff with related learning opportunities in addition to ongoing support for professional development. This enables staff to generate innovative ideas that are well informed and current, which reflect the changing trends and developments at libraries. To familiarize staff with the general process of innovation, for example, a library-wide workshop on design thinking can be offered on a regular basis with library-related examples.[15] Such a workshop introduces staff to useful methods and stages for creative problem-solving, which is key to innovation. Libraries can organize various demo and hands-on training sessions focused on emerging technologies. This will make staff more confident about incorporating new technologies into library services and operations. Libraries should also allow their staff the freedom to develop and present their ideas and offer needed resources to test out those ideas. Specific mechanisms that enable and facilitate staff's participation could be very helpful. For example, libraries can provide their staff with time to observe the library's routine processes, workflows, services, and the user behavior and discover unaddressed needs, which can form the very basis of innovative ideas. A well-known example of this is Google's 20 percent time, with which Google allows its employees to spend 20 percent of their work time on exploratory or experimental projects of their choice.

The staff at a library with an established culture that promotes and supports creativity is likely to generate a lot more innovative ideas than those at a library without such a culture. Setting a clear direction to establish such a culture and maintaining it over time would be the responsibility of library administrators. In this context, Evener points out that to cultivate creativity in staff, library administrators should promote growth mindsets, reward experimentation, and practice discovery skills along with library staff, and McGregor emphasizes the change theories' focus on the leaders' need to pay attention to staff's learning and development for successful change management.[16]

If facilitating innovation is an important part of leadership, leaders must be able to address people's natural resistance to change and obtain staff buy-in. Achieving staff buy-in is necessary for the success of any innovation, but it is not easily done. This explains why the ability to successfully form and achieve staff buy-in is a highly sought-after quality for library administrators and managers. In staff buy-in, however, contrasting views are often expressed. Library administrators tend to bemoan their staff's unwillingness to change and resistance to innovation. On the other hand, many library workers express innovation fatigue. Innovation fatigue is observed when staff lose interest in the innovation agenda from the leadership and no longer actively commit to efforts. Staff at a library where innovation fatigue sets in are tired of and unmotivated by innovation projects that come one after another without a clear vision from the top. Overall, they feel that innovative efforts in the past produced little value and things are unlikely to change. Where does innovation fatigue originate and why is it frequently seen at libraries?

To expedite change and innovation, many library administrators opt to import innovations made at other libraries directly into their own. But when such importing is done without sufficient care, it can backfire and cause innovation fatigue. Reflecting on her own experience, Mosley describes how such a scenario plays out at libraries:

> If one comes back from every conference or educational opportunity with the best new "innovation" since sliced bread and an insistence that it has to be done NOW, one seriously risks losing credibility and equity as a leader. The first reason relates to change fatigue among staff. This occurs when staff are faced by so many changes that their resilience begins to be unable to work through the cycle of emotions that are necessary in engaging and adopting a change. In time, one will begin to face stronger and stronger resistance to moving a change forward. This can have a significant organizational impact when the change is truly an important one, but staff are so disenfranchised that the change initiative is doomed before it can begin. The second concern is that when one is constantly bringing back a new direction or initiative, there is a stronger likelihood that one has not carried a prior change through the full process of mature implementation, including assessment and evaluation of the change to determine if it accomplished what was originally intended and to make appropriate follow-up adjustments.[17]

Many library workers will find this scenario familiar. The intention of the library administrator is likely to be adding innovations to her library as quickly as possible. But the library staff are overwhelmed; the outcomes of many innovative projects are not evaluated in a proper and timely manner; consequently, the purpose, benefits, and positive/negative impact of those projects are neither clearly understood nor felt by staff. The library staff begins to dread another innovation directive coming down from the top and to doubt the overall value of the library's innovative efforts. As a result, a library administrator's attempt to speed up innovation and change ironically ends up slowing down innovation itself by causing her staff's disenfranchisement.

This conflicting dynamic is likely due to the discrepancy between the mental model of a library in the administrator's mind and the reality of everyday work that library staff deal with. Today's leaders want to replicate the speed and style of innovation seen at successful small technology start-up companies, and library administrators are no exception. They often wish libraries to operate more like those technology start-ups that quickly change their directions and produce many radical innovations. However, libraries and tech start-ups have few similarities in their organizational characters. It is well known that small start-ups serve as better incubators for innovation than larger and more mature organizations. Its small size makes a start-up nimble. With small staff, start-up companies can accomplish communication and idea-sharing much more easily and quickly. Their lack of complex workflows, processes, policies, a less hierarchical reporting structure, and a less formal decision-making procedure allow their staff to pursue innovative work with more freedom, speed, and authority.

In a larger and more mature organization, the situation is reversed, however. To support the routine operation, the staff must closely follow many workflows, processes, and policies. The staff spend most of their time managing and maintaining existing services and products. This is time-consuming and leaves little time for other work such as pursuing ideas of innovation. Since a library is a larger organization, any proposed change requires sufficient discussion and full communication, so that it can successfully cascade into all units, whose work is often closely intertwined. A larger and more mature organization moves more slowly because it has many moving parts, and following formal processes and procedures keeps those parts in good coordination. Given the character of libraries as a more complex and mature organization, it is no surprise that innovation takes a longer time and achieving staff buy-in is more difficult. If library leaders do not fully understand the nature of libraries as a mature organization and try to simply mimic a start-up by cutting short the full communication cycle, forgoing an established decision-making procedure, pursuing projects without gathering sufficient input from staff, and so on, they are likely to generate chaos and confusion instead of innovation. Such a leadership style would be counterproductive in a mature organization such as a library.

The idea of speeding up innovation by importing solutions from peer institutions also does not quite accord with the spirit of innovation. Creative problem solving is the core of innovation; copying something is the opposite. Furthermore, top-down innovation directives can be perceived as avoiding more challenging foundational tasks, such as enabling the participative engagement of the staff about innovative projects and establishing a working environment that values and supports library staff as a source of innovation. These tasks are laborious but necessary to building a library's capacity to perform as an innovative organization over time, whereas simply transplanting innovations from other libraries presents only a facade of innovation.

What can bridge the gap between library workers' innovation fatigue and library administrators' push for expediting innovation? Mosley suggests that library administrators should thoughtfully review and assess their ideas without making assumptions, take more care when presenting them to their staff, and go through the process of thoughtful consideration and engaged communication with staff even if it takes time.[18] Participative engagement provides leaders with an opportunity to communicate with staff about their vision for innovation in the context of the library and its parent institution and the value each innovation project creates. It also offers library staff a chance to better understand how each innovation project aligns with the library's strategic priorities and the broader goals of its parent institution and what the project's expected positive short-term and long-term impacts are. Skipping this step does not save time and only undermines a library's innovative efforts in the long run. In addition, an emotional connection plays a key role in staff's mentally processing, accepting, and engaging with a change.[19] Therefore, library leaders must pay close attention to establishing a positive emotional connection with innovative projects in staff's minds early on. The more value library staff see in the library's innovation projects and the more control and influence they feel they can exert over the library's innovative efforts, the more quickly and willingly they will embrace the library's innovative efforts.

In moving the library forward on the innovation front, the responsibilities of a library leader are:

1. to present and communicate a clear vision and effective strategies to staff;
2. to ensure that staff understand the key context and the goal of each innovative project;
3. to establish a positive emotional connection with innovative projects in staff's mind and achieve staff buy-in;
4. to provide support for staff so that they can perform and innovate at their best;
5. to manage and allocate workloads and resources appropriately; and
6. to evaluate each innovative project's outcome and assess its impact at its completion against the original vision, thereby creating a feedback loop for better future decisions.

When library leaders fulfill these responsibilities, they will be able to fully engage their staff and prevent innovation fatigue. It is to be noted that these responsibilities of a library leader apply to all projects, not just to innovation projects. The only differentiating factor between leadership for innovation and general leadership may be a clear vision for innovation for a given library. But no matter how great a vision for innovation may be, the progress of innovation will be inevitably impeded if a leader lacks the qualities of generally effective leadership—such as establishing a shared goal, strategic thinking, open communication, trustworthiness, reliability, social skills to motivate and facilitate collaboration, and the ability to gain staff buy-in. Not everyone with great leadership skills may be good at driving innovation, but no one with poor leadership skills can succeed at making an organization innovative.

INNOVATION STRATEGIES FROM WHERE YOU ARE

Frontline Library Staff

Frontline library staff should be able to actively participate in innovative projects from the beginning and be invited to review and determine the details of the project that are closely related to their work. This allows them to not only contribute their experience and knowledge about the library's daily work processes and unique elements but also flag any potential issues in advance, which can turn into bigger problems down the road. They should also seek and create the opportunities to shape and steer the project in the most suitable direction for the local context beyond merely providing feedback. Frontline staff should request that library administration provide appropriate learning opportunities and supporting mechanisms for innovation, so that they can more easily contribute toward the library's innovative efforts. They should prompt senior administrators to clearly communicate the context of the library' innovative efforts, how their success adds value, how they relate to frontline staff's daily responsibilities, and how each innovative project aligns with the library's general strategic plan at a higher level, whenever such communication is missing. Various leadership skills—such as being proactive, timely communication, effective negotiation, and taking an initiative—will serve them well in navigating this process successfully.

Sometimes, frontline staff directly affected by a library's innovative project end up discovering its full details only right before the implementation. This is not desirable, but they can still volunteer to come up with a concrete plan to monitor how the new project plays out in their daily work and make note of the aspects in which it performs well and poorly. Since an innovative project carries more risks, it often gets added as a pilot on top of the preexisting work of staff without workload adjustment. A pilot is great for testing the water for a short period, but it cannot go on permanently. Without a built-in evaluation timeline, it can meet a slow death due to various issues, such as low user adoption or the decrease of funding and other resources. When those happen, frontline staff can end up bearing the brunt of resolving the initial disruption caused by the pilot and managing the subsequent impact from the project faltering. By requesting that some form of formal evaluation be built into the schedule of all innovative projects, they can minimize disruption and help the library take necessary steps to move the pilot to the next phase: operationalization or sunsetting.

Middle Managers

In library innovation, the greatest challenge for middle managers is balancing their staff's everyday work and needs with the innovation mandate from the top. In general, the more clarity that exists in the shared understanding of a library's overall vision and strategic directions by library staff and the library administration, the easier this challenge becomes for middle managers to meet. The same applies to the library's overall norms of trust, open communication, and collaboration. When these are already well established in the library's work environment and overall culture, middle managers can facilitate and oversee the library's innovative efforts with ease. When those elements are not in place, however, trying to establish them in their units within their power becomes the work that takes up a lot of effort on middle managers' part.

The best strategy to promote innovation for middle managers is to make innovation an important consideration in every project and to provide their staff with a big picture that clearly connects the project with the library's innovation agenda. This information enables their staff to more easily brainstorm and propose innovative ideas that align well with the strategic goals of both the library and the unit. The goal is to make this process a routine step in everything that staff does, so that the innovation mindset comes naturally to them. Middle managers can also further expedite this process by proactively creating an inventory of routine work processes and identifying areas for innovation. Discuss those with staff and ask for ideas. Many times, staff will come back with creative ideas that they already had in mind but couldn't pursue for various reasons. At that point, middle managers simply need to provide necessary resources for staff to develop those ideas into testable solutions and encourage piloting them at a small scale. When this cycle is repeated over time, they will gain trust from staff, and this adds momentum to staff's participation in and contribution toward the library's innovative efforts. What is crucial is building an overall culture in which staff naturally pay attention to various pain points in library work processes and services and enjoy solving problems through collaborative innovation. Such a culture is essential to successful innovation and takes time to grow and establish. Middle managers can play a vital role in building such a culture.

In managing up, middle managers need to keep senior administrators well informed about emerging trends and related potential innovations and, at the same time, keep them fully grounded in the reality of the library's current operations and services. Middle managers should also gently guide senior administrators to engage in participative and open communication and discussion with staff as much as possible. The less barriers and the more clarity and openness exist in communication between senior administrators and frontline staff, the more quickly and smoothly innovation takes form at a library. Middle managers can play a key role in shifting their library into this optimal state.

Another important responsibility of middle managers is to advocate for frontline staff. Middle managers should take concrete measures to provide staff with relevant learning opportunities, freedom, and resources necessary to innovate. At the same time, they should also ensure that staff are not overwhelmed by extra work generated by high-priority innovation projects and that all projects are given a timeline for assessment. Only those projects that are evaluated as successful should be continued after their pilot stage, and unsuccessful ones should be officially closed with the sharing of the lessons learned. In addition, middle managers can coach those staff members who are less motivated to participate in the library's innovative efforts by showing them how their career development can go side by side with their participation. Lastly, middle managers should make efforts to establish appropriate measures to recognize and reward high-performing staff or teams. Examples of such measures include an award, a news feature in the library newsletter, and recognition in a staff member's annual performance evaluation. Those measures help frontline staff feel appreciated and create a virtuous circle for the library's future innovative efforts.

Since middle managers work in the middle, they are put in a unique position where they are asked to do a lot of heavy-lifting in forming staff buy-in by coordinating effective communication, clarification, and negotiation between library administrators and frontline staff. Depending on how well middle managers play this role, a library's innovative efforts can thrive or falter. This important and challenging work of middle managers consists of many thankless chores and often invisible labor in managing differing visions and emotional reactions to change from both library administrators and staff and needs to be properly supported and acknowledged.

Senior Administrators

Library administrators have more formal authority in making decisions about the library's innovation agenda in comparison to middle managers and frontline staff. Consequently, their thorough understanding of the challenges to innovation is crucial, particularly the one related to "recognizing the difference between a true shift that represents an emerging trend or a strategic new direction and positioning one's library in alignment with it, as opposed to a fad or one-off improvement that sounds like a really impressive idea but yields little or no actual long-term impact or applied transferability to other institutions," as Mosley puts it.[20] For this, administrators must have a clear long-term vision of what innovation in their libraries should look like and be able to present short-term strategies designed to be effective in the library's specific operational context, including the parent institution's political landscape, the library's funding, its organizational culture, its current infrastructure, the current capacity of its staff for innovation, and the needs of the library patron community that the library serves and its readiness to adopt innovations. Leaders successful in leading innovation advance their aspirational vision through strategies grounded in reality. They must also be sensitive to the sustainability of innovative projects and make timely decisions about their operationalization or termination after the initial pilot stage, so that the library's efforts for innovation stay optimized at all times.

It goes without saying that administrators must clearly articulate their vision and strategies to obtain staff buy-in. Only when they can effectively communicate and create a momentum for innovation through participative engagement with staff, library administrators can take their vision and strategies off the ground and get them executed. Therefore, they must pay close attention to their communication about innovation and make full use of their leadership skills—such as effective communication, negotiation, consensus-building, empathy, and establishing the baseline norms of trust and collaboration—in achieving staff buy-in. Administrators who want to see innovation immediately in their libraries may get frustrated by the amount of time required to fully communicate with staff, get their feedback, and obtain staff buy-in regarding the library's innovative efforts. But allowing time for staff to think through, digest, and process proposed changes before starting to work on innovation prepares them to be more focused and effective in the following stages of the library's innovation process. It also enables administrators to set a positive tone in staff's perception about innovation and associated emotions. People's perception of change and associated emotions plays a role in the success of change as important as the change itself. Leaders successful in leading innovation address those aspects of change in a straightforward manner, thereby helping staff overcome the fear of uncertainty, learn how they can be part of the library's innovative efforts, and see the value of innovation more clearly.

Lastly, senior administrators must keep a proper balance between the library's everyday work and its innovation efforts, supporting and rewarding staff equitably. Since many library administrators consider innovation to be their top priority, they also tend to allocate more resources and support toward those who are tasked to work on innovative projects. Senior administrators should ensure that those opportunities are not concentrated on a select group of people, since that can create discontent in other staff and have a limiting impact on the library's innovative efforts. Most of all, library leaders must recognize value in all types of library work. Only when the groundwork of a library is solidly maintained and continued can its innovative efforts bloom.

CONCLUSION

In this chapter, I discussed how leadership relates to innovation, what makes something truly innovative along with some common misconceptions about what counts as innovation, and how library leaders can foster innovation by staff while avoiding innovation fatigue and successfully achieving staff buy-in. This should give readers a good idea of what genuine innovation means in the library context, common challenges that libraries experience in moving toward innovation, and how leadership skills can be used to meet those challenges. In the preceding section, I went over some specific leadership strategies that library professionals can utilize to actively engage in, facilitate, and sustain their libraries' innovative efforts from the positions that they occupy. One may think that only senior administrators with the formal authority to allocate fiscal and human resources have a role to play in bringing out innovations. But this is not true. Everyone at a library can and should have a say in how its innovative efforts are shaped, piloted, implemented, evaluated, and operationalized.

The key is to identify what unique role one can play given one's knowledge, skills, and interests in one's current position at the library. Different positions in a library's organizational structure—such as a frontline library professional, a middle manager, or a senior administrator—present possibilities to play different leadership roles and to uniquely contribute toward the library's innovative efforts. The effective use of leadership skills at all levels is crucial to bringing success to those efforts. Whether one is a library director, an interlibrary loan coordinator, a reference librarian, or the head of the IT department, everyone at a library should actively participate in deciding how, when, where, and for whom a library innovates and aim to lead the library's innovative efforts from where they are.

NOTES

1. This is also how today's leadership came to be tightly linked to not just management but *change* management and how innovation came to be often seen as one of the goals of organizational change in libraries. For an example, see Felicity McGregor, "Quality Management/ Change Management: Two Sides of the Same Coin?" (paper presented at *the 25th Conference of the International Association of Technological University Libraries*, Krakow University of Technology, Krakow, Poland, 3 June 2004), https://docs.lib.purdue.edu/iatul/2004/papers/12.

2. Lisa German and Beth Sandore Namachchivaya, "Innovation and R&D, SPEC Kit 339" (Association of Research Libraries, December 24, 2013), https://publications.arl.org /Innovation-R&D-SPEC-Kit-339/, 11.

3. Curtis Brundy, "Academic Libraries and Innovation: A Literature Review," *Journal of Library Innovation* 6, no. 1 (2015): 22–39, https://sites.google.com/site/journaloflibraryinnova tion/vol-6-no-1-2015.

4. Michelle Boisvenue-Fox and Kristin Meyer, "Not What You Expected: Implementing Design Thinking as a Leadership Practice," in *Supporting Entrepreneurship and Innovation*, ed. Janet A. Crum and Samantha Schmehl Hines, vol. 40 (Bingley, UK: Emerald Publishing Limited, 2019), 7–20, https://doi.org/10.1108/S0732-067120190000040009.

5. Murtaza Ashiq et al., "Academic Library Leadership in the Dawn of the New Millennium: A Systematic Literature Review," *The Journal of Academic Librarianship* 47, no. 3 (May 1, 2021): 102355, https://doi.org/10.1016/j.acalib.2021.102355.

6. Dorothy Leonard-Barton and Walter C. Swap, *When Sparks Fly: Igniting Creativity in Groups* (Boston, MA: Harvard Business School Press, 1999), 7.

7. Ronald C. Jantz, "A Framework for Studying Organizational Innovation in Research Libraries," *College & Research Libraries* 73, no. 6 (November 2012): 528, https://crl.acrl.org /index.php/crl/article/view/16264.

8. Fariborz Damanpour, "Organizational Complexity and Innovation: Developing and Testing Multiple Contingency Models," *Management Science* 42, no. 5 (1996): 698–99, https://doi.org/10.1287/mnsc.42.5.693.

9. Richard L. Daft, "A Dual-Core Model of Organizational Innovation," *Academy of Management Journal* 21 (1978): 195–96.

10. Clayton M. Christensen, Efosa Ojomo, and Karen Dillon, *The Prosperity Paradox: How Innovation Can Lift Nations Out of Poverty* (New York, NY: Harper Business, 2019), quoted in David W. Lewis, "Innovation and Growth: Applying Clayton M. Christensen's Theories to Academic Libraries," *Library Leadership & Management* 34, no. 1 (January 2020): 2.

11. David W. Lewis, "Innovation and Growth," 4.

12. Design thinking, which emphasizes a human-centered approach to creative problem-solving, focuses on discovering or reframing people's unmet needs and is a popular and effective methodology for developing innovative solutions. For several examples of non-technological innovations created this way, see Tim Brown and Jocelyn Wyatt, "Design Thinking for Social Innovation," *Stanford Social Innovation Review*, Winter 2010, 30–35, https://ssir.org /articles/entry/design_thinking_for_social_innovation.

13. It would be helpful to distinguish technology-related innovation from technology-driven innovation. Observing this same confusion about the relationship between technology and innovation, Corrall and Jolly noted that when an innovation brings a new way of doing things and its significance lies in the social rather than the technical dimension such as the open-source software movement and open-access initiatives, that significance of the social

dimension must be properly acknowledged. See Sheila Corrall and Liz Jolly, "Innovations in Learning and Teaching in Academic Libraries: Alignment, Collaboration, and the Social Turn," *New Review of Academic Librarianship* 25, nos. 2–4 (April 2019): 113–28.

14. Kathryn J. Deiss, "Innovation and Strategy: Risk and Choice in Shaping User-Centered Libraries," *Library Trends* 53, no. 1 (2004): 18, https://www.ideals.illinois.edu/handle/2142/1717.

15. About how the design thinking and the human computer interaction approach can be used at libraries, see Boisvenue-Fox and Meyer, "Not What You Expected," 7–20; Alma Leora Culén and Andrea A. Gasparini, "HCI and Design Thinking: Effects on Innovation in the Academic Library," in *Proceedings of the IADIS International Conference Interfaces and Human Computer Interaction* (Las Palmas de Gran Canaria, Spain: International Conferences on Interfaces and Human Computer Interaction, 2015), 3–10, https://www.duo.uio.no/handle/10852/46216.

16. Julie Evener, "Innovation in the Library: How to Engage Employees, Cultivate Creativity, and Create Buy-In for New Ideas," *College & Undergraduate Libraries* 22, nos. 3–4 (July 2015): 296–31, https://doi.org/10.1080/10691316.2015.1060142; McGregor, "Quality Management/Change Management," 6.

17. Pixey Anne Mosley, "Engaging Leadership: Bringing Back 'Innovation,'" *Library Leadership & Management* 27, nos. 1/2 (January 2013): 2.

18. Mosley, "Engaging Leadership: Bringing Back 'Innovation,'" 3–5.

19. Ibid., 5.

20. Ibid., 1.

BIBLIOGRAPHY

Ashiq, Murtaza, Shafiq Ur Rehman, Muhammad Safdar, and Haider Ali. "Academic Library Leadership in the Dawn of the New Millennium: A Systematic Literature Review." *The Journal of Academic Librarianship* 47, no 3 (2021): 102355. https://doi.org/10.1016/j.acalib.2021.102355.

Boisvenue-Fox, Michelle, and Kristin Meyer. "Not What You Expected: Implementing Design Thinking as a Leadership Practice." In *Supporting Entrepreneurship and Innovation*, edited by Janet A. Crum and Samantha Schmehl Hines, 7–20, Volume 40 of Advances in Library Administration and Organization. Bingley, UK: Emerald Publishing Limited, 2019. https://doi.org/10.1108/S0732-067120190000040009.

Brown, Tim, and Jocelyn Wyatt. "Design Thinking for Social Innovation." *Stanford Social Innovation Review*, Winter 2010.

Brundy, Curtis. "Academic Libraries and Innovation: A Literature Review." *Journal of Library Innovation* 6, no. 1 (2015): 22–39. https://sites.google.com/site/journaloflibraryinnovation/vol-6-no-1-2015.

Corrall, Sheila, and Liz Jolly. "Innovations in Learning and Teaching in Academic Libraries: Alignment, Collaboration, and the Social Turn." *New Review of Academic Librarianship* 25, nos. 2–4 (2019): 113–28.

Culén, Alma Leora, and Andrea A. Gasparini. "HCI and Design Thinking: Effects on Innovation in the Academic Library." In *Proceedings of the IADIS International Conference Interfaces and Human Computer Interaction*, 3–10. Las Palmas de Gran Canaria, Spain: International

Association for Development of the Information Society, 2015. https://www.duo.uio.no /handle/10852/46216.

Daft, Richard L. "A Dual-Core Model of Organizational Innovation." *The Academy of Management Journal* 21, no. 2 (1978): 193–210. https://doi.org/10.2307/255754.

Damanpour, Fariborz. "Organizational Complexity and Innovation: Developing and Testing Multiple Contingency Models." *Management Science* 42, no. 5 (1996): 693–716. https:// doi.org/10.1287/mnsc.42.5.693.

Deiss, Kathryn J. "Innovation and Strategy: Risk and Choice in Shaping User-Centered Libraries." *Library Trends* 53, no. 1 (2004): 17–32.

Evener, Julie. "Innovation in the Library: How to Engage Employees, Cultivate Creativity, and Create Buy-In for New Ideas." *College & Undergraduate Libraries* 22, nos. 3–4 (2015): 296–311.

German, Lisa, and Beth Sandore Namachchivaya. "Innovation and R&D, SPEC Kit 339." Washington, DC: Association of Research Libraries, 2013. https://publications.arl.org /Innovation-R&D-SPEC-Kit-339/.

Jantz, Ronald C. "A Framework for Studying Organizational Innovation in Research Libraries." *College & Research Libraries* 73, no. 6 (2012): 525–41.

Leonard-Barton, Dorothy, and Walter C. Swap. *When Sparks Fly: Igniting Creativity in Groups.* Boston: Harvard Business School Press, 1999.

Lewis, David W. "Innovation and Growth: Applying Clayton M. Christensen's Theories to Academic Libraries." *Library Leadership & Management* 34, no. 1 (2020): 1–13.

McGregor, Felicity. "Quality Management/Change Management: Two Sides of the Same Coin?" In *Proceedings of the 25th Conference of the International Association of Technological University Libraries.* Volume 14. London, UK: British Library, 2004. https://docs.lib .purdue.edu/iatul/2004/papers/12.

Mosley, Pixey Anne. "Engaging Leadership: Bringing Back 'Innovation.'" *Library Leadership & Management* 27, nos. 1/2 (2013): 1–5.

3

Bringing Experiential Learning to Campus

How to Develop Partnerships and Implement Immersive Learning Experiences

Chris Holthe and Andrew See

As an educational model experiential learning has existed for decades with its practical applications in the context of higher education having been well documented. This chapter will explore the intersections of experiential learning theory and library program operations as demonstrated by the Experiential Learning program at the Northern Arizona University Cline Library. Leveraging our years of combined experience with experiential learning spaces and services including makerspaces, extended reality labs, and multimedia creation studios, this chapter will provide readers with practical examples that will afford them a better understanding of how to develop and operationalize experiential learning programs at scale. Readers will take away knowledge on how to build strong campus partnerships, how to work with faculty to integrate experiential programming and services into the curricula, and how to develop new and creative ways to grow and sustain their own experiential learning program.

EXPERIENTIAL LEARNING IN EDUCATION

Experiential learning in education, particularly on academic campuses, has been detailed extensively in educational literature and encompasses a wide breadth of disciplines. Historically, Experiential Learning Theory (ELT) owes its foundations to twentieth-century scholars John Dewey, Kurt Lewin, and Jean Piaget; while perhaps the most impactful and heavily cited scholarship comes from the work of experiential learning pioneer David Kolb. In his work as an educational theorist, Kolb defines experiential learning as "the process whereby knowledge is created through the transformation of experience."[1] Expanding upon this, Alice and David Kolb later write, "ELT is a holistic theory of learning that identifies learning style differences among different academic specialties, it is not surprising to see that ELT research is highly interdisciplinary, addressing learning and educational issues in many fields."[2]

Kolb also suggests that experiential learning can be reliably applied and assessed in the context of higher education and that ELT synthesizes the interdisciplinary nature of higher education. Additionally, he concludes that "structured exercises and role plays, gaming simulations, and other forms of experience-based education are playing a larger role in the curricula of undergraduate and professional programs."[3] Indeed, recent research which leverages the Kolb model to introduce an experience-based robotics project to engineering students indicates that this methodology has a positive effect on the formative assessment of knowledge.[4]

APPLICATIONS AND BENEFITS

In recent years, immersive technologies have steadily grown in both relevance and use, and as such have enabled academic communities to explore innovative approaches to problem solving and knowledge generation. With makerspaces providing access to rapid prototyping technologies and extended reality labs adding new, even more immersive dimensionalities to their knowledge building programs, today's academic communities are increasingly able to leverage contemporary technologies in their application of ELT in order to empower students to learn by doing. In their literature review, Ford and Minshall indicate that in terms of post-secondary education, the adoption of 3D printing is best represented in universities where "the neutral, non-departmental space allows interactions between students from different faculties and extra-curricular use."[5] In one of their many examples demonstrating the burgeoning use of 3D printing in higher education, Ford and Minshall chiefly note the technology's promising application in robotics education.[6]

In terms of extended reality (XR) technologies and their application in higher education, Curcio, Depace, and Norlund point out that their use can contribute to motivation, engagement, and critical thinking in students.[7] Ludlow indicates that VR applications offer new opportunities to increase the range of hands-on activities offered in the classroom (particularly academic concepts and social and communication skills).[8] Examples of such applications include the successful use of XR in neurosurgical training[9] and in engineering disciplines, where students are afforded the opportunity to engage with simulated engineering challenges that they would otherwise be unable to experience in a real-world environment.[10]

While rapid prototyping and immersive XR technologies naturally lend themselves to pedagogies in STEM fields, experiential learning is a truly interdisciplinary pedagogical approach to learning. Indeed, there are numerous examples of multidisciplinary applications for such technologies, including those in the arts and humanities. For instance, Lugmayr and Teras discuss VR applications in the digital humanities; immersing students in the daily life of a Parisian during the French Revolution.[11] Similarly, Crompton, Siemens, and Lane describe several examples of

3D printing technologies applied to sculpture,[12] Huson demonstrates the effectiveness of 3D printing in the field of ceramics,[13] and Paradis discusses the successful integration of VR into digital Archaeology.[14]

EXPERIENTIAL LEARNING AT CLINE LIBRARY

Academic libraries parallel the interdisciplinary nature of ELT by acting as centers of intellectual inquiry—holistically meeting needs of their academic communities. In particular, modern academic libraries often act as inclusive centers for experience-based programming and technologies, thereby providing students, faculty, and staff with the resources necessary for their academic success. Northern Arizona University's (NAU) Cline Library, located in Flagstaff, Arizona, is an excellent example of this trend. NAU is a public university offering on-campus and online courses to more than thirty thousand undergraduate and graduate students. The library's achievements toward its current experiential learning program began in 2012 when The Studios were launched as part of a phased campus learning spaces project. Programmatically, The Studios (a suite of multimedia production spaces and an accompanying media lab) were designed as the nucleus for learning activities related to advanced media creation. This space was coupled with an equipment lending program that includes digital cameras, microphones, and multimedia accessories. The Studios allow NAU affiliates to learn, explore, and share through the creation of rich multimedia projects from ideation to production and post production.

As early as 2017, the Cline Library had fully deployed The MakerLab, a multidisciplinary collaborative workspace allowing the NAU and Flagstaff community to learn, explore, discover, and create in ways that foster imagination, promote creativity, and solve real-world problems. The MakerLab's equipment supports hi-tech to low-tech making and discovery options including a MakerBot Innovation Center™ consisting of twenty 3D printers, 3D scanners, electronic prototyping kits, and a variety of crafting tools and supplies. The MakerLab facilitates the design and creation of personal and academic projects, group projects and assignments, and experience-based instruction sessions and workshops.

Subsequently, the library partnered with faculty in the NAU School of Communication in 2018 to design and build The Virtual Reality Learning Studio; a place where students can learn and explore in immersive environments using the latest virtual reality technologies. Built as a suite of three Oculus Rift™ consoles, The VR Studio allows individual students and small classes to engage with virtual experiences for leisure, or as part of immersive assignments. At this time the library also collaborated with the NAU School of Communication to embed VR technologies into interdisciplinary curricula. In particular, the library joined an existing partnership between the school's Advanced Media Lab (AML) and the Chemistry Department to help implement an interactive ChemVR app, which allowed organic chemistry students to manipulate molecular structures in virtual space. Though extensive re-

Figure 3.1. NAU student admiring a 3D printed T-Rex skull in the Cline Library MakerLab.
Image courtesy of Northern Arizona University Marketing.

search into the efficacy of the app had already been conducted by the AML, with the construction of The VR Studio Chemistry faculty could now leverage the facility to provide scalable access to VR technologies for larger courses.

Along with the construction of The Virtual Reality Learning Studio, the library simultaneously built the One Button Studio; a video recording studio allowing users to easily create high-quality recordings for presentations, lectures, interviews, and so on. The room, derived from a Penn State design, is equipped with an integrated HD camera, shotgun microphone, professional lighting, presenter screen, and green screen, which are all activated by inserting a flash drive into the control podium and pressing "one button" (a floor mounted foot pedal). Expanding the capabilities of the library's Photography Studio, the One Button Studio enables users to experience multimedia production and editing firsthand and allows them to apply these technologies in their projects. These spaces have been utilized by academic courses, student groups, campus organizations, and, most notably, by faculty developing multimedia content for their online courses.

By 2019, with the library's experiential learning spaces continuing to expand, the Cline Library established a new experiential learning (EL) librarian position in the hopes of more holistically coordinating the programming and management of these spaces. The EL librarian would oversee, expand, and promote the library's efforts to provide outstanding immersive experiences in all of the library's creation spaces. The EL librarian would also partner with the library's Teaching, Learning, and Research Services unit and other stakeholders, to design and deliver experiential learning programming that supports and enriches NAU's curricular and research activities. With the successful appointment of the EL librarian in the fall of 2019, the library was positioned to substantially expand its experiential learning program in a more coordinated and strategic manner. This allowed the library to successfully pursue grant funding to fund a new Extended Reality Creation Studio. The studio, building off of the success of The Virtual Reality Learning Studio, allows the NAU community to design, build, and test educational experiences using virtual and augmented reality tools. This program also offers a selection of XR classroom kits for use by NAU and Flagstaff-area K–12 instructors, thus enabling them to bring XR experiences into their classrooms.

BUILDING PRODUCTIVE CAMPUS PARTNERSHIPS

Advocating for Experiential Learning

The ongoing success of any experiential learning program is dependent on strong collaborations with campus partners. These partnerships can provide guidance and technical expertise, magnify marketing efforts, stimulate financial support, and make possible a myriad of programming opportunities. However, in order to benefit from such fruitful relationships, library staff must first be able to successfully advocate for experiential learning on campus. Advocacy starts by developing institutional knowledge of experiential pedagogies, technologies, and their applications. While this knowledge can be developed through the exploration of literature, conference proceedings, and trade publications, effective advocacy relies on one's personal experience with the use of immersive technologies. Trade conferences and maker fairs are excellent places for library staff to get hands-on experience with a wide assortment of immersive technologies. Once this base knowledge has been established, the first audience for any experiential learning advocacy should be colleagues at all levels of the organization—from library administrators to subject librarians and frontline student staff. In many cases these staff members can become powerful allies who can intensify enthusiasm, encourage buy-in from partners, and leverage their campus connections to help structure, support, and promote an experiential learning program. Moreover, a complex system of internal advocacy serves to orient the library as a hub for experiential learning on campus which can add authority to the development of future partnerships.

Identifying Potential Partners

Once a foundation of support for experiential learning has been developed within the library or organization, the next step is to begin exploring connections with other campus units. Building connections with groups that share similar goals and methods not only leads to more fruitful collaborations but also opens potential avenues for the sharing of resources and expertise. To foster such connections, library staff should begin by examining the institution closely in order to develop an informal catalog of departments, units, organizations, or committees that are working towards similar goals. Library staff must take time to connect with program administrators, tour their experiential learning spaces, test out available technologies, and learn about their services. This process will help develop a firmer understanding of what's being done on campus, who is doing it, and what they are offering to users.

Identifying campus units with similar goals can often point to another powerful set of potential partners: faculty champions. As experiential learning pedagogies grow more ubiquitous in higher education an increasing number of faculty are beginning to recognize and embrace immersive technologies in the classroom. These faculty members—often representing engineering and other STEM disciplines but also present in the humanities, the arts, education, and communication—are frequently active with immersive programming and are strong advocates for experiential learning. Locating these individuals might prove challenging for library staff but nevertheless can result in powerful partnerships and provide excellent opportunities for embedding experiential learning into the curriculum.

Another potentially fruitful avenue for developing campus partnerships is to reach out to academic and non-academic student organizations and clubs. Taking advantage of student groups allows the library to leverage their membership base, communication infrastructure, event calendar, and inherent enthusiasm. These organizations might include maker and crafting clubs, engineering societies, cultural associations, or other niche groups that present opportunities for coordinating events and programs. Student groups are excellent partners for developing experiential activities or projects, planning unique events, and promoting library resources to students and faculty.

Fostering Successful Partnerships

Partnerships are vital to the continued growth of an experiential learning program and, as such, it is extremely important for the library to carefully nurture these relationships. It is crucial for staff to approach all interactions with current and potential partners with both a sense of humility and a cooperative, "this is how I can help you" spirit. This mindset will help the library avoid stepping on toes, harming egos, or placing burdens on potential collaborators. Library staff should be cognizant of differing workplace cultures and levels of investment and anticipate the need for compromise, adaptation, and flexibility. Once this initial, authentic connection has demonstrated the partnership's value, more mutually beneficial collaborations can be built around mutual respect and an appreciation of shared goals.

One of the largest concerns that campus partners often express when dealing with academic libraries is an unease over encroachment upon the associated departments' sphere of influence. Academic programs often regard themselves as the primary authority regarding a given technology or service and can view library attempts at programmatic expansion as intrusions into their territory. This is a situation in which internal advocacy, mixed with a healthy dose of empathy, can help persuade and disarm these potential detractors. It is important for staff to remind these partners that academic libraries are well positioned and capable of providing cross-campus, multidisciplinary access that more insulated departments cannot. Moreover, libraries often represent centralized meeting places and serve as the focus for research, programming, and technology. While these elements clearly orient the library as a natural hub for experiential learning programs, and can therefore offer a lot to partnering organizations, it is nevertheless a good idea for partners to clearly define expected roles, responsibilities, and objectives.

Above all, enduring and productive partnerships are built on continual, but constructive, communication. When partnering with individual groups or faculty members, staff should check in regularly, share updates and progress reports, ask productive questions, and celebrate shared successes. With more complex relationships the library might consider forming a cross-campus taskforce, working group, or standing committee. At the same time library staff should be cognizant of over-burdening their partners and carefully structure all forms of communication. As communication channels strengthen and intensify, so too will the resulting associations. In time, more intimate collaborations such as co-teaching workshops, co-developing courses, and coauthoring articles or conference presentations can serve to further enrich relationships.

DEVELOPING AN EXPERIENTIAL LEARNING PROGRAM

Performing a Needs-Based Analysis

Enthusiasm around experiential pedagogies and immersive technologies makes it easy for the library to rush headlong into program development. However, doing so without proper planning can result in short-lived and ineffective programs. An ideal place to start this process is by investigating experiential learning programs at peer institutions. While evaluating the successes and failures of other libraries might help inspire programming ideas, endorse technology purchases, and frame service structures, it is nevertheless vital to ensure that any program is customized for the desired users. One way to avoid creating a program that is ineffective is to start with an assessment of the current knowledge, abilities, and interests of potential users in order to determine their needs. This assessment also promotes consideration about the scope and objectives of any proposed experiential learning program.

Principal to a well-informed experiential learning program is the development of a method for analyzing the personal, academic, and career needs of users. This analysis can take many forms, but should consider the following questions:

- What learning experiences, skills training, or services do students need to better complete their coursework, projects, or research assignments?

- What practical skills or technologies (hardware and software) will allow students to be competitive in the job market for their fields?

There are many methods that the library can employ to answer these questions; for example, user needs can often be inferred from desk interactions or surveys. Staff should keep in mind, however, that while directly surveying students is important to developing an engaging program, many students do not actually know what they need. Consulting with liaison librarians, faculty partners, academic departments, and university career services can often point out where students' abilities are lacking and provide a broader understanding of their needs. These consultations can take the form of one-on-one meetings, forums, focus groups, or questionnaires. While surveys are quick and cost-effective ways of gathering information, direct contact with faculty can help contextualize responses and often generates more thoughtful ideas that can directly lead to purchase suggestions, service recommendations, and partnership opportunities.

Once library staff have developed a clearer awareness of experiential learning activities on campus and considered the needs of their users the library can now start thinking about how its services can fill the gaps. Perhaps there is a key technology, program, or service the library could provide that other programs do not. Maybe there are resources on campus that are only available to certain disciplines which all students would benefit from. There might even be event opportunities that merge immersive technologies with the library's collections. Thoughtful reflections on all of these factors will allow the library to develop a robust and effective experiential learning program.

Operationalizing an Experiential Learning Program

Once user needs have been analyzed and considered, library staff can begin to implement their experiential learning program. This program can take many different forms based on the needs and capabilities of the institution, but most often will involve the design of spaces and services, procurement of equipment, and the development of library programming. Since time, budget, and staffing constraints can often limit the breadth of library programs, it is vital for staff to consider the most efficient ways to implement EL. This often means expanding upon what the library currently offers as opposed to implementing something entirely new.

Where space is concerned, most modern library spaces can be easily leveraged for experiential learning activities. Indeed, the majority of experiential activities and technologies are relatively mobile and do not require a dedicated space. Instead, equipment can be kept in nearby storage carts and transported across the library as necessary. In some cases, however, semi-permanent EL spaces may be more effective, but should be large enough to support course instruction and group events while also being easily monitored to protect users and secure equipment. These spaces likewise require adequate power and data connectivity, nearby storage options, and furniture that supports both instruction and open usage. Most of these requirements can be met by meeting rooms, classrooms, or even open computing areas. Regardless of the location, it is important for the library to both physically and programmatically define the space. Users should be able to quickly understand proper usage of the space through signage and organization. Likewise, staff should be made aware of the intended outcomes of the space and be able to effectively supervise and maintain its use.

Once space has been allocated the technologies that the space will support can be considered. This may range from rapid prototyping tools (3D printers, 3D scanners, CNC machines, microelectronics, etc.) to multimedia equipment (cameras, recording studios, editing equipment, etc.), or even extended reality hardware (virtual/augmented reality headsets, motion capture equipment, etc.). The specific tools selected will vary widely and will primarily be influenced by the program's budget as well as the needs and capabilities of users. However, no matter which tools or technologies are incorporated into EL spaces, effective training and support are the most crucial factors to promoting use. This means that library staff must invest considerable effort into learning the technologies and developing a wide range of training materials, including: in-person training sessions, point-of-use user manuals, video tutorials, and even project guides in a variety of skill levels. Likewise, staff should be available in some in-person capacity, or by appointment, to assist users with both introductory and advanced use of equipment. Incorporating these support services from the onset will help foster a more robust, effective, and valuable EL program that can magnify the competencies of users.

Finally, a robust experiential learning program must also integrate educational programming as a central feature of its design. Experiential learning is not simply a method for self-directed discovery using immersive technologies, but is instead an approach to teaching which should focus on "hands-on exercises and projects where students develop skills and problem solving."[15] As such, the library's EL services should be regularly and thoughtfully incorporated into larger academic and creative learning opportunities. These opportunities can take the form of course-imbedded instruction, hands-on workshops, or even recreational programs such as XR-enhanced events, hackathons, or design competitions. No matter the format, attendees of these programs should be prompted to apply and demonstrate what they have learned, often by completing a given project. Workshops with deliverable objects—such as fabricating a car from craft supplies, scripting and recording a video skit, designing and printing a 3D keychain, or creating an immersive work of VR art—can successfully introduce attendees to novel technologies in a new and exciting way while also developing a wide range of skills. Moreover, designing these tasks to correspond with course-based learning objectives is a powerful way to serve the needs of students and embed an EL program into the institution's curriculum.

Embedding Experiential Learning into the Curriculum

Once a library's experiential learning program has been operationalized, the next objective should be to embed that program into the curriculum. By integrating EL spaces, services, and programming into academic coursework it is easier to demonstrate the program's value, promote student success, and ensure the program's long-term viability. By this stage library staff have hopefully identified a number of faculty champions who can provide excellent opportunities for experience-based curriculum development. However, in order to increase the library's impact, programs should be designed to reach faculty in as many disciplines as possible. This expansion is often impeded by the fact that both experiential learning and immersive technologies may be new concepts to many conventional instructors who are often reluctant to incorporate them into their courses. Many instructors may not see the value immersive technologies can offer their students or indeed may not want to put in the effort to adjust their courses.

To combat this reluctance, library staff should consider reaching out to faculty groups and offering to host workshops that demonstrate the benefits of experiential learning. This is a great opportunity for staff to communicate the value of EL for teaching and learning, as well as to demonstrate the potential for increased student engagement and achievement. These training opportunities should enable faculty to experience the outcomes of immersive technologies themselves, and provide ample evidence through specific examples and case studies. For example, in 2017, Cline Library staff partnered with faculty from NAU's Department of Theatre to 3D print a prop for a production of Shakespeare's *King John*. In this play the character of Limoges is beheaded, and in order to bring this scene to life the library's MakerLab used 3D scanners and printers to create a realistic facsimile of the actor's head. Describing examples such as this, while not always directly applicable to every discipline, can successfully demonstrate the broad capabilities of immersive technologies and start to cultivate faculty interest.

Another solution to overcoming faculty reluctance is to start small. Liaison librarians and faculty partners can be leveraged to facilitate introductions and to seek out opportunities to augment major course assignments with immersive technologies. This may include, for example, something as simple as converting a written assignment into a more interactive medium. Cline Library regularly supports VR-enhanced writing assignments for a number of our courses. In one particular assignment, students from Spanish 201 used Google Earth VR™ to physically explore Spanish speaking cities, the experience of which they then incorporated into creative writing assignments including a travel brochure and reflective essay. At this early stage, library staff should be prepared to locate immersive experiences that suit a given subject, brainstorm unique ways of teaching using those experiences, and provide training on the technologies involved. In another instance, in partnership with our engineering librarian, the Cline Library's Experiential Learning Unit successfully transitioned a civil engineering research assignment into a video-based case study. Library staff partnered with the faculty member in order to provide instruction on proper research strategies, promote good video recording and editing techniques, provide tours of our recording studios, and develop a useful online guide.

Figure 3.2. NAU student exploring Google Earth VR™ street view in the Cline Library VR Studio.
Image courtesy of Northern Arizona University Marketing.

If faculty are not ready to commit fully to experiential learning opportunities in their classes, suggesting immersive activities as an optional format to a given assignment can often overcome objections. Faculty might be persuaded to accept 3D designed and printed projects in place of traditional formats, or to allow multimedia submissions for creative writing or presentation assignments. Likewise, art faculty might consider accepting virtual art and design applications in place of physical media. For example, each semester Cline Library partners with faculty in the NAU School of Communication to support immersive assignments for the VC345 Motion Design Topics course. As part of their final assignment, students in this course use the library's VR Studio to design VR creatures which they then process as 3D models for printing on the library's 3D printers. Once faculty can see the engagement that immersive assignments like these can foster, and the innovative results, they will be more likely to engage with experiential teaching methods and assignments.

By integrating the library's EL program into the curriculum, and by using these techniques to overcome faculty hesitance, campus recognition and appreciation of the library's experiential learning program will deepen. As this influence continues to develop the program's success will further attract attention, collaboration, and investment. Indeed, some faculty may eventually begin to approach the library with collaboration opportunities of their own, from assignment design to research projects and even grant opportunities.

Sustaining an Experiential Learning Program

While planning and operationalizing an experiential learning program can be difficult, sustaining the program can often be even more demanding. Indeed, there exist a series of common challenges related to managing immersive, tech-rich services that, if not met, can create inefficiencies that result in unsuccessful programs. In order to overcome these challenges library administration must employ strategies to avoid burnout and innovation fatigue among staff, ensure scalability of services, thoughtfully consider technology purchases and associated budget implications, and protect library assets through effective maintenance of experiential learning spaces.

The demands related to implementing services that involve emerging technologies, particularly as they pertain to the experiential learning initiatives outlined in this chapter, can often seem interminable. In many cases librarians who have painstakingly researched, acquired, developed, and operationalized a new piece of technology might quickly be faced with the unfortunate reality that the technology has since become obsolete. Moreover, the ever-evolving nature of the tech market can also make simply staying up to date with current technology trends extremely taxing. These constant, and often very rapid, technological changes can easily contribute to workplace burnout among library staff. However, empathetic administrators can often help to alleviate this phenomenon by applying a more strategic approach to operationalizing their experiential learning spaces and programs. In tech-rich spaces it is often beneficial to start small, focusing on a clear and concise service plan that emphasizes the library's strategic goals and user needs rather than purchasing high-end technologies without a coherent plan for their use and maintenance. Administration might also consider creating a staff position whose primary responsibility is the visioning, coordination, and management of the experiential learning program. Doing so will allow the institution to take a more considered approach to its experiential learning services that not only avoids a reliance on non-specialized staff, but also avoids the potential for investing in short-lived technological trends.

Taking time to consider the scalability of operations will also help to reduce the demands placed on library staff while also creating a more sustainable program overall. Purchasing cutting edge, high-profile technologies can often seem enticing to administrators, but without well-considered and established operations even the most exciting new technologies can leave staff and end users with a bad experience. Libraries should consider starting off by planning and developing a solid operational delivery method. Once this operational bedrock is established it can then be leveraged for many new technologies and can help in lowering innovation fatigue in librarians. Library staff should also keep in mind that high-tech purchases can often place the library into an often-volatile consumer ecosystem. Not only is this ecosystem in a constant state of flux, with new manufacturers entering the market one month and disappearing the next, but in order to remain marketable most tech companies design their products for individual consumers rather than for larger organizations. All of these factors mean that library staff must strongly consider sustainability before purchasing any piece of hardware. It is important that library staff invest time in keeping abreast of technology changes by reading trade publications and blogs and by attending tech-focused conferences, especially when new products are set to be released. When purchasing, staff should consider whether the technology fits into their service plan, whether the manufacturer is well established and reliable (particularly if the institution intends to rely on a single manufacturer), whether the device itself demonstrates longevity and durability, and whether staff are adequately able to manage and maintain that device. In general, the library should avoid investing in specialized, professional-grade equipment that may be too complicated for general use and therefore will have limited applications. These strategies will also help regulate the scalability of EL services once the popularity of experiential learning programming begins to expand across the campus community.

A key element of ensuring program sustainability is being aware of financial demands that experiential learning initiatives place on library budgets. Indeed, the initial overhead cost for high-end technologies can be particularly daunting, especially when significant budgetary constraints often prohibit substantive growth to experiential learning programs. As such, libraries should actively seek out opportunities for grant funding to help support the development of their program. Beyond the initial upfront cost for purchasing new equipment, administrators will need to remain cognizant that every new piece of technology also comes with a number of hidden costs. Indeed, administrators should anticipate a great deal of wear and tear on all equipment and budget accordingly. Repairing or replacing damaged equipment can often be more expensive than the initial purchase, especially considering that repairing high-end technologies typically requires advanced mechanical knowledge that most librarians do not possess. In some cases, libraries might consider service or maintenance contracts with manufacturers in order to help alleviate this burden. Such contracts may result in more upfront expenditures and can limit program flexibility, but often guarantee a more scalable EL operation moving forward. However, while designating a set amount of funding to be used for replacement components and equipment upgrades is ideal, it is not always practical. This is especially true for novel technologies (such as XR headsets) that are constantly being discontinued and replaced with newer, non-backwards compatible models. This means that when it comes time to buy replacement components, they may no longer be available. As such, keeping ready-to-replace backup equipment and components should be heavily considered in the initial budgeting process.

Beyond budgetary considerations, it is also important that staff are aware of the hardware and system requirements that they will have to maintain as part of any technology equipment purchase. As Cross notes, "some of the more challenging emerging technologies require product registration, maintenance, upkeep, cleaning, and consumable components."[16] Likewise, it is important to understand the account requirements for all devices and develop methods for tracking email addresses, passwords, and account information. More specifically, product registration, especially for large quantities of items, can require multiple accounts and email addresses that should be centrally managed and stored. This is particularly vital as these requirements vary widely among devices and manufacturers and may result in a considerable amount of additional work. Similarly, in order to maintain library equipment and reduce expenditures, it is important that library staff set expectations for the use and management of all EL spaces and technologies. Depending on the location of EL spaces, they can often fail to be used for their intended purposes, especially if there is not enough support in the space to make it truly functional. Because of this it is important to post expected user behaviors and to clearly sign all equipment. Likewise, staff should either oversee the space or conduct regular walkthroughs, or space checks, if the space is unstaffed. This should include performing weekly maintenance and cleaning activities. By approaching all of these challenges to program sustainability with a set of well considered and clearly defined strategies, the library is more likely to cultivate a robust, successful, and enduring experiential learning program.

LEVERAGING SUCCESS TO BUILD NEW PARTNERSHIPS

External Community Connections

Though the Cline Library serves, as its primary focus, the academic needs of Northern Arizona University, both the library and the institution as a whole are nevertheless committed to a larger role within Northern Arizona. Indeed, many academic libraries serve as beacons of community engagement, foundations for the preservation of local history, and as central locations for partnerships with local institutions, businesses, schools, government and nonprofit organizations, and native nations. As a result, university-community collaborations are common across academic institutions. Such collaborations are ideal avenues for expanding an experiential learning program beyond the walls of the library, and as an EL program continues to develop, library staff will be presented with ample opportunities to expand the library's programmatic reach into the broader external community.

One example of such an opportunity is the Cline Library's partnership with Upward Bound, a local program that provides college preparatory assistance to high school students from disadvantaged backgrounds and/or who will be first-generation college graduates. Each summer the library partners with the NAU Upward Bound Math-Science (UBMS) Summer Academy to provide spaces, services, and learning experiences for UBMS students. Library staff also consult with UBMS administrators to conceptualize and design immersive "Tech Time" group projects in support of established learning outcomes. Most notably, in the summer of 2019, the library leveraged the entirety of its experiential learning program to support a project which tasked students to develop a screenplay based on a popular movie or book and then create a five- to six-minute video using the library's video production technology. The assignment also required a prop that was designed using VR or 3D design software and then printed by the library's MakerLab. According to the UBMS director, the students rated their tech-time experience as the most useful and fun out of their entire six-week summer program.

Another potential avenue for intercollegiate and community-based experiential programming is demonstrated by the Cline Library's partnership with a Flagstaff-area elementary school in the winter of 2020. As part of a STEAM initiative at the school, students in a second-grade class were assigned a project whereby they researched different countries and cultures across the globe. Once the final projects were presented, the Cline Library invited the class into the Virtual Reality Learning Studio to experience their selected country, or cultural icon, in an immersive virtual space using Google Earth VR™. Based on their project topics, students virtually visited the Eiffel Tower, the Pyramids of Giza, the Base Camp at Mount Everest, the crater of a volcano in Costa Rica, and the Great Wall of China, among other locations. Using the studio's display screens associated with each VR console, peers could also participate in the experience. According to their teacher, the children highly valued their experience and were able to better connect with the subject matter. This example demonstrates the potential for libraries and library staff to leverage their internal experiential learning programs for the benefit of their larger communities and, in so doing, further expand their impact.

CONCLUSION

As academic libraries, and indeed higher education in general, continue to see a demand for experiential and immersive learning opportunities in their curriculum, the necessity for libraries to continue to lead EL initiatives will require a more holistic and scalable re-envisioning of the programs and spaces that libraries provide. At Cline Library, our experiential learning program has become an integral component in our process to re-envision a modern twenty-first-century library. In the spring of 2019, when the library was approved to begin a master planning process, the head of user services and experience, and experiential learning librarian, leveraged this opportunity to begin strategic planning for the convergence of its immersive learning services and programs into a more integrated center for experiential learning. As a result, The Creation Commons was conceptually designed and, as of this writing, is included as a critical component in the library's master redesign plan. The Creation Commons' mission is to:

> Support the academic and personal success of our users, cultivate a technologically skilled 21st-century workforce, and stimulate academic innovation by integrating making, multimedia production, and advanced technologies into the culture of the Northern Arizona University community.

This conceptual space programmatically links all of the library's experiential services and programs—in operation as well as physical location—and expands on them to include:

- a robust service and user support desk;
- a conference room for consultation and project design;

- a re-envisioned and expanded MakerLab;
- a Media Instruction lab; and
- enhanced multimedia creation studios including recording studios, photography and videography suite, and XR studios (including both VR and AR technologies).

With this foundational infrastructure in place, the Cline Library will be well-suited to continue to act as a centralized campus resource; providing service and support as new immersive technologies emerge. Indeed, this initiative demonstrates the importance of academic libraries in continuing to explore and redefine experiential learning programs in order to meet the academic, research, and creative needs of their communities.

NOTES

1. David Kolb, *Experiential Learning: Experience as the Source of Learning and Development* (Englewood Cliffs, NJ: Prentice-Hall, 1984), 41.

2. Alice Y. Kolb and David A. Kolb, "Learning Styles and Learning Spaces: Enhancing Experiential Learning in Higher Education," *Academy of Management Learning & Education* 4, no. 2 (2005): 4.

3. Kolb, *Experiential Learning*, 4.

4. Mohd F. Ibrahim et al., "Strengthening Programming Skills among Engineering Students through Experiential Learning Based Robotics Project," *International Journal of Evaluation and Research in Education* 9, no. 4 (2020): 945.

5. Simon Ford and Tim Minshall, "Invited Review Article: Where and How 3D Printing Is Used in Teaching and Education," *Additive Manufacturing* 25 (2019): 134.

6. Ford and Minshall, "Invited Review Article," 133.

7. Igor D. D. Curcio, Anna Dipace, and Anita Norlund, "Virtual Realities and Education," *Research on Education and Media* 8, no. 2 (2017): 66.

8. Barbara L. Ludlow, "Virtual Reality: Emerging Applications and Future Directions," *Rural Special Education Quarterly* 34, no. 3 (2015): 6.

9. Antonio Bernardo, "Virtual Reality and Simulation in Neurosurgical Training," *World Neurosurgery* 106 (2017): 1015–29.

10. Abdul-Hadi G. Abulrub, Alex N. Atteridge, and Mark A. Williams, "Virtual Reality in Engineering Education: The Future of Creative Learning," in *2011 IEEE Global Engineering Education Conference* (2011): 751–57.

11. Artur Lugmayr and Marko Teras, "Immersive Interactive Technologies in Digital Humanities: A Review and Basic Concepts," in *Proceedings of the Third International Workshop on Immersive Media Experiences* (Brisbane: October 2015): 33.

12. Constance Crompton, Ray Siemens, and Richard Lane, "Fabrication and Research-Creation in the Arts and Humanities," in *Doing Digital Humanities* eds. Constance Crompton, Richard J. Lane, and Ray Siemens (New York: Routledge, 2016): 349–63.

13. David Huson, "3D Printing of Ceramics for Design Concept Modeling," in *Proceedings of the NIP & Digital Fabrication Conference* (Minneapolis, MN: 2011): 815–18.

14. M. A. Paradis et al. "Making Virtual Archaeology Great Again (without Scientific Compromise)," *International Archives of the Photogrammetry, Remote Sensing, and Spatial Information Sciences* 42, no. 2 (2019): 879–86.

15. Emma Cross and Ryan Tucci, "The Emerging Technology Collection at Carleton University Library: Supporting Experiential Learning in the University Curriculum," *Partnership: The Canadian Journal of Library and Information Practice and Research* 12, no. 1 (2017): 2.

16. Emma Cross and Ryan Tucci, "The Emerging Technology Collection at Carleton University Library," 1.

BIBLIOGRAPHY

Abulrub, Abdul-Hadi G., Alex N. Atteridge, and Mark A. Williams. "Virtual Reality in Engineering Education: The Future of Creative Learning." In *2011 IEEE Global Engineering Education Conference* (Amman, Jordan: 2011): 751–57.

Bernardo, Antonio. "Virtual Reality and Simulation in Neurosurgical Training." *World Neurosurgery* 106 (2017): 1015–29.

Crompton, Constance, Ray Siemens, and Richard Lane. "Fabrication and Research-Creation in the Arts and Humanities." In *Doing Digital Humanities*, edited by Constance Crompton, Richard J Lane, Ray Siemens, 349–63. New York: Routledge, 2016.

Cross, Emma, and Ryan Tucci. "The Emerging Technology Collection at Carleton University Library: Supporting Experiential Learning in the University Curriculum." *Partnership: The Canadian Journal of Library and Information Practice and Research* 12, no. 1 (2017): n.p. https://doi.org/10.21083/partnership.v12i1.3917.

Curcio, Igor D. D., Anna Dipace, and Anita Norlund. "Virtual Realities and Education." *Research on Education and Media* 8, no. 2 (2017): 60–68. https://doi.org/10.1515/rem-2016-0019.

Ford, Simon, and Tim Minshall. "Invited Review Article: Where and How 3D Printing Is Used in Teaching and Education." *Additive Manufacturing* 25 (2019): 131–50.

Huson, David. "3D Printing of Ceramics for Design Concept Modeling." In *Proceedings of the NIP & Digital Fabrication Conference* (Minneapolis, MN: 2011): 815–18.

Ibrahim, Mohd F., Aqilah B. Huddin, Fazida H. Hashim, Mardina Abdullah, Ashrani A. Abd Rahni, Seri M. Mustaza, Aini Hussain, and Mohd Hairia Mod Zaman. "Strengthening Programming Skills Among Engineering Students Through Experiential Learning Based Robotics Project." *International Journal of Evaluation and Research in Education* 9, no. 4 (2020): 939–46.

Kolb, David. *Experiential Learning: Experience as the Source of Learning and Development.* Englewood Cliffs, NJ: Prentice-Hall, 1984.

Kolb, Alice Y., and David A. Kolb. "Learning Styles and Learning Spaces: Enhancing Experiential Learning in Higher Education." *Academy of Management Learning & Education* 4, no. 2 (2005): 193–212.

Ludlow, Barbara L. "Virtual Reality: Emerging Applications and Future Directions." *Rural Special Education Quarterly* 34, no. 3 (2015): 3–10.

Lugmayr, Artur, and Marko Teras. "Immersive Interactive Technologies in Digital Humanities: A Review and Basic Concepts." In *Proceedings of the Third International Workshop on Immersive Media Experiences* (Brisbane: October 2015): 31–36.

Paradis, Marie-Anne, Théophane Nicolas, Ronan Gaugne, Jean-Baptiste Barreau, Réginald Auger, and Valérie Gouranton. "Making Virtual Archaeology Great Again (Without Scientific Compromise)." *International Archives of the Photogrammetry, Remote Sensing, and Spatial Information Sciences* 42, no. 2 (2019): 879–86.

Section 2

EXAMPLES AND CASE STUDIES

4

Leading by Design

Building an Experiential Studio to Support Interdisciplinary Learning

Emily S. Darowski, Matt Armstrong, and Leanna Fry

As the information and technology landscape has shifted, academic libraries have been called on to dedicate resources and personnel to innovation.[1] In 2001, Neal encouraged academic libraries to radically shift and envision libraries as spaces for both information consumption and production.[2] Libraries, he imagined, would "function as campus hubs for working with faculty on the integration of technology and electronic resources into teaching and research."[3] Similarly, Sommerville and Collins discussed the importance of using collaborative design with campus partners to ensure that academic library spaces are learner-centered.[4] In other words, experiential learning has become a key goal in the development of library spaces and programs.[5] The library should be a space where "students turn information into knowledge through social interactions that engage and excite students' learning purposes."[6] Libraries have responded to the call to evolve and provide campus learning and creativity spaces. Students are no longer only using libraries to find information; they are using them to create it. New library spaces include innovation commons, makerspaces, technology lending programs, dedicated creativity and innovation spaces, and centers for entrepreneurship education.[7]

The Brigham Young University (BYU) Library is the center of campus both geographically and metaphorically. It was natural for the library to partner with other campus entities to create a space to support experiential learning, beginning with a pilot program called the Creativity, Innovation, and Design (CID) Studio. Several earlier papers discussed assessments, design pedagogy, and library services related to the pilot.[8] We pick up where these articles left off, outlining the process of transitioning from the pilot to a remodeled space with formalized oversight and services. Now officially named the Fritz and Gladys Burns Experiential Studio, it is colloquially referred to as the Experiential Studio. The studio is a uniquely-designed classroom where instructors and students can learn in an interdisciplinary, library-integrated, hands-on environment. It includes a large teaching area and two breakout rooms. Users have access to prototyping materials, media-creation software, and collaboration tools. Evolving the studio from a makeshift pilot project to a permanent feature within the library involved a years-long process of planning and implementing, developing sustainable support, and ongoing assessment:

- 2013: studio vision and partnerships formed
- 2014–2019: courses taught and assessed in pilot studio
- 2015–2018: funding obtained and remodel plans formalized
- 2019: studio remodeled and administrative processes updated
- 2020: Experiential Studio opened; processes implemented, supported, and assessed

This chapter narratively discusses this process and reviews its successes and challenges. We write as current and former members of the studio's steering committee, relying on our own recollection, internal committee minutes and reports, and personal communication with other library personnel involved in the transition. We hope this case study helps other librarians successfully integrate similar spaces into their library services.

PLAN

In 2013, BYU hired Dr. Jennifer Paustenbaugh as the university librarian. Under her leadership, the library's strategic directions came to include "providing spaces that facilitate collaboration, experimentation, creation, and discovery [and] fostering deep collaboration that produces new knowledge (research) and facilitates learning."[9] Paustenbaugh's vision for transformed library spaces led to key campus partnerships.

Partnerships

Paustenbaugh and other library administrators connected with campus members of a newly formed CID Group.[10] The CID Group included faculty and administrative employees from advertising, business, education, and technology. Members believed that students need collaborative classroom experiences that develop critical thinking, creative problem solving, and interdisciplinary teamwork.[11] They were particularly interested in courses that used design thinking—an iterative process involving empathy, ideation, prototyping, and testing—to develop innovative solutions to real-world social problems. Furthermore, they wanted to find classrooms on campus that facilitated active learning.

Library administrators recognized their overlapping interests and saw an opportunity to develop this kind of classroom in the library. Both parties believed that if students from many disciplines took a course in the neutral territory of the library, it would foster a more collaborative environment.[12] For inspiration, Paustenbaugh, CID members, and others visited the design school at Stanford, well known for its focus on design thinking and interdisciplinary work.[13] Then, library administrators approved setting up the pilot CID Studio. Library stacks management removed several collection shelves to make room.[14] Facility managers put up temporary divider walls to create a teaching space and filled it with surplus chairs and tables. The walls enclosed several study rooms that became breakout rooms for group coursework. As the pilot studio launched, the partnership between library administrators and CID members translated into a studio steering committee. They put out a call to all faculty in the CID Group, inviting them to apply to teach a course in the studio starting January 2014. Applications needed to demonstrate that instructors would utilize design thinking and facilitate social innovation through project-based learning. Instructors were also asked to implement their courses with the help of librarians. Beyond reviewing applications, the steering committee helped plan assessments and advocated for future improvements.

The steering committee's composition has changed over time. Library administrators eventually took on oversight roles and asked subject librarians to be the primary library representatives on the committee. Non-library members have included teaching faculty and administrative employees, several who were affiliated with other experiential learning initiatives on campus (e.g., BYU's Ballard Center for Social Impact). At one point when BYU administrators provided feedback about the studio, they asked for clearer connections to campus curriculum goals and more committee involvement from teaching faculty.[15] After this, several non-library faculty took a greater lead on the steering committee. These faculty were still involved with the CID Group and in that realm redoubled work related to curriculum. Their efforts resulted in a design thinking minor at BYU, which became a clear indicator to BYU administrators that there would always be a set of courses well-suited for the studio.

Non-library committee members helped shape the vision and success of the studio through their leadership, enthusiasm, and expertise. However, they did not always understand library bureaucracy and communication channels; librarians on the committee noticed a disconnect forming between the steering committee and the library-at-large.[16] For example, these librarians heard library colleagues express concerns about the purpose of and long-term plans for the studio. They also noted that the steering committee had no formally approved charge, no guidelines for membership rotation, and no posted meeting minutes on the library's intranet. They advocated for regular communication between the committee and library leadership, worked to establish a charge and consistent record keeping,[17] and presented at several meetings to reconnect library employees with the history and vision of the studio.

Changes in the steering committee illustrate the real challenges of balancing interests and expectations when partnering with campus entities. On the one hand, BYU administrators wanted non-library faculty involvement in the studio because they and their students would be the primary users. On the other hand, library administrators needed library employees at the forefront of the committee to ensure library interests and policies were fully represented and acted upon and because the library would ultimately implement and support the space and associated services. Although the committee currently leans toward library oversight, relationships with non-library members remain collegial. Non-library members who are actively pursuing experiential learning in their teaching or other duties bring important perspectives and insights to the committee.

Funding

To determine the success of the pilot, the library's assessment team surveyed faculty and students during the first year of use; they conducted interviews and focus groups as well.[18] Across fifteen courses, participants were from nine disciplines, including business, education, fine arts and communication, and engineering. Results indicated that courses were learner-centered and collaborative. Students felt high levels of autonomy, motivation, and investment in their project-based coursework. However, assessment data identified the need for a larger walled-off space, cohesive but flexible furniture, and greater access to specialized tools and materials. While courses continued to use the pilot space, the steering committee began seeking means to expand and improve the studio. Between bureaucratic processes and other challenges, securing funding was a hurry-up-and-wait process lasting from 2015 to 2018.

Some committee members had connections with potential donors, and they brought one into discussions about the studio. The donor had strong opinions about the purpose of the studio and wanted it placed in a prominent location on the ground floor of the library.[19] Although the amount of funding and scale of improvements would have been substantial, library administrators became cautious about how donor relationships could affect the library's continued oversight of the studio. In the end, funding through this donor did not move forward. This situation highlights the importance of keeping library strategic priorities in mind during dialogue with donors; it is important to balance the need for funding with the need for libraries to maintain autonomy over their space.

Despite this setback, the steering committee worked with a BYU architect to develop floor plans and estimated costs for a remodel of the existing pilot space. They went through several iterations and incorporated informal feedback from faculty and students who had used the pilot studio. With the intention to pay for the remodel with residual donor funds from another project, library administrators requested approval to complete a capital improvement project of this size through BYU's 2016 annual resource planning.[20] Although approval from the resource planning team came in January 2017, several hurdles remained: ensuring a permanent studio would align with overall library building plans, getting permission from the donor to use their residual funds, and requesting funds for technology equipment.

First, knowing the overall library footprint was unlikely to increase, Paustenbaugh had brought in an architectural consultant team to study the building and provide guiding principles (e.g., improving sightlines) for phased remodeling. Because the studio remodel was already approved through the resource planning process, it was considered an active project that could move forward outside of the phased time-lines. However, library administrators formed a temporary planning team to discuss placement of services and future needs for the floor where the studio was situated. The studio was already near software training and media production services. Plans were in motion to move high-fidelity makerspace tools to that floor as well. Ulti-mately, the team saw no red flags associated with remodeling the studio in the same place, although it was clear that a full floor plan would need to facilitate synergy between the studio and nearby services.

Second, funds for technology equipment were not included in the architect's remodel estimate. BYU's Office of Information Technology (OIT) typically funds technology needs across campus and commits to periodic updates, but requests must go through an application process. Although OIT had approved a request to fund audiovisual technology in a portion of the studio, other requests had not been approved yet. Fortunately, another library technology project approved by OIT was deemed unnecessary. OIT leaders wanted to expand technology-rich collaborative spaces on campus, so they allowed these funds to be diverted to the studio, which ensured that the remodel and associated technology could advance on the same timeline.

Third, the library needed to go through the Philanthropies Department of the Church of Jesus Christ of Latter-day Saints to get permission to use the donor's residual funds.[21] The department had recently undergone an administrative reorgani-zation and policy changes. Adjustments to these changes slowed down communica-tion such that the donor liaison was unable to contact the donor representative until late 2018.[22] The donor representative communicated support within a month and requested that the studio be named after the donor family. On the final work order, construction, electrical, and furniture costs amounted to approximately $283,000.[23] This dollar amount does not include OIT technology costs; we did not get campus permission to share this detail.

Remodel

Behind this positive forward movement was a significant stressor: the resource planning approval expired after three years, or the end of 2019. At this point, there was a year left before the approval expired, which meant everything had to come together very quickly. The steering committee, architect, and library facility manag-ers reviewed the existing remodel plans and consulted informally with several faculty who had regularly taught in the studio. The 2,300 square foot plans included an active classroom with seating for up to fifty-four individuals, two breakout rooms with seating for about fifteen each, and a prototyping makerspace for low- to mid-fidelity supplies. See figures 4.1 and 4.2 for photographs of the remodeled studio. Although timing was not ideal, the team made several adjustments to benefit the studio in the long term:

Figure 4.1.   Pictures of the three rooms within the Experiential Studio. A is the active classroom. B is the collaborative breakout room. C is the presentation breakout room. Both breakout rooms are entered from the left-hand side of the active classroom. The locked storage room is at the far back left of the active classroom. The makerspace area is located at the top right of the active classroom.
Images by Matt Armstrong.

Figure 4.2.   Makerspace area located within the Experiential Studio's active classroom. Image A showcases open and lockable cubbies for storing student projects. Image B shows one side of the maker supply cart. Image C shows a wide-angle view of the makerspace which also includes a worktable, desk, and paper supplies.
Images by Matt Armstrong.

- They changed the orientation of the breakout rooms so each would have doors on two sides. Library patrons liked using the breakout rooms for group study, and instructors often had to ask them to leave before or during their course. This design change allowed people to enter the breakout rooms from within or outside the studio. Thus, when instructors only need the active classroom, patrons can enter the breakout rooms from outside the studio, which keeps these rooms in use and minimizes distraction.
- They added a storage room after users reminded them that many projects needed a locked space for project work.[24] The team recognized it could also house portable whiteboards and other supplies.
- Feedback from users also led the group to make one breakout room a flexible, collaborative space and the other a conference room where course groups could hold client meetings when partnering with outside entities on projects.

After solidifying the floor plan, the steering committee and architect made decisions about chairs, tables, and other flexible furniture, including what color palettes would create an energetic environment in the studio. They also chose a cart for prototyping supplies and planned shelving for paper supplies and cubby storage in the makerspace area.

One of the last details was deciding on a permanent name for the studio and getting it approved through several administrative levels. The steering committee disliked that the pilot became known by the acronym CID Studio because it lacked inherent meaning about the space's purpose. They brainstormed new names by consulting with library administrators, colleagues from nearby services, faculty who had taught in the studio, and library student employees. A 2016 address by BYU president Kevin J. Worthen also influenced the name selection. Worthen had called on-campus personnel to inspire learning and increase student participation in experiences like mentored research and internships.[25] He later established an Office of Experiential Learning to formalize this campus initiative. Worthen's call expanded the steering committee's vision for the studio.[26] When the pilot began, the committee recruited faculty to teach design thinking and social innovation courses in the studio. After his address, the committee recruited faculty to teach any type of active learning or project-based course. Besides aligning with campus priorities, the committee felt strongly that the broadened framework would increase the potential user base of the studio. The chosen name—the Fritz and Gladys Burns Experiential Studio—more clearly communicated this framework.

Many individuals helped make the remodeled studio a reality. Library administrators facilitated communication and funding opportunities with BYU administrators. The steering committee met frequently, remained optimistic through years of uncertainty, and communicated with stakeholders throughout the process. Library stacks management devoted many hours on a tight timetable to densely pack collections and remove shelving for the studio's expanded footprint. The architect patiently modified the remodel plans several times. Library facility managers worked behind the scenes and coordinated efforts with the construction team. Library and campus technology teams collaborated to install technology and make sure it would run smoothly. Overall, the entire planning process required vision, productive partnerships, a clear understanding of campus funding avenues and approval processes, and adapting to changing timelines and priorities.

IMPLEMENT

Once construction began in 2019, steering committee members turned their attention to streamlining administrative processes and developing outreach and marketing strategies. These preparations reflected the overall goal to see the studio utilized as much as possible when it reopened. Although some of these details may be specific to the Experiential Studio at BYU, they can help other librarians identify processes, policies, and strategies relevant to implementing analogous spaces in their libraries.

Administrative Processes

Because committee members had expanded what kinds of courses instructors could teach in the studio, they needed to revise the application. The new online application asks faculty to provide the following information:

- course information (e.g., general description of content)
- scheduling details (e.g., day/time of course, what studio rooms to reserve, special technology or makerspace needs)
- interdisciplinary nature of course (e.g., curriculum covering different disciplines, co-instructors from different disciplines, students from different majors)
- plans for library integration (e.g., use of library collections and services, collaboration with library personnel)
- use of experiential learning, creativity, and collaboration (e.g., use of pedagogies that encourage creativity, degree of collaborative project-based learning, how learning outcomes tie to experiential learning)

The application links directly to a rubric that details how the steering committee scores and weighs responses to each question. For example, within the library integration section, collaborating with library personnel—and communicating with them ahead of completing the application—scores higher than simply planning to use library collections. Beyond revising the application content, the steering committee planned more consistent timelines for sending out calls for applications, reviewing them, and announcing accepted courses.

Although priority for studio use has always gone to instructors teaching in the space, the committee did not want the studio sitting empty outside of scheduled courses. Library information technology personnel (LIT) adapted an online calendar system so library staff could block off time for scheduled courses and others could easily make one-time reservations. LIT also installed small screens outside of each studio room to display reservations for each day. Even when unscheduled, the studio remains unlocked so patrons can walk in and use the rooms.

To establish standard studio guidelines, the committee drafted a room use agreement and approved it through library administration. It provides general information about the studio rooms and what prototyping supplies, tools, and technology are available. It also covers scheduling parameters, food restrictions, instructions to reset the studio after use, and safety precautions about certain makerspace tools. Finally, the agreement indicates who to contact about studio questions.

Outreach and Marketing

Formalizing administrative details in parallel with construction took the guesswork out of how the committee would implement the new studio once it reopened. It allowed the committee to turn their attention to outreach and marketing. For an online presence, the committee wanted to transition away from using a LibGuide that was not intuitive to find from the main library webpage. Instead, the committee partnered with LIT to list the Experiential Studio on the library's "Places" webpage with a link to a studio homepage that describes the studio and provides a virtual tour. The homepage links out to the reservation system, teaching application, room use agreement, and related library services.[27] As an example of in-person outreach, the committee got a slot on the agenda of a campus-wide Experiential Learning Summit. One committee member briefly spotlighted the remodeled studio and its purpose; other committee members distributed informational fliers.

The committee decided to do a soft launch of the studio in January 2020 since they expected construction to end in late December and could not fit outreach opportunities into the holiday and semester break. Committee members specifically asked instructors who had taught in the pilot studio to apply so they could compare past and new experiences. Five courses used the remodeled studio that first semester, which included more than one hundred and fifty students from twenty different majors. Three courses hosted by the Design Department focused on creating technology-based user experiences, such as one course that worked on designing digital tools for emergency preparedness. The other two courses from Business and Entrepreneurship were team-based, one focusing on product development and the other on creating resources for international business. A soft launch, although not ideal, allowed the committee to troubleshoot technology, room resources, and scheduling.

Meanwhile, the steering committee began preparations for other outreach efforts in anticipation of a full launch in fall 2020. During the pilot, the steering committee primarily communicated to faculty through CID email lists. After the remodel, the committee started coordinating with the library public relations manager to send calls for applications through campus-wide communications. As had been done in the pilot, committee members discussed creating videos featuring aspects of various courses, not only to preserve a history of studio courses but also to use for promotion and outreach. Unfortunately, the COVID-19 pandemic changed everything. All BYU courses went online in March 2020 and continued online through spring and summer terms. By fall semester, BYU opted for online, hybrid, and limited in-person course offerings. This pattern continued through spring and summer of 2021. Some instructors with smaller courses applied and used the studio during this time but with limited seating for social distancing. When campus shifts to a new normal, the steering committee will pick up marketing and outreach plans so the studio becomes known as a thriving, innovative space for learning on campus.

SUPPORT

The steering committee knew their efforts alone could not fully support the studio beyond the pilot. They advocated for a position that could coordinate day-to-day operations and act as an ex-officio member of the committee. An opening for the library's online learning supervisor became available and library administrators approved adding studio support to the job description. The Experiential Studio and Online Learning supervisor started as a 3/4-time staff position, but library administrators made it a full-time administrative position once it became clear that the reopened studio would benefit from consistent oversight. Around this time, library administrators also set aside an ongoing supplies budget for the Experiential Studio and Online Learning. It started out as a shared budget of $1,000 and was later increased to $1,500. The majority of purchases have been for cables, adapters, and prototyping supplies. The supervisor also has $8,000 to pay a student assistant who helps with organizing the studio and supporting instructors.

Although the studio does not have a staffed help desk, the supervisor and student employee are easily accessible with offices located just outside the studio. Additionally, either the studio supervisor or student assistant attends the first few sessions of each class to make sure instructors are comfortable using the technology and makerspace in the studio. Studio staff also strive to increase the quality of experiential learning, library integration, and interdisciplinary collaboration within courses using the studio. Up to this point, their support has been sufficient; however, when the campus reaches new norms after the pandemic and studio use likely increases, the supervisor will request additional student employees.

Technology and Supplies

The studio contains eleven screens, wireless projection software, and Zoom connection features. Each breakout room has one screen, and the active classroom has nine. The system is built so that up to four individuals can wirelessly share personal devices to one screen. Any screen—even when displaying four personal devices—can be duplicated on the other eight screens in the room. Studio staff keep a large variety of low- and mid-fidelity prototyping materials stocked in the studio. Cardboard and foam board are staples, so studio staff regularly pull materials from recycling and retired library signs. Cutting tools are available (e.g., cardboard knives, rotary cutters) along with cardboard screws, hinges, and rivets. Other makerspace supplies include paper of various colors and weights, craft supplies (e.g., pipe cleaners), and office supplies (e.g., rubber bands, rulers). Digital prototyping options include free templates for websites, apps, and smartwatches, as well as digital drawing stencils. Students can use high-fidelity prototyping services (e.g., 3D printing, laser cutting) near the studio on the same floor.

Design courses are the most likely to use the makerspace area, like one business development course that used materials to iterate new product designs and prepare to market them. Other courses can creatively use the makerspace too. For instance, students in a language course utilized supplies to create a Korean market where students practiced vocabulary. In the future, studio staff hope to inspire more ways of using prototyping materials to enhance active learning. Storage options allow users to keep ongoing work in the studio, including brainstorming materials, prototypes, and portable whiteboards with content that needs to be saved. This kind of course support ensures that students and instructors do not need to keep track of and transport portions of their projects between class and home.

Experiential Learning

Many faculty who apply to teach in the studio are well focused on experiential learning, particularly because the collaborative and flexible atmosphere attracts instructors who already use active-learning pedagogies. One recent course involved students creating resources for international business students, including podcasts and tutorials. For courses that are not inherently experiential, there are many strategies to increase this type of learning. During the pilot, one mutually beneficial strategy was using library-centric projects to engage students in active learning.[28] For example, one course conducted an evaluation of learning spaces in the library, while another innovation course designed and tested a student study carrel that library facility managers later used to replace old carrels throughout the library.

Studio staff have also encouraged experiential learning by holding workshops during course sessions. Workshop topics have included systems design, design thinking, and problem framing. Recently, the studio supervisor tested training on soft skills such as empathy, team building, and self-awareness. Since course instructors need to focus on delivering curriculum content, providing these short, interspersed discussions and assignments received positive feedback. As studio staff and librarians liaise with more instructors and other campus entities interested in the studio, these kinds of co-teaching opportunities will increase and facilitate experiential learning.

Library Integration

The studio's purpose goes beyond providing a space for coursetime. A primary objective of hosting the studio in the library is to connect instructors with library resources and build collaborations with library personnel. The kinds of connections just described demonstrate how library integration can enrich and deepen learning experiences. The revised application encourages instructors to put more thought into library integration, but there is still room to grow. Some instructors have a difficult time expanding beyond the librarian's traditional role of giving one brief presentation on databases. Several efforts have been helpful in achieving our goal of increasing library integration:

- *Providing feedback with application results.* The steering committee recently began providing feedback about the quality of applications rather than a simple approval or rejection. Courses that generally meet studio criteria but need more specific plans (e.g., about library integration strategies) are accepted on a contingent basis.
- *Planning consultation meetings.* Planning pre-semester meetings with instructors whose applications were accepted, the studio supervisor, and subject librarians has been valuable. Instructors send their syllabi, then everyone discusses ideas for library integration and collaboration. The next improvement is developing how the studio supervisor will follow up on plans and commitments related to library integration.
- *Being present in courses.* The studio supervisor plans to spend time in each course throughout the semester, not just during the first few sessions. Seeing students in action helps the supervisor identify opportunities for library-course support and collaborations. For example, the studio supervisor learned one course was unaware of nearby media production and software training, so he connected students with those services.

Interdisciplinary Collaboration

The most interdisciplinary courses are those with instructors from multiple departments and students from multiple majors. However, given the structure of university curriculum, not many instructors can officially team teach, and not all courses fit required or elective courses for multiple majors. In these cases, instructors can invite guest lecturers to teach different disciplinary perspectives. Instructors can also develop course projects that require drawing on skills and knowledge from multiple disciplines. Likewise, the steering committee plays a role in establishing the interdisciplinary atmosphere of the studio. One way the committee does this is by maintaining the studio's neutrality. Rules on not saving anything on installed white boards or walls help students feel comfortable to fully use the studio. Additionally, the committee strives to accept a variety of courses into the studio. The new application rubric weights a course that has never used the studio slightly more than a repeat course. Courses taught in the studio since the reopening are more diverse (e.g., nursing, history, Korean), which suggests that adapted administrative processes, outreach strategies, and support efforts are working.

ASSESS

As library spaces have evolved, assessment of these spaces has come to the forefront. It is critical to demonstrate the value of changes and the impact on users.[29] The steering committee has established qualitative and quantitative methods to assess the remodeled studio and is particularly cognizant of assessing the three guiding principles of library integration, experiential learning, and interdisciplinarity. In addition to observations and tracking usage of various studio features and supplies, the committee distributes surveys to instructors and students after a semester in the studio.

Survey comments from students and instructors are enthusiastic about the new studio and have provided constructive feedback. For example, students and instructors expressed concern with the glass walls and doors that separate the breakout rooms from the active classroom. The glass promotes cohesion within the studio, but the doors have already needed repairs and they do not provide as much soundproofing as other materials. Instructors tend to reserve the whole studio no matter the size of their course so that others do not reserve the breakout rooms and cause noise disturbances. Instructors also requested a projector—an item included in the original remodel plan that went unfunded by OIT—to supplement use of monitors throughout the studio. Based on feedback received each semester, the steering committee has made immediate changes (e.g., buying adaptor cords for screens, adding requested maker supplies, improving onboarding for instructors) and has advocated for resources that will enhance the space (e.g., soundproofing, more storage options, better audio for a blended learning environment). These examples demonstrate that even after a major remodel, fine tuning is still necessary. Future assessment plans include evaluating the functionality of the scheduling screens and the usefulness of the studio website. In totality, early assessments by faculty, students, and librarians are overwhelmingly positive.

CONCLUSION

BYU's Office of Experiential Learning states, "Experiential learning at BYU should develop disciplinary skills and practice, foster broad, boundary-crossing professional competencies, inspire greater learning, and imbue habits of lifelong learning in students. We believe these purposes are most successfully achieved through a process of intention, integration, and reflection."[30] The purpose of the Experiential Studio is intentionally aligned with university aims and initiatives. Being situated in the library allows greater integration between disciplines and with library collections, resources, and services. Students completing coursework in the studio have increased opportunities to reflect on how their experiences impact professional skills and ongoing learning. In the one and a half years since the remodel launch, instructors have taught a total of nineteen courses in the Experiential Studio, about six each semester. Eleven of these were courses that had never used the studio during the pilot. About five hundred students from more than forty majors participated across all courses. We look forward to seeing the growth and potential of the studio outside of the pandemic. Reflecting on our experiences, we offer the following takeaways and recommendations for those at any stage of developing a similar space:

- Map your goals to broader campus initiatives.
- Identify partners who advocate passionately for your project.
- Balance diverse needs while maintaining library oversight.
- Communicate regularly with stakeholders at all levels.
- Determine appropriate funding avenues and explore these early on.
- Pilot your project and make meaningful adjustments.
- Develop clear policies and procedures for implementation.
- Focus on deep library integration into the user experience.
- Collect data over time that measures the project's value and impact.
- Document user experiences for outreach and preservation purposes.
- Expect uncertainty, delays, and changing needs.
- Stay optimistic and persevere.

Developing experiential learning spaces within libraries is a significant undertaking that encompasses evolving partnerships, multiple planning iterations, and trial-and-error implementation efforts. Once established, these spaces require ongoing critical assessment to keep the initiative relevant and ensure it meets user needs. These efforts are rewarding, however, and place libraries in a position to have a greater influence on students learning outcomes and professional advancement.

NOTES

1. Shea-Tinn Yeh and Zhiping Walter, "Critical Success Factors for Integrated Library System Implementation in Academic Libraries: A Qualitative Study," *Information Technology and Libraries* 35, no. 3 (2016): 27–42.

2. James G. Neal, "The Entrepreneurial Imperative: Advancing from Incremental to Radical Change in the Academic Library," *portal: Libraries and Academy* 1, no. 1 (2001): 2, doi: 10.1353/pla.2001.0006.

3. Ibid.

4. Mary M. Somerville and Lydia Collins, "Collaborative Design: A Learner-Centered Library Planning Approach," *The Electronic Library* 26, no. 6 (2008): 805, doi:10.1108 /02640470810921592.

5. Emma Cross and Ryan Tucci, "The Emerging Technology Collection at Carleton University Library: Supporting Experiential Learning in the University Curriculum," *Partnership:*

The Canadian Journal of Library and Information Practice and Research 12, no. 1 (2017): 1–19, doi:10.21083/partnership.v12i1.3917; Fay Q. Miller, "Encountering Relatable Information in Experiential Learning Spaces: A Partnership Framework for Research Information Specialists and Early Career Researchers," *Journal of Documentation* 75, no. 3 (2019): 517–29.

6. Somerville and Collins, "Collaborative Design," 805.

7. Patrick Tod Colegrove, "Editorial Thoughts: Rise of the Innovation Commons," *Information Technology and Libraries* 34, no. 3 (2015): 2–5, doi.org/10.6017/ital.v34i3.8919; Janet L. Balas, "Do Makerspaces Add Value to Libraries?" *Computers in Libraries* 32, no. 9, (2012): 33; Anne Marie Lynn Davis, "Current Trends and Goals in the Development of Makerspaces at New England College and Research Libraries," *Information Technology and Libraries* 37, no. 2 (June 2018): 94–117, doi:10.6017/ital.v37i2.9825; Anne Wong and Helen Partridge, "Making as Learning: Makerspaces in Universities," *Australian Academic & Research Libraries* 47, no. 3 (2016): 143–59, doi:10.1080/00048623.2016.1228163; Cross and Tucci, "The Emerging Technology Collection at Carleton University Library," 1–19; Mark Bieraugel and Stern Niell, "Ascending Bloom's Pyramid: Fostering Student Creativity and Innovation in Academic Library Spaces," *College & Research Libraries* 78, no. 1 (2017): 35–52, doi:10.5860/crl.78.1.35; Wes Edens and Allison Leaming Malecki, "Entrepreneurship Initiatives in Academic Libraries," *Public Services Quarterly* 16, no. 2 (2020): 107–11, doi:10.1 080/15228959.2020.1736707; Jared Hoppenfeld and Elizabeth Malafi, "Engaging Entrepreneurs in Academic and Public Libraries," *Reference Services Review* 43, no. 3 (2015): 379–99, doi:10.1108/RSR-02-2015-0011; Risa M. Lumley, "A Coworking Project in the Campus Library: Supporting and Modeling Entrepreneurial Activity in the Academic Library," *New Review of Academic Librarianship* 20, no. 1 (2014): 49–65, doi.org/10.1080/13614533.201 3.850101; Jennifer Nichols, Marijel Melo, and Jason Dewland, "Unifying Space and Service for Makers Entrepreneurs, and Digital Scholars," *portal: Libraries and the Academy* 17, no. 2 (2017): 363–74, doi:10.1353/pla.2017.0022.

8. Holt Zaugg and Melissa C. Warr, "Integrating a Creativity, Innovation, and Design Studio within an Academic Library," *Library Management* 39, nos. 3/4 (2018): 172–87, doi .org/10.1108/LM-09-2017-0091; Peter J. Rich, Richard E. West, and Melissa Warr, "Innovating How We Teach Collaborative Design Through Studio-Based Pedagogy," in *Educational Media and Technology Yearbook*, eds. M. Orey and R. Branch (Switzerland: Springer, 2015): 147–63, doi:10.1007/978-3-319-14188-6_11; Richard E. West, "Breaking Down Walls to Creativity through Interdisciplinary Design," *Educational Technology* 56, no. 6 (2016): 47–52, https://www.jstor.org/stable/44430508l; Elizabeth Smart, Emily S. Darowski, and Matt Armstrong, "Inspiration, Ideation, and Implementation: Library Integration with Design Thinking Courses," in *Recasting the Narrative: The Proceedings of the ACRL 2019 Conference*, eds. Dawn M. Mueller, (Cleveland, OH: Association of College & Research Libraries, April 10–13, 2019): 356–68, http://www.ala.org/acrl/sites/ala.org.acrl/files/content/conferences /confsandpreconfs/2019/InspirationIdeationImplementation.pdf.

9. "Strategic Directions," BYU Library, accessed April 30. 2021, http://lib.byu.edu /about/strategic-directions/.

10. Smart, Darowski, and Armstrong, "Inspiration, Ideation, and Implementation," 359; Zaugg and Warr, "Integrating a Creativity," 173–74.

11. S. Adams Becker et al., *NMC Horizon Report: 2017 Higher Education Edition* (Austin, TX: The New Media Consortium, 2017): 6–9, http://www.learntechlib.org/p/174879/; Michael Jones et al., "The Hard Truth about Soft Skills: What Recruiters Look for in Business Graduates," *College Student Journal* 50, no. 3 (Fall 2016): 424–26.

12. Smart, Darowski, and Armstrong, "Inspiration, Ideation, and Implementation," 359.

13. Ibid.

14. Zaugg and Warr, "Integrating a Creativity," 174.

15. C. Jeffrey Belliston, email messages to author, April 19 and April 26, 2021.

16. Smart, Darowski, and Armstrong, "Inspiration, Ideation, and Implementation," 363–64.

17. Ibid., 361–64.

18. Zaugg and Warr, "Integrating a Creativity," 176–79.

19. Belliston, email messages to author, April 19 and April 26, 2021.

20. Ibid.

21. Cali O'Connell, email messages to author, April 21 and April 26, 2021.

22. Ibid.

23. Allen Arnoldsen, email message to author, August 2, 2021.

24. This change happened after the Smart et al. (2019) report.

25. Kevin J. Worthen, "Inspiring Learning" (speech, Brigham Young University, Provo, UT, August 22, 2016), https://speeches.byu.edu/talks/kevin-j-worthen/inspiring-learning/; David A. Kolb, *Experiential Learning: Experience as the Source of Learning and Development* (Cranbury, NJ: Pearson Education, 2014): 3–4.

26. Smart, Darowski, and Armstrong, "Inspiration, Ideation, and Implementation," 361.

27. "Places," BYU Library, accessed April 30, 2021, https://lib.byu.edu/places/; "Experiential Studio," BYU Library, accessed April 30, 2021, https://lib.byu.edu/services/experiential-studio/.

28. Smart, Darowski, and Armstrong, "Inspiration, Ideation, and Implementation," 364.

29. Gricel Dominguez, "Beyond Gate Counts: Seating Studies and Observations to Assess Library Space Usage," *New Library World* 117, nos. 5/6 (2016): 321–28, doi:10.1108/NLW-08-2015-0058; Joseph R. Matthews, "Assessing Library Contributions to University Outcomes: The Need for Individual Student Level Data," *Library Management* 33, nos. 6/7 (2012): 389–402, doi:10.1108/01435121211266203; Luiza Baptista Melo, Tatiana Sanches, Gaspar Matos, and Patrícia Torres, "Assessing the Impact of Academic Library Spaces on Users' Behavior with the ISO16439: 2014 (E)," *Qualitative and Quantitative Methods in Libraries* 6, no. 3 (2017): 467–78, http://hdl.handle.net/10451/37371; Susan E. Montgomery, "Library Space Assessment: User Learning Behaviors in the Library," *The Journal of Academic Librarianship* 40, no. 1 (2014): 70–75, doi:10.1016/j.acalib.2013.11.003; Danuta A. Nitecki, "Space Assessment as a Venue for Defining the Academic Library," *The Library Quarterly: Information, Community, Policy* 81, no. 1 (2011): 27–59, https://www.jstor.org/stable/10.1086/657446.

30. "Cycle of Inspiring Learning," BYU Experiential Learning and Internships, Brigham Young University, accessed April 30, 2021, https://experience.byu.edu/cycle-of-inspiring-learning.

BIBLIOGRAPHY

Balas, Janet L. "Do Makerspaces Add Value to Libraries?" *Computers in Libraries* 32, no. 9 (2012): 33.

Becker, Samantha Adams, M. Cummins, A. Davis, A. Freeman, C. Glesinger Hall, and V. Ananthanarayanan. *NMC Horizon Report: 2017 Higher Education Edition* (Austin, TX: The New Media Consortium, 2017). https://www.learntechlib.org/p/174879/.

Bieraugel, Mark, and Stern Neill. "Ascending Bloom's Pyramid: Fostering Student Creativity and Innovation in Academic Library Spaces." *College & Research Libraries* 78, no. 1 (2017): 35–52. doi:10.5860/crl.78.1.35.

BYU Experiential Learning and Internships. "Cycle of Inspiring Learning." Accessed April 30, 2021. https://experience.byu.edu/cycle-of-inspiring-learning.

BYU Library. "Experiential Studio." Accessed April 30, 2021. https://lib.byu.edu/services /experiential-studio/.

———. "Places." Accessed April 30, 2021. https://lib.byu.edu/places/.

———. "Strategic Directions." Accessed April 30, 2021. https://lib.byu.edu/about/strategic -directions/.

Colegrove, Patrick Tod. "Editorial Thoughts: Rise of the Innovation Commons." *Information Technology and Libraries* 34, no. 3 (2015): 2–5. doi:10.6017/ital.v34i3.8919.

Cross, Emma, and Ryan Tucci. "The Emerging Technology Collection at Carleton University Library: Supporting Experiential Learning in the University Curriculum." *Partnership: The Canadian Journal of Library and Information Practice and Research* 12, no. 1 (2017): 1–19. doi:10.21083/partnership.v12i1.3917.

Davis, Ann Marie L. "Current Trends and Goals in the Development of Makerspaces at New England College and Research Libraries." *Information Technology and Libraries* 37, no. 2 (June 2018): 94–117. doi:10.6017/ital.v37i2.9825.

Dominguez, Gricel. "Beyond Gate Counts: Seating Studies and Observations to Assess Library Space Usage." *New Library World* 117, nos. 5/6 (2016): 321–28. doi:10.1108 /NLW-08-2015-0058.

Edens, Wes, and Allison Leaming Malecki. "Entrepreneurship Initiatives in Academic Libraries." *Public Services Quarterly* 16, no. 2 (2020): 107–11. doi:10.1080/15228959.2020.17 36707.

Hoppenfeld, Jared, and Elizabeth Malafi. "Engaging with Entrepreneurs in Academic and Public Libraries." *Reference Services Review* 43, no. 3 (2015): 379–99. doi:10.1108/RSR -02-2015-0011.

Jones, Michael, Cindi Baldi, Carl Phillips, and Avinash Waikar. "The Hard Truth about Soft Skills: What Recruiters Look for in Business Graduates." *College Student Journal* 50, no. 3 (Fall 2016): 422–28.

Kolb, David A. *Experiential learning: Experience as the Source of Learning and Development.* Cranbury: NJ: Pearson Education, 2014.

Lumley, Risa M. "A Coworking Project in the Campus Library: Supporting and Modeling Entrepreneurial Activity in the Academic Library." *New Review of Academic Librarianship* 20, no. 1 (2014): 49–65. doi:10.1080/13614533.2013.850101.

Matthews, Joseph R. "Assessing Library Contributions to University Outcomes: The Need for Individual Student Level Data." *Library Management* 33, nos. 6/7 (2012): 389–402. doi:10.1108/01435121211266203.

Melo, Luiza Baptista, Tatiana Sanches, Gaspar Matos, and Patrícia Torres. "Assessing the Impact of Academic Library Spaces on Users' Behavior with the ISO16439: 2014 (E)." *Qualitative and Quantitative Methods in Libraries* 6, no. 3 (2017): 467–78. http://hdl .handle.net/10451/37371.

Miller, Faye Q. "Encountering Relatable Information in Experiential Learning Spaces: A Partnership Framework for Research Information Specialists and Early Career Researchers." *Journal of Documentation* 75, no. 3 (2019): 517–29. doi:10.1108/JD-05-2018-0069.

Montgomery, Susan E. "Library Space Assessment: User Learning Behaviors in the Library." *The Journal of Academic Librarianship* 40, no. 1 (2014): 70–75. doi:10.1016/j .acalib.2013.11.003.

Neal, James G. "The Entrepreneurial Imperative Advancing from Incremental to Radical Change in the Academic Library." *portal: Libraries and the Academy* 1, no. 1 (2001): 1–13. doi:10.1353/pla.2001.0006.

Nichols, Jennifer, Marijel Melo, and Jason Dewland. "Unifying Space and Service for Makers, Entrepreneurs, and Digital Scholars." *portal: Libraries and the Academy* 17, no. 2 (2017): 363–74. doi:10.1353/pla.2017.0022.

Nitecki, Danuta A. "Space Assessment as a Venue for Defining the Academic Library." *The Library Quarterly* 81, no. 1 (2011): 27–59. https://www.jstor.org/stable/10.1086/657446.

Rich, Peter J., Richard E. West, and Melissa Warr. "Innovating How We Teach Collaborative Design Through Studio-Based Pedagogy." In *Educational Media and Technology Yearbook: Volume 39*, edited by M. Orey and R. Branch, 147–63. Switzerland: Springer, 2015. doi:10.1007/978-3-319-14188-6_11.

Smart, Elizabeth, Emily S. Darowski, and Matt Armstrong. "Inspiration, Ideation, and Implementation: Library Integration with Design Thinking Courses." In *Recasting the Narrative: The Proceedings of the ACRL 2019 Conference*, edited by Dawn M. Mueller, 356–68. Cleveland: Association of College and Research Libraries, 2019. http://www.ala .org/acrl/sites/ala.org.acrl/files/content/conferences/confsandpreconfs/2019/Inspiration IdeationImplementation.pdf.

Somerville, Mary M., and Lydia Collins. "Collaborative Design: A Learner-Centered Library Planning Approach." *The Electronic Library* 26, no. 6 (2008): 803–20. doi:10.1108 /02640470810921592.

West, Richard E. "Breaking Down Walls to Creativity Through Interdisciplinary Design." *Educational Technology* 56, no. 6 (2016): 47–52. http://www.jstor.org/stable/44430508.

Wong, Anne, and Helen Partridge. "Making as Learning: Makerspaces in Universities." *Australian Academic & Research Libraries* 47, no. 3 (2016): 143–59: doi:10.1080/00048623 .2016.1228163.

Worthen, Kevin J. "Inspiring Learning." Speech given at the BYU University Conference, Provo, UT, August 22, 2016. https://speeches.byu.edu/talks/kevin-j-worthen/inspiring -learning/.

Yeh, Shea-Tinn, and Zhiping Walter. "Critical Success Factors for Integrated Library System Implementation in Academic Libraries: A Qualitative Study." *Information Technology and Libraries* 35, no. 3 (2016): 27–42. doi:10.6017/ital.v35i3.9255.

Zaugg, Holt, and Melissa C. Warr, "Integrating a Creativity, Innovation, and Design Studio within an Academic Library." *Library Management* 39, nos. 3/4 (2018): 172–87. doi:10.1108/LM-09-2017-0091.

5

Creative Deconstruction

Using Zines to Teach the ACRL Framework

Stefanie Hilles

When the Association of College and Research Libraries (ACRL) replaced the prescriptive "Information Literacy Competency Standards for Higher Education" (the Standards) with the "Framework for Information Literacy for Higher Education" (the Framework) in 2016, it created new opportunities to engage with information literacy in non-traditional ways. Instead of a checklist of skills to master, there are now core competencies and threshold concepts that both encourage and allow us to go beyond simple skills acquisition and teach students information literacy through creative making and experiential learning. The Framework has been described as more "flexible,"[1] "theoretical,"[2] and "constructivist"[3] than its predecessor and an opportunity to depart from the traditional "sage on the stage" method of instruction.[4] In fact, the Framework's "development seems to be, in part, a recognition and response to criticisms that those earlier conceptualizations [the Standards] were too focused on tasks and processes rather than critical thinking."[5] The more abstract and conceptual nature of the Framework, as well as its emphasis on transferable threshold concepts, broaden the idea of what information literacy instruction is and how it can be taught.

In this chapter, I will investigate how one-shot zine making workshops can be used to teach students in a variety of disciplines the frames "Authority is Constructed and Contextual" and "Information Has Value" through the creative process, experiential learning, and visual literacy. Zines, which students make as part of the session, not only provide excellent opportunities for experiential learning[6] while engaging in the creative process, they are tied to critical theory, critical pedagogy, and critical information literacy. Likewise, the Framework is also linked to these critical practices, especially the frames "Authority is Constructed and Contextual" and Information Has Value." Both zines and these two frames, like critical theory, are inherently intertwined with power, privilege, and authority. "Zines give librarians an opportunity to 'move away from the demonstration of technical search processes and simplistic claims that certain sources are 'authoritative' because authorities have decided they are' and to make the questioning of authority explicit."[7] Zine-making also teaches students that the information they create is valuable and initiates discussions about copyright, fair use, and public domain.[8]

THE "ACRL FRAMEWORK FOR INFORMATION LITERACY," EXPERIENTIAL LEARNING, AND CREATIVITY

While there was hesitancy and concern about embracing the Framework when it was first published,[9] a 2021 study found that 71 percent of librarians now use it as the basis for their information literacy instruction.[10] A survey of the recent literature demonstrates how experiential learning can be adopted to teach the Framework, from using Reddit to show "Authority is Constructed and Contextual[11] to having students submit academic conference proposals to teach "Scholarship as Conversation."[12]

"The ACRL Framework encourages creativity and offers an opportunity to simultaneously teach visual literacy, information literacy, and transferrable design skills through information creation."[13] Art librarians, who often work with creative populations, provide precedent for how creative processes and experiential learning can be used to teach the Framework. In fact, Garcia and Labatte argue that the Framework's threshold concepts make information literacy more applicable and relatable to art students than ever before.[14] Examples include using digital images of medieval manuscripts and the creation of embroidery patterns to teach "Searching as Strategic Exploration" and "Information Has Value,"[15] relating studio critique practices to "Scholarship as Conversation,"[16] applying "Scholarship as Conversation" to art made in the classroom to understand its "artistic, cultural, historical, political, and social contexts,"[17] and using the Framework to teach critical visual literacy skills to overturn stereotypes typically found in comics and animation.[18] Creative practices like these can be applied to disciplines outside the studio arts to engage students with information literacy in non-traditional ways. Keeran, Bowers, Crowe, and Kor demonstrate that creative practices can be expanded beyond the art classroom when they use the frames "Authority is Constructed and Contextual," "Research as Inquiry," and "Searching as Strategic Exploration" to teach non-studio art students how to read images.[19] Zines are another way that we can creatively engage students in a variety of disciplines with the Framework.

THE "ACRL FRAMEWORK FOR INFORMATION LITERACY," ZINES, AND THEIR RELATIONSHIP TO CRITICAL PEDAGOGY AND CRITICAL INFORMATION LITERACY

Critical theory investigates how social, societal, cultural, economic, and political structures operate within systems of power, privilege, and oppression. The use of critical theory as a guiding principle, and its subsets critical pedagogy and critical information literacy, predate ACRL's adoption of the Framework, "arriv[ing] as part of the maturing of the information literacy movement, a natural growth in understanding literacy as a contested social construction, rather than as a naturally occurring phenomenon."[20] Many librarians who practiced critical approaches to pedagogy and information literacy embraced the Framework upon its arrival,[21] seeing it as liberating.[22]

"Authority is Constructed and Contextual," one of the most heavily debated frames,[23] is where critical theory is most clearly seen in the Framework. This frame is "rooted in critical information literacy and invites both students and educators to interrogate the context surrounding information and reveal the systems of privilege and oppression at work."[24] Previous to the Framework, students were given a checklist to confirm authority but weren't asked to think about how authority is granted and participates in power structures.[25] "Critical information literacy problematizes these traditional criteria by evaluating authority through a lens that takes into account sociopolitical factors that prioritize certain voices over others along lines of race, gender, class, and abledness, among others."[26]

According to the Framework, when students internalize the idea that "Authority is Constructed and Contextual," they "recognize that authoritative content may be packaged formally or informally and may include sources of all media types" and "question traditional notions of granting authority and recognize the value of diverse ideas and worldviews."[27] Zines are an excellent medium for exploring these ideas because they serve as voices for counterculture movements, exist outside traditional publishing systems, and challenge power structures. In addition, their do-it-yourself (DIY), collage-like aesthetic is informal and directly deconstructs authority though design elements. Zines also teach students that information is political.[28]

Like "Authority is Constructed and Contextual," "Information Has Value" is indebted to critical theory and critical information literacy, "acknowledg[ing] that bias, privilege, and power are implicated in the production of information."[29] According to this frame, students should "understand how and why some individuals or groups of individuals may be underrepresented or systematically marginalized within the systems that produce and disseminate information" and "see themselves as contributors to the information marketplace rather than only consumers of it."[30] An awareness of copyright, fair use, and public domain are also aspects of this frame. Through zines, "students can examine how knowledge is constructed, and the social positions and intent of those who produce and disseminate information."[31] Students can also learn about copyright, fair use, and the public domain, either through discussion on how they relate to zines in general or through experiential learning and asking students to apply copyright, fair use, and public domain considerations to their own zines.

WHAT IS A ZINE?

In his often-cited book, *Notes from Underground: Zines and the Politics of Alternative Culture*, Stephen Duncombe defines zines as, "noncommercial, nonprofessional, small-circulation magazines which their creators produce, publish, and distribute themselves."[32] Zines are handmade, often with a DIY or collage-like aesthetic, and they use both text and image to make meaning. Content can either be original, as in created by the author or artist, or appropriated from another source, as with collage. Subjects are various, running the gambit from diary-like perzines (short for personal zines), to music, creative writing, art, comics, politics, and social justice. Zines can be written by a single author or created as a collaborative project. While many zines have a photocopied aesthetic and are bound with staples, some are more elaborate and include things like inserts, stitched binding, and other printing processes, like risograph, a type of printer/photocopier known for its bright, yet pastel color palette and associated with zinemaking. Most importantly for their application to the Framework, both historical and contemporary zines exist outside popular publishing systems, are not motivated by profit, and are associated with countercultures and alternative voices. As a result, zines are free to both question authority and subvert power and privilege, linking them to critical theory and the frames "Authority is Constructed and Contextual" and "Information Has Value."

The Comet, published in Chicago in the 1930s, is typically acknowledged as the first zine. Edited by Raymond Palmer, it was intended as a way for science fiction fans to communicate; the letters section of the zine was especially important.[33] However, while *The Comet* might be the first zine proper, independent self-publishing intended to subvert the status quo and advance counterculture ideas has been around since the beginning of mainstream publishing in the Western world. Not long after the invention of movable type in the West[34] and the printing of the *Gutenberg Bible* from 1454 to 1455, Martin Luther self-published his *Ninety-Five Theses* in 1517 starting the Protestant Reformation. The broadsides and pamphlets of both the American and French Revolutions, like Thomas Paine's *Common Sense* from 1775–1776, which argued for American independence from British rule, are other examples.[35] In fact, Seth Friedman, publisher of *Factsheet Five*, an influential zine review publication, is quoted in *Time* as saying, "Benjamin Franklin made zines. He published his own thoughts using his own printing presses. It wasn't the magazine business. He did it all on his own.[36] Dada, Surrealist, and Futurist artist journals of the early 1900s are also seen as predecessors.[37] Since their inception, zines have featured alternative voices and counterculture ideas.

After their official birth with the publication of *The Comet* in the 1930s, zines became a central part of the 1970s punk movement, which also defined itself as being anti-authority. Usually focused on music and the punk scene, the punks' DIY style consisting of collage, Sharpie marker, and a photocopied aesthetic, has become closely associated with zine construction.[38] Queercore, an offshoot of the punk movement, started publishing queer zines in the 1980s. In the 1990s, Riot Grrrl zines continued the punk aesthetic, DIY attitude, and emphasis on music but took a more specifically feminist approach. In their pages, women are called to challenge patriarchal norms and assert their power by publishing their own zines and starting bands. Contemporary zines have continued activist discourses featuring voices from the LGBTQ+ and BIPOC communities. Examples are numerous and online zine collections dedicated to LGBTQ+ and BIPOC people and topics like the Queer Zine Archive Project (QZAP) and the People of Color (POC) Zine Project now exist, spreading zine culture online and continuing to challenge mainstream values while advocating for change. Both the inherent qualities of zines and their histories make them excellent resources for teaching the *Framework*, particularly the frames "Authority is Constructed and Contextual"[39] and "Information Has Value."[40] Zines focus on counterculture ideas and exist outside mainstream publishing, giving them the ability to recognize, challenge, and deconstruct power, privilege, and authority, central tenets to both critical theory and these frames.

ZINE COLLECTIONS AND INSTRUCTION IN LIBRARIES

Zines' place in libraries is well established. They have been collected since the 1990s,[41] and, by 2018, at least one hundred and fifty American public and academic libraries housed zines in archives or circulating collections.[42] Zines have been used for engagement and instruction in libraries, both in and outside the classroom,[43] in a variety of ways, including: zine readings,[44] zine-making workshops,[45] circulating zine-making kits,[46] and using zines as primary sources.[47] Zines by transgender folks have been used for discussions of Jeffery Eugenies *Middlemarch*, Riot Grrrl zines have been used to teach feminism, and students have used zines as mediums to reinterpret past writing assignments.[48]

More recently, zine instruction both in and outside of libraries, much like the Framework, has been seen through the lens of critical theory. Creasap compared zine-making to feminist pedagogy,[49] a subset of critical pedagogy, and Congdon and Blandy use zines to teach postmodernism in art,[50] which also takes a critical approach to power and privilege while deconstructing traditional authority. Articles that don't reference critical theory explicitly, argue that zines support its main tenants: Moshoula and Desyllas note that zines teach students about "power hierarchies";[51] Wan argues that zines "can open student's eyes to other outlets of information, showing alternative sources and forcing students to see how the accessible information that is often taken for fact also has origins and agendas";[52] and Potter and Sellie state that zines are, "a site for collaborative and critical teaching about the political nature of information."[53] Zines and the frames "Authority is Constructed and Contextual" and "Information Has Value" are rooted in critical theory, critical pedagogy, and critical information literacy. By teaching with zines, we are also teaching these lessons in the Framework.

ZINE INSTRUCTION AT MIAMI UNIVERSITY LIBRARIES

Zine instruction at Miami University Libraries started with a small, uncatalogued collection donated by previous librarians who held drop-in zine-making sessions for students. I began formal instruction in 2017, after a professor expressed interest in using the collection to introduce zines for an assignment requiring students to reinterpret one of their previous writings in a new medium. Through word of mouth and advertising on faculty listservs, workshops expanded beyond English and creative writing classes and now include a range of disciplines like women and gender studies, teacher education, disability studies, and communication design. Student groups focused on social justice issues, like Spectrum and Colored Lens, have also requested workshops for their events. Given the success of the workshops, I organized the informal zine collection into a teaching archive aimed at supporting instruction named the Wertz Art and Architecture Library Zine Archive.

Workshops begin with a think-pair-share activity where students interact with zines from the archive and make observations about their qualities, whether that be subject matter, aesthetics, intended audience, and/or construction. Five zines are placed on a table of three to four students. Students get one minute to look at each zine, passing them around their table. After viewing the zines individually, students discuss their observations with their group and we engage in a classwide discussion. Following the think-pair-share activity, I give students a short lecture on zine histories, topics, and aesthetics.

The remainder of the workshop is dedicated to zine-making. I provide supplies like glue, markers, crayons, scissors, stencils, and collage materials and show students how to fold an 8.5" × 11" sheet of paper into an 8-page mini-zine. I also tailor workshops to specific instructor requests. Some classes make a collaborative zine instead of individual ones or focus on a particular topic relevant to course content. For example, women and gender studies classes will have more of an emphasis on the Riot Grrrl movement while art classes learn more about artist journals as zine predecessors. Workshops don't require any advance work on the part of the students, although if a professor requests a pre-workshop reading, I give them the first chapter of Stephen Duncombe's *Notes from the Underground: Zines and the Politics of Alternative Culture* as an introduction.

After students make their zines, they have the option of adding them to the archive. Created as a collection to support workshop instruction, I divided the archive into two main series, a teaching collection composed of purchased and donated hardcopy zines for instructional use and a parallel collection that preserves the zines students make during workshops. Since students often want to keep their hardcopies, their zines are digitized and uploaded to a collection in CONTENTdm, the library's digital collection management system, by the digital collections librarian so originals can be returned. Both series are described at the item level and entered into ArchiveSpace, the library's archival information management system, to aid discoverability.

I designed the components of the workshop to teach students that "Authority is Constructed and Contextual" and "Information Has Value." During the think-pair-share portion, students learn from and about authorities and voices not found in mainstream media. The lecture, which discusses zine histories, exposes students to counterculture ideas and movements. The lecture also focuses on how zine aesthetics reinforce the deconstruction of authority and how appropriation can be used as a tool for subversion, which teaches students visual literacy skills.

Zine aesthetics play an important role in how zines teach the frame "Authority is Constructed and Contextual." Zines are, after all, both art objects and literary texts. Punk design, the DIY, collage-like aesthetic most associated with zines, intentionally undermines authority. During the 1970s, the International Typographic Style reigned supreme in mainstream media. Characterized by the use of the grid as an organizing principle, straightforward objective photography, easy to read typography, and an absence of illustration or decoration, the International Typographic Style valued clarity, logic, and order.[54] Punk design challenges these principles. The use of collage obscures objective photography and the grid as an organizing principle, illustration and decoration are heavily used, and legibility is challenged by handwriting, decorative fonts, and crossed-out words.

Punk aesthetics often rely on a principle called *détournement*, which uses appropriation to turn "known ideas or images into something new and different with the intent to communicate subversive ideas in a familiar guise."[55] In class, we discuss Jamie Reid's famous image on the cover of the Sex Pistol's album *God Save the Queen* as an example of *détournement* being used to undermine authority. The image shows the official Silver Jubilee portrait released by Buckingham Palace for Queen Elizabeth's twenty-fifth year on the throne with the words "God Save the Queen" and "Sex Pistols" collaged over the Queen's eyes and mouth. Reid's use of letters cut from magazines reminds the viewer of ransom notes and overturns the portrait's authority. Placing the text over the Queen's eyes and mouth, which have been ripped away, further suggests that some kind of violence has taken place. The words "God Save the Queen," something that would normally be said in reverence, now has an air of menace. Meaning has been deconstructed.

By discussing how zine aesthetics function, students also learn visual literacy skills. Here, visual literacy "may be said to include not only textual competence but material competence, and ability to read the semiotics of the concrete forms that embody, shape, and condition the meanings of texts."[56] Zine aesthetics can also lead to discussions about how to "critically evaluate media images."[57] Understanding how images make meaning is an essential skill for twenty-firsty-century learners.

After I introduce zines, their histories, and their aesthetics, students make their own. Through the creative process and experiential learning, students not only study power and authority, they take the process one step further by actively deconstructing these narratives. Students "see themselves as contributors to the information marketplace rather than only consumers of it,"[58] one of the dispositions of the frame "Information Has Value." Experiential learning also transcends the "sage on the stage" teaching mentality and facilitates students becoming active agents in their own learning. It allows them to participate in "the active cultural production of information as opposed to passive cultural consumption of that knowledge," one of the goals of the Framework.[59] Moreover, zine-making itself aligns with feminist pedagogy, one of the subsets of critical pedagogy, in three ways: through participatory learning, validation of personal experience, and the development of critical thinking skills.[60]

Once their zines are complete, I give students the option to add them to the digital archive, introducing the elements of copyright and public domain, additional tenants of the frame "Information Has Value." This is a fully voluntary process. Participating students grant Creative Commons Licenses to their zines using a form created in partnership with the scholarly communications librarian. This allows students to choose how, or even if, their zine is added to the collection, reinforcing the idea that their zine, the information they just created, has value. Asking students to add to the archive also emphasizes the fact that they are producers, not just consumers, of information. As Veitch points out, "The zine library allows me to reinforce this by telling students: we want your writing—*your* ideas—for the library collection."[61] Even if students' zines aren't added to an archive, zines still offer opportunities for the discussion of copyright and intellectual property. Since they exist outside traditional publishing systems, many zine creators are anti-copyright. Zines' use of appropriation could also be used to discuss fair use principles as they pertain to criticism and parody. Below, I discuss three specific zine-making assignments that ask students to think about how "Authority is Constructed and Contextual" and "Information Has Value."

Feminist Remix

Feminist Remix was a zine project I did with a women and gender studies class. The workshop followed the typical format, starting with a think-pair-share activity and lecture. During the making portion, each student received a *Vogue* magazine from the 1940s to 1970s weeded from the library's collection. Students were given some time to browse through the magazine for patriarchal and heternormative messages and tasked with making a zine that deconstructed these messages through collage. Below are pages from a zine, *No You Don't Complete Me*, where a student overturned the "women need to be in a relationship to have value" trope they found in their *Vogue*.

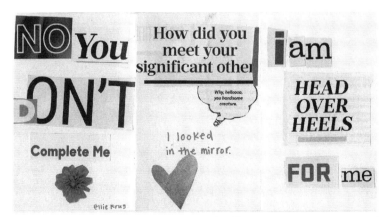

Figure 5.1. *No You Don't Complete Me*, by Ellie Krug, 2019; Wertz Art and Architecture Library Zine Archive, Miami, Ohio.

Deconstructing Disability

Deconstructing Disability was a zine project I did with a disability in literature course that also followed the typical workshop structure. Students came to the library for a zine-making workshop and used what they learned to make longer zines for their final group project and presentation. Each group created a zine that took the perspective of one of the characters with a disability they read about in their course, providing students with the opportunity to experience disability through narrative voice, challenge ableist power structures, and share the experience with others.

Oppressive Advertising

Oppressive Advertising was a zine project I did with a communication design class. Like "Deconstructing Disability," the workshop was in preparation for a larger group project. Students researched the histories of racist and sexist advertising mascots, like Aunt Jemima, Uncle Ben, and Chiquita Banana, and were tasked with overturning and denouncing these stereotypes through their zines. However, unlike the previous two examples, this workshop was held online due to campus shutdowns caused by COVID-19. I gave students links to digital zines for the think-pair-share activity in lieu of hardcopy zines and had them complete their small group discussions in Zoom breakout rooms. Students' final zines, which used bright, yet pastel color palettes reminiscent of risograph printing, were also digital. Instead of making zines during the workshop, I assigned student groups an artwork that used appropriation as a subversive tool, like Kehinde Wiley's *Napoleon Crossing the Alps* from 2005 and Ester Hérnandez's *Sun Mad Raisins* from 1982, then asked them to deconstruct how authority was challenged through visual elements and present their arguments to the class. Below are pages from the zine, *Betty Crocker's Keeping a Woman in the Kitchen*, which appropriates the style of a cookbook to confront the brand's sexism.

Figure 5.2. *Betty Crocker's Keeping a Woman in the Kitchen,* by Emilie Abrams, Cassidy Gebhart, Gracie Glickman, and Coleen Sallot, 2020; Wertz Art and Architecture Library Zine Archive, Miami, Ohio.

Transitioning from in-person to online zine instruction presented some challenges. First and foremost, students weren't able to interact with zines as objects; they missed out on the opportunity to turn pages, feel textures, see staples, and experience the "zine-ness" of zines. Finding digital surrogates was difficult. Many online zine archives had scanned their zines in such a way that they were excellent for printing but lost pagination when viewed online. Issuu, which uses a flipbook format, turned out to be the best place to source digital zines. However, this setback proved fruitful in the long run, as it forced me to reevaluate the way students' zines were scanned for Miami's collection. I, too, had originally scanned zines for printing, not for viewing online and, after realizing the drawbacks to this method, worked with the digital collections librarian to install a flipbook viewer in CONTENTdm. Now our zine collection is formatted for both printing and online viewing.

The other obstacle was online making. During in-person zine workshops, students are able to converse with one another while creating, bounce ideas back and forth, and learn from each other in an organic way. In person, students can casually talk to the person sitting next to them. If they speak while making in Zoom, they are the focus of the entire class. One of the reasons this workshop example didn't involve zine-making until students' final projects was that previous online zine workshops where students were tasked with making zines didn't foster the same community as in-person workshops, resulting in students just silently making zines over Zoom. While I was able to find workable solutions for the think-pair-share activity and lecture, I struggled to translate the making component of zine workshops online.

ASSESSMENT AND FEEDBACK

I assess students both formally and informally to see if they have gained an understanding of the frames "Authority is Constructed" and Contextual and "Information Has Value." Informally, the think-pair-share activity, classroom discussions, and decision to add their zine to the archive show whether students are engaged. Formally, the zines students create, either during the workshops or as part of larger class projects, are also assessed. The vast majority of students are successful; their zines show an understanding of both mainstream power narratives and how they can be challenged, thus demonstrating that "Authority is Constructed and Contextual" and "Information Has Value." "While they [students] may not have been previously aware of zines, they intuitively understand the unconventional, insurgent, and spontaneous structure that characterizes them."[62]

Effective assessment requires knowledge of how power structures function in society. Taking *Betty Crocker's Keeping a Woman in the Kitchen* as an example, we can see that students have used the style and language of a Betty Crocker cookbook and recipe in their zine. The Betty Crocker character was created in 1921 as a female cooking authority. Washburn-Crosby, Betty Crocker's parent company, started receiving cooking questions. Samuel Gale, the advertising director, believed women would be more comfortable taking cooking advice from a woman than someone in his all-male department.[63] Thus, Betty Crocker was born as a female stand-in for male authority. The 1920s also saw the women's suffrage movement and successful ratification of the Nineteenth Amendment allowing women to vote, a direct threat to the patriarchy. Betty Crocker's cookbook, specifically aimed at women, helps to neutralize this threat by reinforcing the patriarchal idea that women belong in the kitchen, cooking for and taking care of men. Using this format to question male authority with a sarcastic recipe for the idea housewife demonstrates that students have understood how the cookbook's authority relates to larger societal power structures while deconstructing them through satire.

Students who have attended workshops frequently request them for their own classes or student groups. Some students have donated zines to the archive, either from their own collections or ones they made after workshop instruction, and one student was inspired to write her senior capstone paper on the history of zines. Faculty also find the workshops beneficial; it's rare for them to request a single workshop. Many return, either on a semesterly basis or when they are teaching another class where zine-making fits the curriculum.

THE FURTHER VALUE OF TEACHING WITH ZINES

Zine workshops also add diversity to library collections and instruction because they feature underrepresented viewpoints. By doing so, zines further relate to and reinforce the frames "Authority is Constructed and Contextual" and "Information Has Value." By including zines in our collections, we demonstrate that different authorities exist and have value, confront biases and traditions that say these voices and objects don't belong in our collections or curriculum, and recognize the role librarians and libraries play in granting authority. Moreover, diversity also relates to critical theory, critical pedagogy, and critical information literacy.

> It is a main tenet of critical information literacy that information literacy instruction should resist the tendency to reinforce and reproduce hegemonic knowledge, and instead nurture students' understandings of how information and knowledge are informed by unequal power relations based on class, race, gender, and sexuality.[64]

Others have argued that zines can go beyond merely making students aware of power relationships and effect social change by "attempt[ing] to dismantle oppressive forms of knowledge systems."[65] Veitch agrees, "zines . . . share resources for creating change, bringing a critical lens into the library where personal narratives are often muffled or muted by the scholarly discourse in which they are embedded."[66] When we teach with zines we not only acknowledge the ways traditional authority is intertwined with privilege and power structures but also introduce students to materials and voices that seek to create social change and show them how they can make these objects themselves.

THE FUTURE OF ZINE INSTRUCTION

The "ACRL Framework for Information Literacy" is inherently tied to critical theory, critical pedagogy, and critical information literacy. The frames "Authority is Constructed and Contextual" and "Information Has Value" are rooted in how power, privilege, and oppression function within information systems. These qualities align with zine culture, histories, and making. By using zines in library instruction, we teach the Framework through experiential learning and the creative process. Moreover, when "we teach our students critical information literacy skills by way of zines, they learn to critically evaluate the establishment itself."[67] Zines have the potential to inspire and affect real change.

Many additional opportunities exist for zines to continue to address diversity, equity, and inclusion (DEI) in the library classroom and beyond. I am currently planning a workshop where zines will be used alongside abolitionist newspapers from Ohio and historical alternative publications created by Miami students housed in special collections in an experience design studio course. Students will learn about these local, underground publications and, after taking the Implicit Association Test (IAT) created by scientists at Harvard University, the University of Virginia, and the University of Washington,[68] create zines addressing their own biases. I will also be using zines, along with artist books and Miami's Native American Women's Playwright Archive, as examples of how art can be used to create social change for a class called "Arts, Advocacy, and Activism." As this chapter has shown, zines are an excellent way to teach the frames "Authority is Constructed and Contextual" and "Information Has Value," thereby demonstrating the power structures inherent in our society. As our profession begins to reckon with its own role in silencing marginalized voices, zine collections and zine instruction are some ways we take steps to create truly diverse, equitable, and inclusive libraries.

NOTES

1. Ian Beilin, "Beyond the Threshold: Conformity, Resistance and the ACRL Information Literacy Framework for Higher Education," *In the Library with the Lead Pipe*, February 25, 2015, http://www.inthelibrarywiththeleadpipe.org/2015/beyond-the-threshold-conformity -resistance-and-the-aclr-information-literacy-framework-for-higher-education/.

2. Ma Lei Hsieh, Patricia H. Dawson, and Sharon Q. Yang, "The ACRL Framework Successes and Challenges since 2016: A Survey," *The Journal of Academic Librarianship* 47, no. 2 (March 2021): 1, https://doi.org/10.1016/j.acalib.2020.102306.

3. Nancy M. Foasberg, "From Standards to Frameworks for IL: How the ACRL Framework Addresses Critiques of the Standards," *Portal: Libraries and the Academy* 15, no. 4 (2015): 702, https://doi.org/10.1353/pla.2015.0045.

4. Colleen Burgess, "Teaching Students, Not Standards: The New ACRL Information Literacy Framework and Threshold Crossings for Instructors," *Partnership: The Canadian Journal of Library and Information Practice and Research* 10, no. 1 (2015): 4, https://doi.org/10.21083 /partnership.v10i1.3440.

5. Laura Saunders and John Budd, "Examining Authority and Reclaiming Expertise," *The Journal of Academic Librarianship* 46, no. 1 (January 2020): 3, https://doi:10.1016/j.acalib.2019.102077.

6. Moshoula Capous Desyllas and Allison Sinclair, "Zine-Making as a Pedagogical Tool for Transformative Learning in Social Work Education," *Social Work Education* 33, no. 3 (June 2013): 296, https://doi.org/10.1080/02615479.2013.805194.

7. Robin Potter and Alycia Sellie, "Zines in the Classroom: Critical Librarianship and Participatory Collections," in *Critical Library Pedagogy Handbook Volume 2: Lesson Plans*, eds. Nicole Pagowsky and Kelly McElroy (Chicago: Association of College and Research Libraries, 2016), 117.

8. Susan Thomas, "Zines for Teaching: A Survey of Pedagogy and Implications for Academic Librarians," *portal: Libraries and the Academy* 18, no. 4 (2018): 751, https://doi.org/10.1353/pla.2018.0043.

9. Beilin, "Beyond the threshold."

10. Hsieh, Dawson, and Yang, "The ACRL Framework Successes and Challenges," 3.

11. Anna M. White, "Reddit as an Analogy for Scholarly Publishing and the Constructed, Contextual Nature of Authority," *Communications in Information Literacy* 13, no. 2 (December 2019): 147–63, https://doi.org/10.15760/comminfolit.2019.13.2.2.

12. Erin Durnham, "Tune Up Your #Critlib Toolkit: Scaffolding Critical Information Literacy Discussions with Upper Level Students" (presentation, LOEX Conference of the Library Orientation Exchange, online, May 11–13, 2020).

13. Krystyna K. Matusiak, Chelsea Heinbach, Anna Harper, and Michael Bovee, "Visual Literacy in Practice: Use of Images in Students' Academic Work," *College & Research Libraries* 80, no. 1 (January 2019): 135, https://doi:10.5860/crl.80.1.123.

14. Larissa Garcia and Jessica Labatte, "Threshold Concepts as Metaphors for the Creative Process: Adapting the Framework for Information Literacy to Studio Art Classes," *Art Documentation: Journal of the Art Libraries Society of North America* 34, no. 2 (September 2015): 237–38, https://doi.org/10.1086/683383.

15. Julie Carmen, "Makerspaces: Combining Information Literacy with Pattern Design for Fiber Art through Digital Images," *Library Trends* 69, no. 3 (2021): 585–611, https://doi.org/10.1353/lib.2021.0005.

16. Larissa Garcia and Ashley Peterson, "Who Invited the Librarian? Studio Critiques as a Site for Information Literacy Education," *Art Libraries Journal* 42, no. 2 (2017): 73–79, https://doi.org/10.1017/alj.2017.6.

17. Lijuan Xu and Nestor Gil, "Librarians as Co-Teachers and Curators: Integrating Information Literacy in a Studio Art Course at a Liberal Arts College," *Art Documentation: Journal of the Art Libraries Society of North America* 36, no. 1 (March 2017): 126, https://doi.org/10.1086/691376.

18. Stephanie Grimm and Amanda Meeks, "Break the Stereotype! Critical Visual Literacy in Art and Design Librarianship," *Art Documentation: Journal of the Art Libraries Society of North America* 36, no. 2 (September 2017): 173–90, https://doi.org/10.1086/694238.

19. Peggy Keeran, Jennifer Bowers, Katherine Crowe, and Kristen Kor. "Using Visual Materials to Teach Information Literacy Outside the Arts Curriculum," *Art Documentation: Journal of the Art Libraries Society of North America* 38, no. 1 (March 2019): 141–58, https://doi.org/10.1086/702894.

20. James Elmborg, "Foreward," *Critical Library Pedagogy Volume 1: Essays and Workbook Activities*, eds. Nicole Pagowsky and Kelly McElroy (Chicago: Association of College and Research Libraries, 2016), ix.

21. Emily Drabinski, "A Kairos of the Critical: Teaching Critically in a Time of Compliance," *Comminfolit* 11, no. 1 (2017): 78, https://doi.org/10.15760/comminfolit.2017.11.1.35.

22. Beilin, "Beyond the threshold."

23. Andrea Baer, "It's All Relative?: Post-Truth Rhetoric, Relativism, and Teaching on 'Authority as Constructed and Contextual,'" *College & Research Libraries News* 79, no. 2 (February 1, 2018): 72, https://doi.org/10.5860/crln.79.2.72.

24. Kevin Seeber, "This Is Really Happening: Criticality and Discussions of Context in ACRL's Framework for Information Literacy," *Comminfolit* 9, no. 2 (2015): 159, https://doi.org/10.15760/comminfolit.2015.9.2.192.

25. Jonathan Cope, "Information Literacy and Social Power," in *Critical Library Instruction: Theories and Method*, eds. Maria T. Accardi, Emily Drabinski, and Alana Kumbier (Duluth, MN: Library Juice Press, 2010): 16.

26. Cope, "Information Literacy and Social Power," 16.

27. Association of College and Research Libraries (ACRL), "Framework for Information Literacy for Higher Education," 2016, http://www.ala.org/acrl/standards/ilframework.

28. Potter and Sellie, "Zines in the Classroom," 117.

29. Foasberg, "From Standards to Frameworks for IL," 709.

30. ACRL, "Framework for Information Literacy."

31. Dawn Stahura, "Filling in the Gaps: Using Zines to Amplify the Voices of People Who Are Silenced in Academic Research," in *The Feminist Reference Desk: Concepts, Critiques, and Conversations*, ed. Maria T. Accardi (Sacramento: Library Juice Press, 2017), 182.

32. Stephen Duncombe, *Notes from the Underground: Zines and the Politics of Alternative Culture* (Portland: Microcosm Publishing, 2017), 9.

33. "The Comet," *Zinewiki*, July 31, 2012, https://zinewiki.com/wiki/The_Comet.

34. Movable type was invented in China c. 1045 by Pi Sheng.

35. Alison Piepmeier, *Girl Zines: Making Media, Doing Feminism* (New York: New York University Press, 2009), 215.

36. David M. Gross, "Zine but Not Heard: Edgy and Underground, Homemade Fanzines Mine Punk-Rock Love and Crepe-Sole Shoes to Make Words on Paper Radical Again," *Time*, September 5, 1994, http://content.time.com/time/subscriber/article/0,33009,981403,00.html.

37. Seth Friedman, *The Factsheet Five Zine Reader* (New York: Three Rivers Press, 1997): 4.

38. While the photocopier is widely associated with zine making, many punk zines and flyers were actually offset printed.

39. Alana Kumbier, interview by Robert Schroeder, *Critical Journeys: How 14 Librarians Came to Embrace Critical Practice* (Sacramento: Library Juice Press, 2014): 164; Thomas, "Zines for Teaching," 751.

40. Ibid.

41. Potter and Sellie, "Zines in the Classroom," 117.

42. Anne Hays, "Zine Authors' Attitudes about Inclusion in Public and Academic Library Collections: A Survey-Based Study," *The Library Quarterly* 88, no. 1 (January 2018): 60. https://doi.org/10.1086/694869.

43. For a literature review of the ways zines have been used in libraries, see Thomas, "Zines for Teaching," 737–58.

44. Madeline Veitch, "Read a Zine, Then Make One, Then Catalog it: Creating a Zine Library at SUNY New Paltz," *The Reading Room* 2, no. 1 (Fall 2016): 93.

45. Potter and Sellie, "Zines in the Classroom," 117–24.

46. Veitch, "Read a Zine," 93.

47. Kelly Wooten, "Zines as Primary Sources," in *Critical Library Pedagogy Handbook Volume 2: Lesson Plans*, eds. Nicole Pagowsky and Kelly McElroy (Chicago: Association of College and Research Libraries, 2016), 95–102.

48. Kelly Wooten, "Feminist Archives: Zines at the Bingham Center," *Feminist Collections* 33, no. 2 (Spring, 2012): 9–12.

49. Kimberly Creasap, "Zine-Making as Feminist Pedagogy," *Feminist Teacher* 24, no. 3 (2014): 155–68, https://doi.org/10.5406/femteacher.24.3.0155.

50. Kristin G. Congdon and Doug Blandy, "Zinesters in the Classroom: Using Zines to Teach about Postmodernism and the Communication of Ideas," *Art Education* 56, no. 3 (May 1, 2003): 44–52.

51. Moshoula and Desyllas, "Zine-Making as a Pedagogical Tool," 296.

52. Amy J. Wan, "Not Just for Kids Anymore: Using Zines in the Classroom," *The Radical Teacher* 55 (Spring 1999): 18.

53. Potter and Sellie, "Zines in the Classroom," 117.

54. Philip B. Meggs and Alston W. Purvis, *Megg's History of Graphic Design* (Hoboken, NJ: John Wiley & Sons, 2016): 397.

55. Stephen J. Eskilson, *Graphic Design: A New History* (New Haven, CT: Yale University Press, 2012): 339.

56. Michele Moyland and Lane Stiles, "Introduction," in *Reading Books: Essays on the Material Text in Literature in America*, eds. Michele Moyland and Lane Stiles (Amherst: University of Massachusetts Press, 1996), 2.

57. Creasap, "Zine-Making as Feminist Pedagogy," 157.

58. ACRL, "Framework for Information Literacy."

59. Stahura, "Filling in the Gaps," 183–84.

60. Creasap, "Zine-Making as Feminist Pedagogy," 155–68.

61. Veitch, "Read a Zine," 87.

62. Congdon and Blandy, "Zinesters in the Classroom," 45.

63. Tori Avery, "Who was Betty Crocker?" last modified February 15, 2003, https://www.pbs.org/food/the-history-kitchen/who-was-betty-crocker/.

64. Beilin, "Beyond the Threshold."

65. Stahura, "Filling the Gaps," 175–76.

66. Veitch, "Read a Zine," 88.

67. Stahura, "Filling in the Gaps," 184.

68. The IAT can be found at https://implicit.harvard.edu/implicit/takeatest.html.

BIBLIOGRAPHY

Association of College and Research Libraries (ACRL). "Framework for Information Literacy for Higher Education." 2016. http://www.ala.org/acrl/standards/ilframework.

Avery, Tori. "Who was Betty Crocker?" Last modified February 15, 2013. https://www.pbs.org/food/the-history-kitchen/who-was-betty-crocker/.

Baer, Andrea. "It's All Relative? Post-Truth Rhetoric, Relativism, and Teaching on 'Authority as Constructed and Contextual.'" *College & Research Libraries News* 79, no. 2 (February 1, 2018): 72–75. https://doi.org/10.5860/crln.79.2.72.

Beilin, Ian. "Beyond the Threshold: Conformity, Resistance and the ACRL Information Literacy Framework for Higher Education." *In The Library with the Lead Pipe* (February 25, 2015). http://www.inthelibrarywiththeleadpipe.org/2015/beyond-the-threshold-conformity -resistance-and-the-aclr-information-literacy-framework-for-higher-education/.

Burgess, Colleen. "Teaching Students, Not Standards: The New ACRL Information Literacy Framework and Threshold Crossings for Instructors." *Partnership: The Canadian Journal of Library and Information Practice and Research* 10, no. 1 (2015): 1–6. https://doi.org/10 .21083/partnership.v10i1.3440.

Carmen, Julie. "Makerspaces: Combining Information Literacy with Pattern Design for Fiber Art through Digital Images." *Library Trends* 69, no. 3 (2021): 585–611. https://doi .org/10.1353/lib.2021.0005.

Creasap, Kimberly. "Zine-Making as Feminist Pedagogy." *Feminist Teacher* 24, no. 3 (2014): 155–68. https://doi.org/10.5406/femteacher.24.3.0155.

"The Comet." *Zinewiki*. Last modified July 31, 2012. https://zinewiki.com/wiki/The_Comet.

Congdon, Kristin G., and Doug Blandy. "Using Zines to Teach about Postmodernism and the Communication of Ideas." *Art Education* 56, no. 3 (May 2003): 44–52. https://www .tandfonline.com/doi/abs/10.1080/00043125.2003.11653501?journalCode=uare20.

Cope, Jonathan. "Information Literacy and Social Power." In *Critical Library Instruction: Theories and Method*, edited by Maria T. Accardi, Emily Drabinski, and Alana Kumbier, 13–27. Duluth, MN: Library Juice Press, 2010.

Desyllas, Moshoula Capous, and Allison Sinclair. "Zine-Making as a Pedagogical Tool for Transformative Learning in Social Work Education." *Social Work Education* 33, no. 3 (June 2013): 296–316. https://doi:10.1080/02615479.2013.805194.

Drabinski, Emily. "A Kairos of the Critical: Teaching Critically in a Time of Compliance." *Comminfolit* 11, no. 1 (2017): 76–94. https://doi.org/10.15760/comminfolit.2017.11.1.35.

Duncombe, Stephen. *Notes from the Underground: Zines and the Politics of Alternative Culture*. Portland, OR: Microcosm Publishing, 2017.

Durnham, Erin. "Tune Up Your #Critlib Toolkit: Scaffolding Critical Information Literacy Discussions with Upper Level Students." Presentation at LOEX Conference of the Library Orientation Exchange, online, May 11–13, 2020.

Elmborg, James. "Foreward." In *Critical Library Pedagogy Volume 1: Essays and Workbook Activities*, edited by Nicole Pagowsky and Kelly McElroy, vii–xiii. Chicago: Association of College and Research Libraries, 2016.

Eskilson, Stephen J. *Graphic Design: A New History*. New Haven, CT: Yale University Press, 2012.

Foasberg, Nancy M. "From Standards to Frameworks for IL: How the ACRL Framework Addresses Critiques of the Standards." *portal: Libraries and the Academy* 15, no. 4 (2015): 699–717. https://doi.org/10.1353/pla.2015.0045.

Friedman, Seth. *The Factsheet Five Zine Reader*. New York: Three Rivers Press, 1997.

Garcia, Larissa, and Ashley Peterson. "Who Invited the Librarian? Studio Critiques as a Site of Information Literacy Education." *Art Libraries Journal* 42, no. 2 (April 2017): 73–79. https://doi:10.1017/alj.2017.6.

Garcia, Larissa, and Jessica Labatte. "Threshold Concepts as Metaphors for the Creative Process: Adapting the Framework for Information Literacy to Studio Art Classes." *Art Documentation: Journal of the Art Libraries Society of North America* 34, no. 2 (September 2015): 235–48. https://doi:10.1086/683383.

Grimm, Stephanie, and Amanda Meeks. "Break the Stereotype! Critical Visual Literacy in Art and Design Librarianship." *Art Documentation: Journal of the Art Libraries Society of North America* 36, no. 2 (September 2017): 173–90. https://doi:10.1086/694238.

Gross, David M. "Zine but Not Heard: Edgy and Underground, Homemade Fanzines Mine Punk-Rock Love and Crepe-Sole Shoes to Make Words on Paper Radical Again." *Time*, September 5, 1994. http://content.time.com/time/subscriber/article/0,33009,981403,00.html.

Hays, Anne. "Zine Authors' Attitudes about Inclusion in Public and Academic Library Collections: A Survey-Based Study." *The Library Quarterly* 88, no. 1 (January 2018): 60–78. https://doi.org/10.1086/694869.

Hsieh, Ma Lei, Patricia H. Dawson, and Sharon Q. Yang. "The ACRL Framework Successes and Challenges since 2016: A Survey." *The Journal of Academic Librarianship* 47, no. 2 (March 2021): 1–10. https://doi.org/10.1016/j.acalib.2020.102306.

Keeran, Peggy, Jennifer Bowers, Katherine Crowe, and Kristen Kor. "Using Visual Materials to Teach Information Literacy Outside the Arts Curriculum." *Art Documentation: Journal of the Art Libraries Society of North America* 38, no. 1 (Spring 2019): 141–58. https://doi.org/10.1086/702894.

Kumbier, Alana. Interview by Robert Schroeder. In *Critical Journeys: How 14 Librarians Came to Embrace Critical Practice*, 155–73. Sacramento: Library Juice Press, 2014.

Matusiak, Krystyna, Chelsea Heinbach, Anna Harper, and Michael Bovee. "Visual Literacy in Practice: Use of Images in Students' Academic Work." *College & Research Libraries* 80, no. 1 (2019): 123–39. https://doi:10.5860/crl.80.1.123.

Meggs, Philip B., and Alston W. Purvis. *Megg's History of Graphic Design.* Hoboken, NJ: John Wiley & Sons, 2016.

Moyland, Michele, and Lane Stiles. "Introduction." In *Reading Books: Essays on the Material Text in Literature in America,* edited by Michele Moyland and Lane Stiles, 1–15. Amherst: University of Massachusetts Press, 1996.

Piepmeier, Alison. *Girl Zines: Making Media, Doing Feminism.* New York: New York University Press, 2009.

Potter, Robin, and Alycia Sellie. "Zines in the Classroom: Critical Librarianship and Participatory Collections." In *Critical Library Pedagogy Handbook Volume 2: Lesson Plans*, edited by Nicole Pagowsky and Kelly McElroy, 117–24. Chicago: Association of College and Research Libraries, 2016.

Saunders, Laura, and John Budd. "Examining Authority and Reclaiming Expertise." *The Journal of Academic Librarianship* 46, no. 1 (January 2020): 1–8. https://doi.org/10.1016/j.acalib.2019.102077.

Seeber, Kevin. "This Is Really Happening: Criticality and Discussions of Context in ACRL's Framework for Information Literacy." *Comminfolit* 9, no. 2 (2015): 157–63. https://doi.org/10.15760/comminfolit.2015.9.2.192.

Stahura, Dawn. "Filling in the Gaps: Using Zines to Amplify the Voices of People Who Are Silenced in Academic Research." In *The Feminist Reference Desk: Concepts, Critiques, and Conversations*, edited by Maria T. Accardi, 175–88. Sacramento: Library Juice Press, 2017.

Thomas, Susan. "Zines for Teaching: A Survey of Pedagogy and Implications for Academic Librarians." *portal: Libraries and the Academy* 18, no. 4 (2018): 737–58. https://doi.org/10.1353/pla.2018.0043.

Veitch, Madeline. "Read a Zine, Then Make One, Then Catalog it: Creating a Zine Library at SUNY New Paltz. *The Reading Room* 2, no. 1 (Fall 2016): 83–101.

Wan, Amy J. "Not Just for Kids Anymore: Using Zines in the Classroom." *The Radical Teacher* 55 (Spring 1999): 15–19.

White, Anna M. "Reddit as an Analogy for Scholarly Publishing and the Constructed, Contextual Nature of Authority." *Communications in Information Literacy* 13, no. 2 (December 2019): 147–63. https://doi.org/10.15760/comminfolit.2019.13.2.2.

Wooten, Kelly. "Feminist Archives: Zines at the Bingham Center." *Feminist Collections* 33, no. 2 (Spring, 2012): 9–12.

Wooten, Kelly. "Zines as Primary Sources." In *Critical Library Pedagogy Handbook Volume 2: Lesson Plans*, edited by. Nicole Pagowsky and Kelly McElroy, 95–102. Chicago: Association of College and Research Libraries, 2016.

Xu, Lijuan, and Nestor Gil. "Librarians as Co-Teachers and Curators: Integrating Information Literacy in a Studio Art Course at a Liberal Arts College." *Art Documentation: Journal of the Art Libraries Society of North America* 36, no. 1 (March 2017): 122–36. https://doi:10.1086/691376.

6

LEGO™, the Library, and a Mastodon Tusk

Undergraduate Research Partnerships in Chemistry

Anne Marie Gruber and Dr. Joshua Sebree

University of Northern Iowa (UNI) is a teaching-focused regional comprehensive university in Cedar Falls, Iowa, with approximately 8,600 full-time equivalency (FTE) students, primarily undergraduate. UNI's Rod Library, UNI Museum (a unit of Rod Library), and the Department of Chemistry and Biochemistry have formed a unique and ongoing partnership to support undergraduate student research in an upper-level course, Instrumental Analysis. Students enrolled in the course, with structured support from the instructor (Sebree) and the chemistry/biochemistry liaison librarian (Gruber), write and carry out individual research proposals using scientific and interdisciplinary literature. Past projects have included chemical analysis of collections housed by the UNI Museum such as a mastodon tusk, historic textiles, and World War II-era brassworks.

After both peer review and review by the instructor and librarian, students revise their proposals and perform the proposed lab work. The project is designed to show students what life as a research primary investigator is like, from developing a grant proposal to giving a poster presentation. Students gain valuable hands-on experience working with lab equipment and are able to use the research instruments themselves after some training that is built into the course. A more typical model would have students work with existing data acquired by the professor. Proposing and carrying out an original research proposal increases the students' scientific literacy. The class is important in providing students with a hands-on research experience that does not require an additional course enrollment or time commitment during a semester break when most students need paid employment. The case study in this chapter focuses on integration of multiple library services within the CURE-based research project in Sebree's upper-level chemistry course, filling a gap in the literature while providing a model that could be adapted to various levels and disciplines.

LITERATURE REVIEW

Course-Based Undergraduate Research Experience (CURE)

This course-based undergraduate research experience (CURE) model is supported by the literature as effective in reducing barriers to research experiences. Because it is incorporated within an existing class, students do not need to worry about juggling the time and financial commitment of unpaid undergraduate research opportunities. Therefore, it can help provide experience for those who would be otherwise under-represented.[1] The literature demonstrates that the CURE model has the potential to help students develop stronger skills in science literacy and data analysis.[2] Waterman and Heemstra, in their 2018 report *Expanding the CURE Model: Course-based Undergraduate Research Experience*, note that CUREs are implemented less frequently in the physical sciences, such as chemistry, when compared with the life sciences.[3] They also address barriers to implementation faculty may encounter and suggest CURE-related professional networks such as CUREnet.[4] Heemstra et al. detail some of the logistical challenges of the CURE model but tout its flexibility in adapting to various groups of students.[5]

Student Success and Experiential Learning

Undergraduate research is considered a high-impact educational practice, dem-onstrated to be positively impactful for student learning.[6] Hands-on components, including those that engage community partners and go beyond traditional lab work, can aid students in understanding and applying challenging course content in the real world. While Towns indicates that a mismatch between science teaching methods and students' preferred learning styles is often reported by students as rea-sons they leave STEM majors,[7] addressing real-world problems in an experiential, hands-on project has been a fairly common model to support student learning in chemistry.[8] Often these models focus on lower-level undergraduate students and/or students who are not chemistry majors, which can be advantageous for recruit-ment and retention of STEM majors. Towns applied Kolb's Experiential Learning Theory to a chemistry context, suggesting diverse teaching methods and caution-ing that sustained implementation is important to connect with students.[9] Nguyen et al. also applies Kolb, detailing a method for evaluating student learning styles and engaging summer research students in primary research and presentations; the authors note that experiential learning can engage those from underrepresented populations in research.[10]

Library Collaboration in Undergraduate Chemistry

Library collaboration in undergraduate chemistry is not uncommon. For example, Mandernach et al. describe a chemistry literature and seminar two-course sequence at James Madison University, team-taught by a chemistry faculty member and a librarian.[11] Lomness et al. incorporate information literacy and writing modules within the learning management system in a first-year high-enrollment chemistry course, allowing for a scalable integration of these foundational concepts. The collaboration includes the chemistry faculty, the chemistry librarian, a writing center manager, and the learning and curriculum support librarian.[12]

Library involvement in lab-based courses appears to be less common. Peters provides an example of a UCLA librarian partnering with faculty, using a train-the-trainer model with teaching assistants to implement a series of guided and structured searching exercises in chemistry lab courses. Faculty feedback indicated students' use of quality information sources improved in subsequent assignments.[13] There are also collaborations in which librarians provide direct instruction on specific chemistry information tools such as SciFinder Scholar.[14] In terms of other library services supporting CURE, archiving and showcasing undergraduate research in institutional repositories is a common practice in a growing number of academic libraries.

CURE and Library Services

While academic librarians do partner with chemistry faculty in lecture, seminar, and lab settings,[15] there is little literature related to such collaborations when it comes to course-integrated undergraduate chemistry research. Often literature searching and library instruction are emphasized, but little is mentioned related to other library services such as research consultations, hosting of research-based events, or archiving student research. Some faculty incorporating CURE-based pedagogy teach information literacy concepts but do not necessarily collaborate with the liaison librarian. Waterman and Heemstra note the potential for increasing workload the CURE model may create for support personnel, including librarians in that category.[16] Heemstra et al. describe thirteen CURE case studies using the CURE model in chemistry courses.[17] Only one, however, a sophomore-level Organic Chemistry Lab course at Hope College, mentions library involvement; in that course, the science librarian spends one hour with students in a literature search workshop covering SciFinder and other library resources, as students spend two of their seven-week lab session in the library for training and proposal preparation. None of the included cases explicitly engage students with higher-order literature review skills via library collaboration.

BACKGROUND

Institutional Setting

The University of Northern Iowa is a regional, comprehensive university located in Cedar Falls, Iowa. It has a Carnegie classification of M1 (Master's Colleges and Universities: Larger Programs). Predominantly an undergraduate teaching-focused institution, UNI's undergraduate enrollment was 7,749 FTE students in 2020–2021.

The Chemistry and Biochemistry program, accredited by the American Chemical Society (ACS), offers five undergraduate majors as well as general education lecture and lab-based courses. There are thirteen full-time faculty with independent research programs covering many fields of chemistry. The department graduates twenty to thirty students per year, many of whom have participated in some variety of hands-on research. There is a robust summer undergraduate research program along with an active chapter of the Student Affiliates of the American Chemical Society.

Course Setting

CHEM 4310: *Instrumental Analysis* is offered each fall semester, and is required for the Chemistry BS and Biochemistry BS degrees, though it is also often used as an elective for Chemistry BA, Biochemistry BA, and Chemistry Teaching BA students. As an upper-level course, students take Instrumental Analysis toward the end of their chemistry curriculum, building upon both theoretical foundations from quantum chemistry and laboratory foundations from quantitative chemical laboratory courses. Enrollment typically ranges from six to sixteen students, with a marked increase in recent years due to the hands-on nature of the course and positive student feedback. Dr. Sebree has been the sole instructor for the past seven years. During that time, he has added real-world research problems, challenging students to use what they learn in class to help a community partner with a research project.

The overarching goal of the course is for the students to learn about the theory and proper use and implementation of scientific equipment for the study of chemical systems. As not every technique can be paired with every chemical system, students are shown how to select a technique appropriate for the object of study to obtain a relevant dataset. Students then learn how to best present the data in written, oral, and visual forms via lab reports, formal proposals, posters, and poster presentations. As interest and enrollment has grown, hands-on time for each student with each instrument has had to be decreased because of a lack of duplicative setups in the department. The addition of a CURE project has helped provide more individualized learning for the students. As their CURE projects are proposed and carried out, each student can get much more hands-on time with individual instruments of their choosing in addition to the traditional, prescriptive "cookbook" style labs.

In some cases, objects of study have been transported to the chemistry lab rooms for analysis; for example, Chinese tapestries and Peruvian pots held by the UNI Museum were transported to chemistry labs for students to investigate. In the event of large or specialized objects of analysis, such as the Museum's eleven-foot-long mastodon tusk, roasted coffee from a local roaster, and rock cores at a local quarry, the class traveled to work onsite with the course partner using portable style instruments. Most recently, students were given the task of crafting field-ready instruments from LEGO™ Mindstorms that were both properly calibrated and portable. Students were able to use high-quality research instruments as needed to capture data in the field that course partners then can use to make decisions.

COURSE RESEARCH PROJECT

Project History and Overview

The initial student research projects (spring 2014 to fall 2016) took the form of fifteen-page white paper proposals and oral presentations on themes such as "Chemistry in Space." The 2017 project "Chemistry of Pluto" was modified to provide students with analog samples from Dr. Sebree's research they could use to acquire data. As the students took ownership of their data, the caliber of the final projects were a significant improvement from prior semesters; therefore, Dr. Sebree decided to keep the hands-on portion of the project in subsequent years. The length of the proposal was shortened but more literature depth was required. It was clear, however, that students needed to gain a better understanding of effective literature review techniques and skills in providing scholarly context, including to a non-scientific audience. Around the same time as these assignment changes, Gruber started as liaison librarian for Chemistry and Biochemistry, strengthening and expanding the existing library partnership in the course that had included one-shot instruction with the prior liaison.

In its current form, the main research project is staged throughout the semester, with support from the instructor and the liaison librarian. Students develop research questions on some aspect of the class research subject and conduct a literature search to form a scholarly foundation. Each student writes an extended outline overviewing the published research and their proposed research to answer their research question(s). To ensure source quality and effective proposals, students are required to meet one-on-one with Gruber prior to submitting outlines to Sebree for grading. Students then write individual research proposals, which must be based on high-quality scholarly research and fall below a strict six-page maximum length. Students must also submit a CV and budget narrative to request supplies.

Each student anonymously peer reviews the work of at least three classmates; the final paper grade consists of 25 percent peer review, 25 percent non-instructor external review (typically liaison librarian and campus STEM coordinator), and 50 percent instructor review. This portion of the exercise is to show the students what life as a research primary investigator (PI) is like and provide experience in giving and receiving detailed feedback. Students then consider the feedback while carrying out their project.

By the end of the semester, each student creates a poster to present at an annual open house hosted by Rod Library. Typically, more than sixty people from across campus and the community have attended; students must share their findings with chemists and non-chemists alike. Research related to the UNI Mastodon Tusk, held by Rod Library's UNI Museum, was particularly popular among both the researchers and audience, and students' tusk-related research has been incorporated into a permanent digital exhibit. Because the final grade incorporates internal and external reviews as well as public voting and instructor review, there is a strong push for the students to hone their public speaking skills with a focus on presenting a complex topic to a general audience.

Learning Outcomes and Assessment

Learning outcomes for the Instrumental Analysis course relate to not only technical skills in using scientific instruments and interpreting data, but also include the domains of science communication and information literacy. The CURE model helps students develop skills that are applicable beyond the lab and beyond graduation; projects require significant critical thinking, creativity, problem solving, communication, and teamwork. Chemistry skills are assessed throughout the course. Students must demonstrate proficient use of instrumentation through lab work and apply those skills to their own research project. Assessment is not based on the results of lab work, but on students' ability to apply lab techniques to their project appropriately and accurately. Inconclusive lab work is acceptable as long as students demonstrate that they used a technique appropriate to their research question and used the instrumentation in keeping with standard protocols. In this way, the assessment of students' chemistry skills takes a process-based approach.

Science communication skills are assessed via multiple methods, as students are expected to communicate their projects at various stages in writing and speaking. Written proposals are intended for a chemistry audience and often include technical language. Proposals are evaluated by the faculty member with librarian input using a rubric to assess both the proper structural formatting (grant authorship) and scientific technical literacy (see table 6.1). A successful proposal is one that demonstrates a high degree of technical knowledge of the subject matter in a concise manner so a scientific audience can understand the proposed work. On the other hand, public presentations are for a non-technical audience. Successful presentations demonstrate students' ability to translate technical information to lay language and think on their feet as they answer questions during the presentation.

Table 6.1. Master Rubric for Evaluating Proposal Structure and Content

Title of Proposal under Review	Title Page (with only name and date [1])
Executive Summary (3 points)	The executive summary is a short summary of the proposal. It should be no more than one paragraph (100–200 words) and should briefly summarize the entire proposal, including: 1. The goal of the study 2. The method to be used 3. A brief justification of what is going to be studied
Introduction (5 points)	In this section should give the background for the system being studied including: 1. A brief history of the scientific interest 2. A brief introduction to the object you are going to study 3. A synopsis of the chemical nature of the part of the object you will be sampling Good arguments include examples of previous work that has been done in this area to backup claims.

Technical Approach (3 points)	This is the description of the setup. What technique(s) is/are being used? How does it work? You should be convinced the writer knows how the instrument works and the running requirements that it needs (sample type, running temperature, signal to noise, etc.).
Instrument Diagram (2 points)	Is there a diagram with all the working parts labeled similar to the exploded diagrams in a textbook (2 points)? Or is it just a basic block diagram (1 point)?
Proposed Research (5 points)	Put it all together. This is where the writer tells what research is going to be done. Examples of "if there is this . . . then results could look like . . . " Figures that demonstrate the expected data would fit well in this section. The writer shows that they have a thorough understanding of the concepts of the experiment and the expected results.
Conclusion (2 points)	This section includes only a few sentences that summarize definitive conclusions from the proposal as a whole.
Works Cited (2 points)	Make sure all the references and figures that are used are properly cited both within the text, and at the end of the proposal using a consistent formal formatting style.
Organization (2 points)	Is the report well organized and easy to follow? Can all the text in the figures/tables be read?
Grantsmanship Score (25)	
Scientific and Technical Merit (5 points)	Proposals are expected to present a clear description of a specific scientific problem and how the attack on this problem will be carried out.
Relevance (5 points)	Is the proposed work relevant to the science goals? How compelling and articulate is the argument presented in the proposal for the relevance of the proposed work?
Academic Qualifications (5 points)	Does the student have the appropriate depth in the subject to accomplish the proposed work? This can be demonstrated through two ways: 1. The implied knowledge of the proposer through the accurate portrayal of the work in the proposal 2. Through the background of the student as described on their CV.
Merit Score (15)	

Source: Anne Marie Gruber and Dr. Joshua Sebree.

Information literacy skills are assessed by the librarian and instructor as they review bibliographies during multiple evaluation processes. Students are generally successful in the project when they find and cite high-quality sources to support their work. The ACRL Framework for Information Literacy for Higher Education[18] and Information Literacy Standards for Science and Engineering/Technology[19] inform the collaboration, but, to date, neither has been explicitly mapped to the course and project learning objectives.

Library Involvement

As the liaison librarian for Chemistry, I (Gruber) have been quite involved in the course over the past six years. I meet with the class during the first week of the semester to lead a hands-on session for students to begin finding literature to support their proposals. Prior to the outline deadline, each student is also required to meet with me for a thirty- to forty-five-minute research consultation. This allows each student one-on-one time to ask any questions about the literature review portion of the project. Questions often relate not only to how to find appropriate literature but also to how to connect published literature to novel areas of research and how to translate scientific concepts for a non-scientific audience. Required consultations early in the research process also encourage students to make continual progress throughout the semester and meet deadlines from the start. I then serve as an "expert reviewer" on the students' proposals as well as on the final poster presentations. I complete a rubric for each proposal, the results of which are incorporated into the instructor grading process. I then complete a feedback form on the students' poster presentations. Because my involvement in this course is fairly extensive and I serve as a liaison for ten departments/programs on campus, careful consideration has been paid to an appropriate and sustainable level. The class enrollment tends to be fairly small (fewer than sixteen students), so it has been manageable to date. The scheduling of the course, typically offered at 8:00 a.m., is helpful because there are only a few other courses I work with offered at that time, and I have no desk staffing responsibilities in the early morning.

There are a number of additional ways I have ensured sustainability. For example, I have streamlined consultations by having students use my existing online appointment scheduler (LibCal) that is available to all students; I add more availability, if needed, as the outline deadline approaches. An early iteration of the project involved me serving, with the campus STEM coordinator, as a facilitator for a peer-review process during class time. While students still review each other's proposals, we no longer attend the class session when this takes place, trimming the time commitment. Some of the evaluative work I do can be done on my own time outside of scheduled sessions; I evaluate proposals during a one-week period, and posters are usually available in advance of the public presentation, so both these activities take place on my own schedule. The only synchronous, scheduled evaluation is of students' oral presentations during the live poster session, and I would plan to attend anyway as a show of support. Some librarian involvement is optional. For example, I choose to participate in a final class wrap-up/celebration session as a way to support the students and congratulate them on their hard work, but this isn't a required part of the collaboration.

Beyond instructional support and consultations, the Rod Library Digital Scholarship Unit is involved, archiving the students' work in a course project collection in the institutional repository.[20] Students are strongly encouraged to archive their full proposals, raw data sets, and final posters, and most choose to do so. Some choose to embargo some of their data so they can publish their findings in a scholarly journal prior to the data being made available to the public.

Additional Partners and Funding

UNI Museum, part of Rod Library, has been a key partner in providing objects of analysis, funding for related research, expert guidance on techniques for working with archival objects of study, and an outlet for some students' research to be shared and placed on permanent display. Museum involvement has been particularly strong during years when students analyzed the mastodon tusk and other objects in the Museum's holdings. The permanent display of the tusk within Museum space is coupled with a digital interactive display sharing the students' research. Additionally, the Museum staff have facilitated permanent display of some Museum objects and student research in high-traffic areas on campus, such as near the university President's Office.

Additional campus departments such as University Relations and Digital Media Studies have been involved with the course. Marcy Seavey, UNI STEM coordinator, who facilitates interdisciplinary STEM collaborations on campus and statewide, has

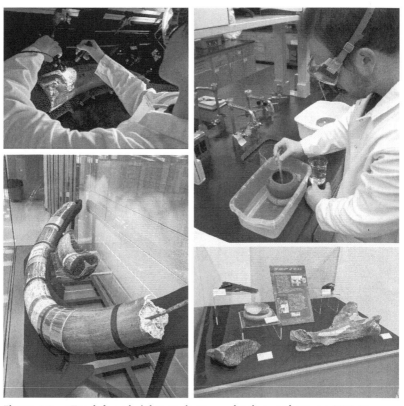

Figure 6.1. (Top left and right) students conducting analyses on UNI Museum objects; (bottom left) UNI Museum mastodon tusk on display; (bottom right) UNI Museum display highlighting student research on various objects.
All images courtesy of Dr. Joshua Sebree.

served as an external reviewer for student proposals and is active in providing feed-back on student projects. During some semesters, community partners from beyond campus have been involved. For example, during fall 2018, students collaborated with a local coffee roaster to test for various compounds, such as caffeine, in coffee brewed at various stages of the roasting process.

Funding sources have included departmental funds and, for the mastodon tusk project, a Carver Foundation grant that the UNI Museum had received to support the tusk's study and conservation. To continue to bolster the strength of the course, supplemental funding was acquired from the Iowa Space Grant Consortium (ISGC). This course directly ties in to support NASA's Office of Education goals to advance STEM education. The course allows for student professional development and ensures that all participants receive a unique STEM experience, opening up the pos-sibility for UNI students to be better informed and competitive when applying for internship and fellowship opportunities. These are key areas identified by the NASA Office of Education for advancing STEM fields in the United States and ensuring that NASA's "education investments are unique and non-duplicative," per the NASA Strategic Plan.[21] The funding of the ISGC grant allowed for the purchase of eleven sets of programmable LEGO™ Mindstorm Kits along with Vernier probes. The interfacing of LEGO™ with probes provided the opportunity for students to not only use traditional benchtop instruments but also to build, program, and calibrate field use instruments.

OUTCOMES

Liaison Librarian Perception

As a liaison librarian for more than ten academic departments/campus programs, I (Gruber) can confidently say the Instrumental Analysis course is the class with which I'm most heavily involved. I appreciate the level of integration, which has evolved organically over time. Significant involvement on my part is possible and manageable because of both a highly collaborative instructor who trusts my expertise and a small class size. While I was hesitant at first to agree to required consultations, students invariably have positive feedback about them, and it's clear these meetings help students move in the right direction as they prepare their project components. Students often schedule more than the one required consultation as they hone out-lines, proposals, posters, and presentations.

I go beyond simple literature searching when assisting students with research. They often struggle to understand what the proposal should include because it's a new type of scientific writing for them. Consultations often consist not just of database and search strategy suggestions but of going through the sections of the instructor-provided outline to help students understand what each entails and how to approach the proposal. Students also experience frustration if they don't find scholarly literature that matches their research topic and chosen technique. Because they are combining objects of study with chemistry techniques in novel ways (such as analyzing a mastodon tusk using near-infrared spectroscopy), students don't often have a sense for what type of literature is relevant to their research. They need help determining not only how to search, but how to select articles that can help form the foundation of their work and connect their own ideas to existing research. Emphasizing interdisciplinary research helps students expand their ideas about what types of sources to include; they are not used to consulting literature outside of chemistry and yet sources in museum studies, conservation sciences, art, history, and even dentistry may lend important information to the research process. Students also need to be explicitly told that sometimes older sources, such as seminal works or those detailing historic preservation methods for museum objects, might be useful; this contradicts their tendency to only seek out newer scholarly articles.

Upper-level chemistry students often have a difficult time translating technical concepts to common language that a non-expert can understand; this is a vital skill not only for the public poster presentations but also because it will translate to future career plans for most students. This course has been an ideal venue for helping students practice skills necessary for effective science communication. Somewhat unexpectedly, I (Gruber) have found myself serving as a non-chemist practice audience for students to workshop their projects. Written proposals require students to articulate why the research matters, and some struggle to do so. I have found that my role with the course and background as a non-chemist means I can help them take a step back from the details of the chemistry techniques and lab work and place their work in a broader context of published research and community impact. If I can't understand what they plan to share in oral poster presentations, they need to more carefully translate their findings into general language. The aspects of this project that require translating chemistry content for the general public have led to more repeated consultations than expected, and I have been surprised that my non-chemist role has been an advantage here.

My most significant takeaway is that the open-ended nature of the research projects is challenging to students, and, while most of them are quite strong in the chemistry content required, they need support to build confidence in the process and to get past any perceived roadblocks. It is advantageous to have a team approach so both the instructor and liaison librarian can provide this support in various ways based on our own areas of expertise. Referrals are common between instructor and librarian; the trust we share ensures that students will get support from the appropriate person.

I have found it particularly gratifying to help students lead their own primary research projects, building confidence and learning to translate complex chemical techniques and new findings to a public audience. One student, Nicole (Bishop) North, won the 2019 Mary Ann Bolton Undergraduate Research Award, a prize Rod Library offers annually. It is also important to note that, as many liaison librarians find, the nature of the relationship with students may differ from their relationship with an instructor; while I do evaluate work in the course, the supportive nature of my role seems to aid in building student trust.

Professor Perception

When initially planning for the implementation of the research component of Instrumental Analysis, I (Sebree) wanted to make sure that my students would gain valuable skills that were cross-disciplinary so that regardless of post-graduation plans, they would have more than just a useful set of analysis skills suited for laboratory work. With my students planning careers that ranged from medical degrees to research to laboratory technicians, the ability to problem-solve and stay up to date with current literature are important skills. While the CURE project was often referred to by students and me as a "crash course in graduate school," the skills that are important in getting funding for a new/relevant project and presenting the results, either to the funders or the general public, are in universal demand. With so many science courses focusing on the "final product" lab reports, there was a skill gap where students were not being exposed to the idea that science is continually evolving and can be pushed forward by anyone with a solid background in scientific literature.

Implementing the model in use now was a multi-year task. The early years were spent crafting the white paper proposal portion of the project. Students were given a theme and tasked with designing a research project that could theoretically be performed, presenting both a mock-rover design and simulated expected data to the public at the end-of-term open house. Once I was satisfied with the clarity of the rubrics and quality of the proposals, I replaced the "simulated" data sets with analog samples students then used to create model data sets. The quality of the work took a significant step up once students were taking ownership of their data and could proudly show that their proposed project could yield actual results.

The final step in moving from simulated research to actual research was simple with the addition of external partners providing the research questions and objects, instead of myself. With the possibility of real results that organizations could act upon, many of the students were intimidated about the work. The increased participation of the liaison librarian, including individual consultations with each student, was a valuable asset in bolstering student confidence and quality of background research. This, in turn, led to better crafted proposals and, ultimately, better science at the end of the CURE project. The sense of accomplishment the students showed at the end of their work truly reflected how much they grew as independent researchers and thinkers. In the years since, I have received many thank you notes calling out the Instrumental Analysis project as one of the key turning points that helped my students have a leg up when applying for jobs and graduate schools.

Student Feedback

Students have found that having an external "client" encourages them to pay particular attention to careful research methods and science communication; the stakes seem higher when the audience goes beyond their instructor.

Gruber sends students who have scheduled consultations with her an optional feedback form. Several chemistry students complete it each fall and responses from students in the Instrumental Analysis course include: "Anne Marie Gruber assisted me with communicating scientific jargon into a more understandable language that allows people with a less scientific background understand the information that was conveyed." Students clearly use the skills they gained in the course in the future. Nicole North, one alum who is now in a chemistry PhD program shared, "I also get to teach honors analytical next semester instead of general chemistry. They do research projects so they need to write proposals. I am incredibly grateful for the experience of having written one in undergrad so I can help the students with theirs." She went on to say, "I just wanted to say thank you. So many of the opportunities that I had in undergrad are really paying off in graduate school."[22]

Another student, Warren Rouse, went on to a PhD program and became the first student in his department ever to win a prestigious National Institutes of Health fellowship that will fully fund his postdoctoral research. He recently contacted Dr. Sebree, sharing, "I found out yesterday that my proposal made it through all the review processes and was selected to be funded. This award is funded by the NCI/NIH and will cover all of my studies for the next five years. Once again, thank you for everything that you taught me in undergrad. I have used many of the skills I gained from your courses to get this award and prove to my PI that I am capable of doing high quality research."[23] While these alumni success stories are not due solely to the Instrumental Analysis course and speak to the overall quality of the UNI Chemistry and Biochemistry experience, the students' experiences in proposal-writing and hands-on research are directly applicable to post-graduation plans and provide the students an advantage with future applications, proposals, and projects.

Partner Feedback

Community partners have enjoyed working with the students and have benefitted from the findings. For example, when students found there was lead but not asbestos in the mastodon tusk, this influenced the conservation techniques and safety measures the UNI Museum and their conservation contractor would then need to follow. The implications are even broader, as museum director Nathan Arndt shares: "How can we help the state best take care of their tusks? This is groundbreaking work that we're hoping to do, to help people maintain their collections across the state. This will show what a modern museum is capable of and how it influences and impacts your life. Doing this will also show people UNI is relevant in the world of academia—we do great things."[24]

STEM coordinator Marcy Seavey recognizes the value of the project to student learning, sharing, "The students in the Instrumental Analysis class communicate, receive and process feedback, and communicate about their project again several times throughout the semester. That is a very different and authentic experience from doing a lab, turning it in, and moving on to the next lab."[25] Seavey goes on to indicate how the high level of work Sebree expects in the course impacts students: "They can explain how their project evolved both from receiving outside and peer reviewer feedback and by incorporating their data. Finally, one of the most difficult obstacles to becoming a PI is writing your first proposal, getting feedback, and knowing what to do with it. These students are two to four years ahead of their peers in that respect."

CHALLENGES

Adapting the fall 2020 course was necessary due to the COVID pandemic, and, while challenging, the transition went smoothly. The course was offered in a flexible format, with all lectures being offered in-person as well as livestreamed so students could choose the option that best fit their needs. Lab sessions were held in-person as normal and scheduled to allow for social distancing. There was less emphasis on group work than pre-pandemic research projects. A focus on LEGO™ Mindstorm projects was a good fit for a hybrid version of the course because there was enough equipment for each student to have a self-contained research kit; students built their own working instrumentation using the kits, which could be taken home if necessary. The public poster session was fully virtual, and students recorded their presentations in advance. The videos were then played for the public audience attendees via Zoom, and a live question and answer session was held with each presenter. Attendees were encouraged to use their microphones or the Zoom chat option to interact with the student researchers. Attendance and engagement was very good, with around forty virtual attendees compared to fifty to seventy-five in-person pre-COVID-19, indicating that a virtual option was appealing to the audience and perhaps allowed people to attend and participate who may not have otherwise.

Library services were adapted so the library instruction session and all consultations were fully virtual using Zoom software. All instructional strategies translated well. One advantage was the ability for students to engage using both their microphone and the Zoom chat as they wished. While students often feel comfortable participating, particularly in small, upper-level classes such as this one, some may prefer to use chat. Gruber had offered Zoom consultations to distance-learning or commuter students in other programs prior to the pandemic, but had not suggested the option to chemistry students since they are usually all on-campus learners. In the future, she will plan to offer both in-person and virtual consultation options for all students because some may appreciate additional flexibility. While students were not asked directly how they felt about the Zoom consultations, Gruber perceived that some found them very convenient; similar to past in-person semesters, several students scheduled more than the one required consultation and commented they found the sessions helpful. It's possible the Zoom option simply made it easier to attend, since going to the library or science building was not required.

CONCLUSION: FUTURE DIRECTIONS

This partnership will continue as long as Sebree teaches the course, and it is clearly effective in helping students gain not only understanding of the necessary chemistry concepts and methods, but also an expanded skill set in finding, evaluating, and using the scholarly literature. Future directions will include more formal surveying of students regarding their feedback about the librarian's involvement. Additionally, with a strong diversity emphasis at UNI, it will be important to better understand the impact of the CURE model on female students, students of color, and those who have been economically disadvantaged. The collaboration will be strengthened by explicitly mapping to information literacy frameworks as well as ensuring assessment on targeted learning practices and dispositions. In addition, it will be helpful to map to the current ACS accreditation standards for undergraduate programs, which are explicit regarding students' skills related to literature searching and management.[26]

Bangera and Brownell call for the CURE model to be adopted for required intro-ductory-level courses[27]; while this upper-level course is successful, it does not address the need for lower-level undergraduates to be introduced to research. Conversations will continue in light of a campus-wide emphasis on diversity and inclusion as well as high-impact practices throughout the curriculum in the UNI Chemistry and Biochemistry program. Rod Library will continue to support and expand services for undergraduate research and experiential learning across various disciplines, and partnerships such as the one described here can serve as a model.

ACKNOWLEDGMENTS

Funding for this project was provided by Iowa Space Grant Consortium under NASA Award No. NNX16AL88H (LEGO™ equipment) and Roy J. Carver Charitable Trust (heritage grant for mastodon tusk study and restoration). The authors extend additional appreciation to Nathan Arndt (UNI Museum), Jed Vander Zanden (Sidecar Coffee), Marcy Seavey (UNI STEM coordinator), Dr. Alexa Sedlacek (associate professor of geology), the Rod Library Dean's Office, and Chris Neuhaus (associate professor of library services).

NOTES

1. Gita Bangera and Sara E. Brownell, "Course-Based Undergraduate Research Experiences Can Make Scientific Research More Inclusive," *CBE—Life Sciences Education* 13, no. 4 (2014): 603, https://doi.org/10.1187/cbe.14-06-0099.

2. Sara E. Brownell et al., "A High-Enrollment Course-Based Undergraduate Research Experience Improves Student Conceptions of Scientific Thinking and Ability to Interpret Data," *CBE—Life Sciences Education* 14, no. 2 (2015): ar21, 8, 10, https://doi.org/10.1187/cbe.14-05-0092.

3. Rory Waterman and Jen Heemstra, *Expanding the CURE Model: Course-Based Undergraduate Research Experience* (Tucson: Research Corporation for Science Advancement, 2018), https://rescorp.org/gdresources/publications/Expanding-the-CURE-Model.pdf.

4. "CUREnet: Course-Based Undergraduate Research Experience," Science Education Resource Center at Carleton College, 2021 https://serc.carleton.edu/curenet/index.html.

5. Jennifer M. Heemstra et al., "Throwing Away the Cookbook: Implementing Course-Based Undergraduate Research Experiences (CUREs) in Chemistry," in *Educational and Outreach Projects from the Cottrell Scholars Collaborative: Volume 1, Undergraduate and Graduate Education*, ed. Rory Waterman and Andrew Feig (Washington DC: American Chemical Society, 2017), 48, https://doi.org/10.1021/bk-2017-1248.ch003.

6. George D. Kuh, "High-Impact Educational Practices: A Brief Overview," Association of American Colleges and Universities, 2008, https://www.aacu.org/node/4084.

7. Marcy Hamby Towns, "Kolb for Chemists: David A. Kolb and Experiential Learning Theory," *Journal of Chemical Education* 78 (2001): 1107, https://doi.org/10.1021/ed078p1107.7.

8. Jennifer A. Dabrowski and Mary E. Manson McManamy, "Design of Culinary Transformations: A Chemistry Course for Nonscience Majors," *Journal of Chemical Education* 97, no. 5 (2020): 1283–88, https://doi.org/10.1021/acs.jchemed.9b00964; Kimberlee Daus and Rachel Rigsby, "The Power of Experiential Learning: Leveraging Your General Education Curriculum to Invigorate Your Chemistry Courses," in *The Promise of Chemical Education: Addressing our Students' Needs*, eds. Kimberlee Daus and Rachel Rigsby (Washington, DC: American Chemical Society, 2015), 101–13, https://doi.org/10.1021/bk-2015-1193.ch008.

9. Towns, "Kolb for Chemists," 1107.

10. Huong Thi Huynh Nguyen et al., "Student-Assisted Research-Focused Experiential Learning in the Bioanalytical Chemistry Curriculum," in *Teaching Bioanalytical Chemistry*, ed. Harvey J. M. Hou (Washington, DC: American Chemical Society, 2013), 257.

11. Meris Mandernach, Yasmeen Shorish, and Barbara A. Reisner, "The Evolution of Library Instruction Delivery in the Chemistry Curriculum Informed by Mixed Assessment Methods," *Issues in Science and Technology Librarianship*, 2014, https://kb.osu.edu/handle/1811/62040.

12. Arielle Lomness et al., "Seizing the Opportunity: Collaborative Creation of Academic Integrity and Information Literacy LMS Modules for Undergraduate Chemistry." *The Journal of Academic Librarianship* 47, no. 3 (2021), https://doi.org/10.1016/j.acalib.2021.102328.

13. Marion C. Peters, "Beyond Google: Integrating Chemical Information into the Undergraduate Chemistry and Biochemistry Curriculum," *Science & Technology Libraries* 30, no. 1 (2011): 84, https://doi.org/10.1080/0194262x.2011.545671.

14. Heemstra et al., "Throwing Away the Cookbook," 33–63.

15. Ignacio J. Ferrer-Vinent et al., "Introducing Scientific Literature to Honors General Chemistry Students: Teaching Information Literacy and the Nature of Research to First-Year Chemistry Students," *Journal of Chemical Education* 92, no. 4 (2015): 617–24 https://doi.org/10.1021/ed500472v; Danielle L. Jacobs, Heather A. Dalal, and Patricia H. Dawson, "Integrating Chemical Information Instruction into the Chemistry Curriculum on Borrowed Time: The Multi-Year Development and Evolution of a Virtual Instructional Tutorial," *Journal of Chemical Education* 93, no. 3 (2016): 452–63, https://doi.org/10.1021/acs.jchemed.5b00427; April Colosimo and Emily Kasuto, "Library Video Tutorials to Support Large Undergraduate Labs: Will They Watch?" *Issues in Science and Technology Librarianship* 68, no. 4 (2012), http://www.istl.org/12-winter/refereed1.html?a_aid=3598aabf; Yasmeen

Shorish and Barbara A. Reisner, "Building Data and Information Literacy in the Undergraduate Chemistry Curriculum," in *Integrating Information Literacy into the Chemistry Curriculum*, eds. Charity F. Lovitt, Kristen Shuyler, and Ye Li (Washington, DC: American Chemical Society, 2016), 31–56, https://doi.org/10.1021/bk-2016-1232.ch002.

16. Waterman and Heemstra, "Expanding the CURE Model," 101.

17. Heemstra et al., "Throwing Away the Cookbook," 33–63.

18. "Framework for Information Literacy for Higher Education," Association of College and Research Libraries, 2015, http://www.ala.org/acrl/sites/ala.org.acrl/files/content/issues /infolit/framework1.pdf.

19. "Information Literacy Standards for Science and Engineering/Technology," Association of College and Research Libraries, last modified June 21, 2018, http://www.ala.org/acrl /standards/infolitscitech.

20. "Chemical Analysis Class Projects," UNI ScholarWorks, 2019, https://scholarworks .uni.edu/chemanalysis.

21. "NASA Strategic Plan 2014," NASA, 2014: 35, https://www.nasa.gov/sites/default /files/files/FY2014_NASA_SP_508c.pdf.

22. Nicole North, email message to author, August, 28, 2019.

23. Warren Rouse, email message to author, January 21, 2021.

24. Nathan Arndt, email message to author, May 3, 2021.

25. Marcy Seavey, email message to the author, May 2, 2021.

26. "ACS Guidelines and Evaluation Procedures for Bachelor's Degree Programs," American Chemical Society, 2015, https://www.acs.org/content/dam/acsorg/about/governance /committees/training/2015-acs-guidelines-for-bachelors-degree-programs.pdf.

27. Bangera and Brownell, "Course-Based Undergraduate Research," 604.

BIBLIOGRAPHY

Bangera, Gita, and Sara E. Brownell. "Course-Based Undergraduate Research Experiences Can Make Scientific Research More Inclusive." *CBE—Life Sciences Education* 13, no. 4 (2014): 602–6. https://doi.org/10.1187/cbe.14-06-0099.

Brownell, Sara E., Daria S. Hekmat-Scafe, Veena Singla, Patricia Chandler Seawell, Jamie F. Conklin Imam, Sarah L. Eddy, Tim Stearns, and Martha S. Cyert. "A High-Enrollment Course-Based Undergraduate Research Experience Improves Student Conceptions of Scientific Thinking and Ability to Interpret Data." *CBE—Life Sciences Education* 14, no. 2 (2015): ar21 https://doi.org/10.1187/cbe.14-05-0092.

Colosimo, April, and Emily Kasuto. "Library Video Tutorials to Support Large Undergraduate Labs: Will They Watch?" *Issues in Science and Technology Librarianship* 68, no. 4 (2012). http://www.istl.org/12-winter/refereed1.html?a_aid=3598aabf.

Dabrowski, Jennifer A., and Mary E. Manson McManamy. "Design of Culinary Transformations: A Chemistry Course for Nonscience Majors." *Journal of Chemical Education* 97, no. 5 (2020): 1283–88. https://doi.org/10.1021/acs.jchemed.9b00964.

Daus, Kimberlee, and Rachel Rigsby. "The Power of Experiential Learning: Leveraging Your General Education Curriculum to Invigorate Your Chemistry Courses." In *The Promise of Chemical Education: Addressing our Students' Needs*, edited by Kimberlee Daus and Rachel Rigsby, 101–13. Washington, DC: American Chemical Society, 2015. https://doi .org/10.1021/bk-2015-1193.ch008.

Ferrer-Vinent, Ignacio J., Margaret Bruehl, Denise Pan, and Galin L. Jones. "Introducing Scientific Literature to Honors General Chemistry Students: Teaching Information Literacy and the Nature of Research to First-Year Chemistry Students." *Journal of Chemical Education* 92, no. 4 (2015): 617–24. https://doi.org/10.1021/ed500472v.

Heemstra, Jennifer M., Rory Waterman, John M. Antos, Penny J. Beuning, Scott K. Bur, Linda Columbus, Andrew L. Feig, Amelia A. Fuller, Jason G. Gillmore, Aaron M. Leconte, Casey H. Londergan, William C. K. Pomerantz, Jennifer A. Prescher, and Levi M. Stanley. "Throwing Away the Cookbook: Implementing Course-Based Undergraduate Research Experiences (CUREs) in Chemistry." In *Educational and Outreach Projects from the Cottrell Scholars Collaborative: Volume 1, Undergraduate and Graduate Education*, edited by Rory Waterman and Andrew Feig, 33–63. Washington DC: American Chemical Society, 2017. https://doi.org/10.1021/bk-2017-1248.ch003.

Jacobs, Danielle L., Heather A. Dalal, and Patricia H. Dawson. "Integrating Chemical Information Instruction into the Chemistry Curriculum on Borrowed Time: The Multiyear Development and Evolution of a Virtual Instructional Tutorial." *Journal of Chemical Education* 93, no. 3 (2016): 452–63. https://doi.org/10.1021/acs.jchemed.5b00427.

Kuh, George. "High-Impact Educational Practices: What They Are, Who Has Access to Them, and Why They Matter." Association of American Colleges and Universities, 2008. https://www.aacu.org/node/4084.

Lomness, Arielle, Sajni Lacey, Amanda Brobbel, and Tamara Freeman. "Seizing the Opportunity: Collaborative Creation of Academic Integrity and Information Literacy LMS Modules for Undergraduate Chemistry." *The Journal of Academic Librarianship* 47, no. 3 (2021): 1–4. https://doi.org/10.1016/j.acalib.2021.102328.

Mandernach, Meris, Yasmeen Shorish, and Barbara A. Reisner. "The Evolution of Library Instruction Delivery in the Chemistry Curriculum Informed by Mixed Assessment Methods." *Issues in Science and Technology Librarianship* 2014. https://kb.osu.edu/handle/1811/62040.

NASA. "NASA Strategic Plan 2014." 2014. https://www.nasa.gov/sites/default/files/files/FY2014_NASA_SP_508c.pdf.

Nguyen, Huong Thi Huynh, Marilyn Arceo, Annika M. Weber, Robert K. Springer, and Grady Hanrahan. "Student-Assisted Research-Focused Experiential Learning in the Bioanalytical Chemistry Curriculum." In *Teaching Bioanalytical Chemistry*, edited by Harvey J. M. Hou, 245–59. Washington, DC: American Chemical Society, 2013.

Peters, Marion C. "Beyond Google: Integrating Chemical Information into the Undergraduate Chemistry and Biochemistry Curriculum." *Science & Technology Libraries* 30, no. 1 (2011): 80–88. https://doi.org/10.1080/0194262x.2011.545671.

Shorish, Yasmeen, and Barbara A. Reisner. "Building Data and Information Literacy in the Undergraduate Chemistry Curriculum." In *Integrating Information Literacy into the Chemistry Curriculum*, edited by Charity F. Lovitt, Kristen Shuyler, and Ye Li, 31–56. Washington, DC: American Chemical Society, 2016. https://doi.org/10.1021/bk-2016-1232.ch002.

Towns, Marcy Hamby. "Kolb for Chemists: David A. Kolb and Experiential Learning Theory." *Journal of Chemical Education* 78 (2001): 1107. https://doi.org/10.1021/ed078p1107.7.

Waterman, Rory, and Jen Heemstra. *Expanding the CURE Model: Course-Based Undergraduate Research Experience*. Tucson: Research Corporation for Science Advancement, 2018. https://rescorp.org/gdresources/publications/Expanding-the-CURE-Model.pdf.

7

Out of the Archives

Making Collections Accessible through the Implementation of a 3D Scanning Lab

Kristi Wyatt and Dr. Zenobie S. Garrett

The University of Oklahoma is home to a collaborative and exploratory team the Bizzell Memorial Library calls the Emerging Technologies (ET) unit. This unit began in 2015 with the goal to explore the impact of new technologies and assist with their implementation and integration into campus research and teaching. As a new unit, the team focused on building faculty relationships through virtual reality (VR) and 3D printing. The team's extensive work in these arenas was welcomed and supported by faculty and students.[1] At the same time, the success of VR and 3D printing highlighted a growing need for 3D assets for VR, web, and printing content as well as for standalone research objects. The expansion of ET's services and personnel in 2018 provided the opportunity to investigate solutions to the expanding demand for 3D content. The authors embarked on a year-long development and exploratory project, which ultimately led to the launch of the 3D scanning lab within the library in the fall of 2019.

As 3D data has become more ubiquitous across disciplines, researchers have responded by acquiring assorted 3D scanning equipment for their personal research and lab use. The challenge of this approach is that the technology and expertise remain siloed within the individual lab, making it inaccessible both within and beyond the department. Furthermore, these researchers may not have background or expertise in 3D scanning methodologies and do not have the time or money to learn them beyond a need-to-know basis. By centralizing access to 3D technology in Bizzell Library we create a robust technological infrastructure that provides equitable access for all researchers on the OU campus. Our primary goal is to increase access to state-of-the-art research techniques while decreasing the financial and temporal barriers researchers face in this area. At the same time, we want to create a new form of collaborative service and research within the library that establishes the library as an active partner in the research process. To do so required us to not only investigate what other academic libraries have been doing but also invest in our own training so that we can provide support, guidance, and instruction across the entire 3D scanning workflow. A literature review indicates that publications mainly discuss 3D printing, modeling, and makerspaces rather than focusing solely on 3D scanning as a generalized service in the library.[2] For example, Dalhousie University describes a pilot project pairing a 3D scanner and 3D printer for patron use at their Help Desk, while University of Nevada writes on supporting 3D modeling to better help those utilizing the 3D printers and scanners in their library makerspace.[3,4] A publication written by Pennsylvania Libraries notes their use of 3D scanning as a public service, allowing patrons to physically check out a scanner (specifically the NextEngine Laser scanner).[5] While there has been increased 3D scanning activity throughout libraries, our lab is dedicated to support for research-specific projects across the university; this topic is almost entirely absent from the literature. We have developed a lab training methodology that focuses on experiential and collaborative learning in order to provide our patrons with robust and long-lasting skill sets. Finally, we wanted to create a research space for us to experiment with 3D scanning techniques and practices, explore the use of 3D scanning across the academic disciplines, and understand the legal and ethical discussions surrounding this rapidly-changing process.

The Lab currently has established working relationships with fifteen OU departments and affiliates. These research collaborations have yielded a variety of scholarly output including presentations, publications, and funding proposals. In 2021, despite COVID-19 restrictions and protocols, the lab demand has increased 58 percent, in part due to greater need for digital assets. Below we will provide a brief overview of the lab's development as a resource for those interested in the decisions we made or those who are going through the process of integrating 3D scanning into library services themselves. We will then present a number of case studies that illustrate not only the benefits of 3D scanning to researchers but what we have learned as part of the collaborative experience.

LAB DEVELOPMENT

We began the development phase by designing a Qualtrics survey to collect information on who was already scanning on campus, what equipment and software they were using, and who had access to the scanning technologies. The survey was sent via email to nine departments in STEM and the humanities across the university. We found less usage with departments as a whole; rather it was individual faculty members who used and/or possessed these technologies. This meant access was extremely restricted, and knowledge of 3D scanning capabilities limited. We also found that in some instances there was a loss of knowledge or expertise due to someone leaving or graduating. Other departments had great interest, but did not have the time, expertise, or the equipment needed. This initial survey gave us a better idea of what kind of impact a 3D scanning lab within the library could have on the campus community. It also provided insight into what equipment and software was already in use and the challenges they presented. This allowed us to understand what technologies the lab should invest in that would be most accessible and most useful as a whole. Moreover, it defined what technologies and workflows faculty who already used 3D scanners might need or want support in and invest in a centralized, stable knowledge base within the library.

We also determined that the 3D scanning process known as photogrammetry had the greatest potential to address unmet needs across the university. Photogrammetry is the technique of extracting 3D measurements from photographs in order to digitally reconstruct an object. For our initial purposes, it offered several advantages. First, the equipment cost was relatively low—our initial investment focused on a DSLR camera and lens, a tripod, clamp lights, cloth backdrops, and a software license for Agisoft Metashape Pro. While some other 3D scanning methods also have low-cost entryways, as a camera-based technology, photogrammetry offers several additional benefits. While the DSLR camera was purchased for photogrammetry, it can also be used to take still photographs for other library activities making it more versatile. Additionally, it is a technology that is more readily accessible to students and faculty at the university. Most have some type of camera at home—whether it is a DSLR, point-and-shoot, or even a phone camera—and have some knowledge, however limited, of taking a photograph. Our library also has cameras available at check-out, which allows those without cameras to still have access to the hardware involved. The ubiquity of cameras in everyday life allows researchers and students to utilize the technology outside of the library's open hours and gives them a point of entry and familiarity as they start out. Photogrammetry is also fairly portable and scalable; cameras and lighting can be taken to objects that are not able to be moved, and photogrammetry can capture a wide range of object sizes, shapes, and surfaces. Moreover, unlike some handheld scanners, photogrammetry has the ability to collect texture and color information and incorporate that into the final model.

Furthermore, photogrammetry presents several advantages in terms of archiving the final model and associated data. Through a photogrammetry training workshop hosted by Cultural Heritage Imaging (CHI), we learned how to use Agisoft Metashape Pro to create high-resolution, research quality models in reproducible ways.[6] This software is somewhat unique among proprietary software because it allows the user the greatest amount of control and transparency in model manipulation. This transparency allows the user to document and archive the processing workflow which is necessary for research usage and reproducibility. However, open-source software for photogrammetry also exists making it a useful method for access purposes.

One of the major issues involved in 3D model archiving is that, currently, there are no set standards regarding acceptable file formats or associated information needed. Much of the work done so far has been led by a variety of working groups and institutions, the most notable being the Smithsonian Digitization Program Office, the Community Standards for 3D Data Preservation (CS3DP), LIB3DVR, and, more recently, Gallery Archive Library and Museum 3D (GLAM3D).[7] These groups have been at the forefront of 3D data preservation and archive discussions defining the relevant metadata and establishing good, better, and best practices. Nevertheless, widely agreed upon standards and their broad adoption is ongoing and may continue to change going forward. One of the strengths of photogrammetry is that while the accepted file format for the model itself is still under debate, the photographs themselves can be saved and archived as DNGs and/or TIFs. This allows them to be easily integrated into existing archive workflows and provides a way of recreating the model if the file format becomes obsolete and/or unsupported.

To test-run the 3D scanning workflow and build a beginner's skillset in photogrammetry, we partnered with the library's Special Collections and with the Oklahoma Archaeological Survey. In fall of 2018, we were able to petition for a small amount of space and equipment to more formalize the service. Our goal with this space was to continue building partnerships and improving skills, but to also use the space as a research and testing area in order to build a development plan for a future 3D scanning lab within the library. The partnerships would be a key part of demonstrating the need and contribution such a service could have to broadening and strengthening the library's role supporting research campus-wide and provide important insight into the diverse needs of researchers using 3D Scanning on campus.

POLICY DEVELOPMENT

We focused our development strategy around the construction of a comprehensive and forward-looking policy that incorporated future development, established assessment strategies for expansion, and created a series of steps to reach that plan. This comprehensive approach, while more challenging, ultimately allowed us to better define our goals and perspectives and create a sounder strategy. We began by breaking down the 3D scanning lifecycle: (1) project development, (2) scanning, (3) processing, (4) archiving, and (5) dissemination. We then used our past and current projects to define key policy points for each phase.

In the development of our lab policy, we wanted to create something beyond the traditional service model in the library. Since 3D scanning is still relatively new, especially in terms of mainstream research, we saw this as an opportunity to build a new vision of what library roles could be in research. At the same time, while we wanted to exploit the possibility of new technology to challenge problematic power structures of access, we were conscious that caution must be taken to not re-encode or validate those traditional structures. Our goal from the outset was the development of an ethically aspirational policy that drove our discussion and outlook. Finally, we wanted the lab to also serve as a research space for the library itself; this included not only creating 3D models for exhibits and outreach but also experimenting with hardware and software, as well as using projects in the lab to explore storage needs and challenges as additoin to metadata collection. To move the lab away from a makerspace model and to ensure its use as a research space, we limited use to research purposes only, although students can still use the makerspace area to scan objects for fun. The lab is open to students, faculty, staff, and affiliated researchers at the University of Oklahoma. As a state institution we also allow collaborations on projects outside of OU that will benefit nonprofit institutions and agencies within Oklahoma.

Typically, we schedule several introductory sessions with the researcher where we work with them one-on-one to teach them the entire 3D scanning workflow, including metadata capture and best practices for archiving and publication. We believe as a lab that experiential learning is a driving force in research and development. By having new researchers scan their objects under our guidance we are not simply providing them with a 3D data set, but also the familiarity and the language to engage 3D research more fully and more often. Those that leave the lab may neither use 3D scanning beyond that instance nor think themselves proficient; however, they do leave our lab with a skillset and experience to build upon and use. As part of our commitment to teaching, we also offer lectures and classroom activities and hope to design workshops for future classroom integration. In the case of larger projects involving faculty and staff (especially those that involve the creation of 3D asset collections for teaching), we create the 3D scans ourselves.

One of the primary research agendas of our lab has been focused on the metadata required to archive 3D objects. We recently started working with the library's director of open initiatives and scholarly communication as well as the university's repository SHAREOK to create a workflow for archiving and publication of 3D models. The advent of technologies such as WebGL have led to a variety of convenient online 3D viewers, from permissively-licensed systems such as Google's "ModelViewer" and the Smithsonian Institution's "Voyager Explorer" (both available under the Apache 2.0 license) to proprietary visualization approaches such as Sketchfab's "3D Viewer."[8] Furthermore, the existence of open-source Web-specific rendering platforms such as "Three.js" and the Microsoft-backed "Babylon.js" have made the creation of bespoke 3D viewers plausible even for organizations with limited development resources.[9] We are currently researching how to implement 3D viewers into the catalog and create 3D content available for check-out. We are also looking for funding to work on a project about accessibility and 3D data.

CASE STUDIES

Our experiential approach to teaching in the lab has increased research opportunities for our community of scholars as well as elevated the role the library plays in research support. The ability to learn the process has increased the research output of our collaborators, and our cooperative model has resulted in long-term projects and returning users. At the same time, the collective approach has allowed us to carry out our own research in tandem with user projects in order to assess our own offerings to make sure we are creating the largest impact we can. The case studies that

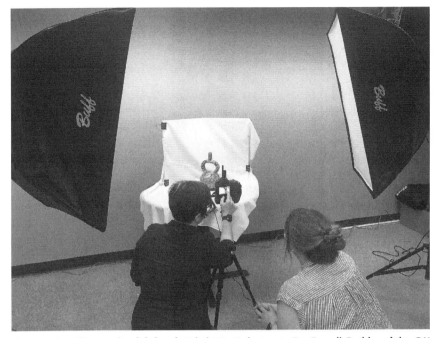

Figure 7.1.   3D scanning lab head, Kristi Wyatt, instructs Dr. Brandi Bethke of the OK Archeological Survey in the process of photogrammetric capture.

follow provide two key insights. First, they provide examples of the impact the 3D scanning lab has had on research in both STEM and humanities disciplines. Second, the case studies illustrate how the lab's success allowed it to grow in four key ways: (1) scaling up our skills, (2) building partnerships, (3) increasing visibility both within and beyond the library, and (4) inclusion in grant proposals. We also briefly discuss the ongoing use of the lab despite the impact of COVID-19. Ultimately, they demonstrate what we learned from these projects in order to grow both the lab and the library's role in campus research.

Skill Building and Scaling Up

One of the biggest impacts 3D scanning projects have had is on our ability to expand our expertise and our ability to support a variety of scanning projects on campus. Building confidence in our skillset was crucial early on and has provided us with a firm foundation to expand our offerings.

History of Science

The University of Oklahoma's Special Collections includes a large corpus focused on the history of science. In addition to its varied print collections, which include a cuneiform brick, the holdings also include a number of scientific instruments. While a library's mission is to promote patron access, issues of preservation limit physical access to the objects in this collection. Early on, we were able to partner with the History of Science collections to scan objects with a wide variety of physical properties. This allowed the library to increase virtual access and availability to the collection and showcase several pieces. Furthermore, the staff now had additional documentation when reviewing the object's state for preservation and conservation. Working on internal projects such as the History of Science Collection enabled us to hone our skills and develop our 3D scanning workflows. The process allowed us to identify and resolve potential challenges such as size restrictions, metadata collection, and costs associated with the 3D scanning process. Partnering internally not only demonstrated the value of the lab to the library's own collections but also provided clear examples to show future campus collaborators.

Law School

In the summer of 2019, we were approached by a member of the law school who wanted to recreate a virtual crime scene for a Trial Techniques course. This project involved the recreation of the scene using physical props and live actors, which we photographed in order to build a 3D model of the crime scene and import it into a virtual environment. Law students can now explore the efficacy of using virtual environments in building and presenting their arguments and the heightened realism they provide to jurors. For our lab, the project gave us the chance to test out scanning an entire environment containing multiple artifacts with an imposed time limit. It also allowed us to troubleshoot the processing and archiving of multiple scans with large file sizes.

This project also provided a unique opportunity to examine the validity of 3D models to stand in for their real-world counterparts. The key issues from the court's perspective "center on the integrity and sufficiency of the data obtained and used (whether the simulation included all the necessary data, and whether it included any unreliable data), the reliability of the software program that crunched the data and generated the simulation," and if the model could somehow induce unfair prejudice or misleading evidence.[10] Such concerns about the accuracy and validity of 3D models exist beyond the courtroom, as researchers grapple with how to create an accurate 3D model as well as how to demonstrate that the model is a credible representation of its real-world counterpart. This forced us to examine the definition and parameters of accuracy across research disciplines and to explore workflows that could capture the effects of software manipulation. The need to quantify the error in the models reinforced the benefits of the Cultural Heritage Imaging (CHI) workflow and the selection of photogrammetry and the Agisoft Metashape Pro software. The CHI image capture workflow was designed by the Bureau of Land Management and is software independent. The workflow consists of both guidelines for camera settings and capture methods to allow for a repeatable and scalable photogrammetric model. The workflow also allows us to identify and isolate which 3D data extracted from the photographs have the least amount of error. Data points with higher amounts of error are then removed in order to reduce error in the final 3D model.

Partnerships

The partnerships we have built via the 3D scanning lab have not only increased user numbers but also the number of repeat users. Our success has not only helped us maintain existing faculty/student relationships but also created paths for new ones. Faculty partners have sent multiple students to our lab for instruction and support. Furthermore, many of the pilot projects we have done with faculty have yielded ongoing endeavors.

Archaeological Survey

One of our long-term partnerships has been with the Oklahoma Archeological Survey. We have collaborated with them on a number of community outreach events as well as several research projects. One of these research projects involved the creating 3D models of horse bones prior to analysis that required a small sample of the bone to be removed. The finite and fragile nature of the archaeological record makes this type of destructive analysis problematic, despite its ability to provide additional information about the artifacts. These artifacts and the associated models were part of a larger project involving multiple stakeholders, including the Archeological Survey, the Max Planck Institute, and the Wichita and Affiliated tribes. The variety of stakeholders highlighted the importance of consistent communication to build trust. Departments that come to us for assistance need to be comfortable and confident in our abilities to help them with their research goals and having open lines of communication allows for that and it keeps them coming back. Moreover, as creators of research products, we as librarians can be involved in the data management process earlier and form stronger collaborations between the library and research partners.

Department of Anthropology

Early on in our development, we reached out to a faculty member in the Department of Anthropology. In this case, the faculty member was interested in exploring 3D scanning as a non-destructive method for analysis as well as for its potential in outreach and education. The faculty member recruited an undergraduate student to work with us in the lab to test out how 3D scanning could add to archaeological research. Additionally, the faculty member wanted to make the 3D nature of their data more accessible and tangible to both research and public audiences. After a semester of working in our lab, the student was able to create models on his own. He was also able to present his research in the lab at OU's undergraduate research conference, for which he won an award. At the same time, their project allowed us to learn several lessons. We were able to test out and receive feedback on our teaching methodology in the lab. Working with them also allowed us to understand how often, when, and why the lab would be used. This provided us key information for projecting future development potential and needs, but more immediately it provided us with a successful use case to illustrate the value such a lab could have.

Building on this initial success, the faculty member and undergraduate student were able to apply for additional funding to continue the project via a new initiative in the library, Digital Scholarship Fellowships. The goal of this project was to test alternative models to develop a more "field-friendly" photogrammetry workflow as well as learning how to archive and present 3D model data using FAIR principles. These principles were developed in order to provide guidance on data management and sustainability by emphasizing the key aspects all data should have: (1) it should be **F**indable, (2) it should be **A**ccessible, (3) it should be **I**nteroperable, and (4) it should be **R**eusable. They were first published in 2016 and have been internationally adopted by numerous library organizations.[11] At the same time, this growth in scope allowed us to gather new data for the lab, such as testing a variety of software and hardware to develop a capture process that is easily accessible and affordable. This project provided us valuable information and insight into the strengths and challenges of different hardwares and softwares, which allows us to better serve the community. It has also allowed us to expand our offering by providing detailed teaching and support on the documentation and archiving of 3D data. This is something that our lab has explicitly explored as part of our own research agenda and this project provides feedback on what will work and what needs to be implemented to allow researchers to effectively and easily implement this type of data collection in their own work.

Growing Visibility

Through word of mouth, our evolving faculty relationships have grown and extended beyond our main campus to our Health Sciences campus. Acting on the suggestion of a faculty member we had previously worked with, a graduate from the College of Allied Health's Department of Communication Sciences and Disorders at the Oklahoma City campus. They approached the lab to see if we could create a 3D model of an existing ear mold impression, which could be used to 3D print a model of the ear for training purposes. The ears will be used to create a head/ear task trainer to allow audiology students to practice audiology skills related to hearing aids, without potential harm to patients. The project connected the researcher to the technical expertise needed and allowed the department to develop safer training methods. For us, the project demonstrated the multidisciplinary success that our work had in the university community and its needs.

Engineering

A group of engineering students working on a capstone project contacted us about scanning an individual sitting in a racing seat; although they would normally utilize

CAD software, modeling a person would have been too time consuming. After the initial consultation, we determined that they could derive a workable model with one of the makerspace scanners and did not need to use photogrammetry. Within the next hour, the group of students had scanned and created a workable model of an individual sitting in a racing seat. Having this model allowed the students to have a better understanding of the interior driving space they were custom building. Once the model was completed and in their hands, they could inspect, measure, and annotate it any time during the car's fabrication. The scanning process allowed the students to not only learn a new skill but also saved them time in their project without outsourcing the learning aspect to someone else.

The following semester, we were again contacted by a different group of engineering students working on their capstone project. They had heard about the success of the other group and wanted to create a model of a motorcycle engine for their project. Their project had greater precision needs and so we suggested that they use photogrammetry to capture the engine. We walked them through the process and stood by to offer advice and direction as they photographed the engine and then worked with them to process the images. A few weeks later, we were again contacted by them because there were some issues with the measurements of the engine model in the software. We were able to troubleshoot with them to find the error and correct it. The experience highlighted the lab's ability to contribute to major undergraduate research projects. The word-of-mouth knowledge of the lab illustrated how effective the lab was at providing not only tools but also knowledge and training that was useful enough for students to tell others about their success. It also demonstrated how 3D modeling can benefit researchers by cutting down on the model creation time, allowing them to advance their research faster.

Environmental Studies

As part of our campaign to make people more aware of the 3D scanning lab, we spent some time creating a new web page for the lab on the library website. We tried to anticipate what search terms people might use who would be looking for more information about the lab or who might not know about the lab itself but wanted information on 3D scanning. We then included key phrases on the page as well as links to current research collaborations. We also worked with other staff in the library to create links on relevant library pages to the 3D scanning lab.

Our efforts to increase the virtual visibility of the lab saw quick results. In November of 2019, we received a consultation appointment from a postdoc who had found out about the lab solely from web searching. The postdoc had created the appointment to learn more about 3D scanning technology because they were interested in using it as part of their digital forestry research. Much of their research focused on using laser scanners and they were interested in learning more about the capabilities of photogrammetry to complement laser scanning techniques. The initial consultation led to an additional intensive training session where we worked with the visiting scholar to teach them the method of capture and analysis and to test out the method's ability to capture the necessary information from a modeled tree. The postdoc was very excited about the results, as the model proved successful and demonstrated the potential for photogrammetry to add to their research. Although their visiting scholar status at OU was almost finished, they expressed a willingness to keep in touch at their future research institution as well as a desire to continue collaboration and coauthorship. The project generated a particularly useful dataset for photo processing training since it was small enough to manage in an entire sitting. The project also demonstrated our ability to provide a useful service to the visiting scholar community—a community in the research world whose transience can impose particular challenges on research support and outreach.

Beyond the Library

In addition to researchers at OU, the lab has also successfully collaborated with researchers at other institutions in Oklahoma. Shortly after our website went live, we were contacted by an undergraduate from the University of Science and Arts of Oklahoma, which is approximately forty-five minutes southeast of OU's Norman campus. She had found us online and wanted to incorporate photogrammetry into her senior thesis project, but her school did not have the equipment or personnel resources for her to learn more about the process. We were able to meet up with her online and in the lab to teach her the entire photogrammetric process. This collaboration demonstrated that the lab could not only democratize access to resources on the OU campus, but could play a role in a larger research network. The access to the lab and its ability to reach beyond its front door is part of what makes it successful.

Uncas Star Chart

This is an ongoing project with the Sam Noble Museum of Natural History to create 3D models of a sixty-plus piece artifact found in Uncas, Oklahoma. Along with scanning and creating 3D models, they also wanted 3D printed replicas for use in the classroom. The 3D models offer both a preservation record for the museum and virtual access—meaning, patrons can explore the artifacts and move them around on a screen while the integrity of the real artifacts remain intact. The 3D printed replicas allow for hands-on experience in the classroom. Students can recreate the chart layout and get an idea of the texture and other topographic characteristics of the artifact. Off-site projects like these demonstrate the utility of having a portable 3D scanning technique like photogrammetry. This allows us to access objects that may be difficult or too fragile to move from their current locations. This mobility also increases our ability to collaborate with researchers and does not impose additional stress on or challenges to them.

Inclusion in Grant Proposals

As our expertise has grown, faculty from both the Architecture and Construction Science Departments have approached us to collaboratively write National Endowment for the Humanities (NEH) grant proposals involving 3D scanning. Our involvement in these proposals includes advising on the capture and workflow processes, publication of the models, and data storage and archiving. At times, financial support from stakeholders is requested for our staff time, (i.e., one of us creating the scan, equipment such as a new scanner(s), and general library maintenance of digital storage). Involvement in grant projects as integrated members of the research teams helps establish the library as research peers and co-creators of knowledge within the campus community.

COVID-19

In the midst of the pandemic, we were approached by the Western History Collection of OU Libraries to scan selected objects for an art history professor. This request came about as course instruction was being moved online, and in-person visits to collections were being cancelled. The selected objects were from the St. Louis World's Fair collection and consisted of a variety of objects such as a belt buckle, medallion, advertising plate, and a few other items. This allowed both professor and students to maintain their coursework without sacrificing a chance to view the objects they were studying. Having the artifacts available for viewing online gives the students the ability to return to the object, as needed. The pandemic highlighted the ability of the lab to expand the digital collections available to faculty and students for course instruction. Beyond the immediacy of the pandemic, online learning continues to be a major push of many academic institutions. Our experiences in the lab have highlighted the need for the digitization of research objects as part of online learning environments.

QUANTIFYING SUCCESS

The 3D scanning lab's work, to date, has included researchers of all ranks across fifteen OU divisions (see table 7.1) plus collaborations with researchers beyond the OU campus. As part of our development plan, we worked with other librarians to design a booking system for the lab via Spaces in LibCal. This allowed us to track a variety of user metrics and measure who used the lab and how they used it. We are able to not only identify areas for growth and development but also document the impact we have on research support.

Our first full year saw twelve unique users in the lab with a total of fifty-five bookings for a time-slot average of three hours. In 2020, these numbers increased to fifteen unique users and eighty-seven total bookings. These numbers represented an increase in usage of approximately 58 percent, and this increase happened despite the

Table 7.1. 3D Scanning Lab Campus Collaborators

Division/Unit	No. of Researchers and Rank
Department of Anthropology	1 associate professor, 2 assistant professors, 1 undergraduate
OK Archeological Survey	1 research faculty, 1 senior researcher
Department of Classics and Letters	1 professor
College of Law	1 director
Health Science Center	1 associate professor, 1 associate dean, 1 graduate student
Sam Noble—Archaeology	1 associate curator, 1 professor emerita
Sam Noble—Vertebrate Paleontology	1 fossil preparator, 1 head of exhibits
Sam Noble—Mammalogy	1 curatorial associate
Architecture	1 professor
Western History Collections	1 librarian
History of Science Collections	1 associate professor
College of Engineering	10–15 undergraduates, 1 assistant professor
Fred Jones Jr. Museum of Art—Department of Learning and Engagement	1 director, 2 staff
Construction Science	1 associate professor
Environmental Studies	1 postdoctoral student

Created by Kristi Wyatt and Zenobie Garrett.

closure of the lab from March throughAugust 2020 due to COVID-19. In terms of scholarly outputs for our collaborators, research in the lab has yielded nine conference presentations and posters, six outreach programs, four funding proposals, three classroom integrations, three capstone projects, two publications, and one graduate thesis, to date (our partridge in a pear tree is currently in transit).

The success of the lab with faculty and students has resulted in internal growth. The increased usage of the lab in a single year has allowed us to petition for student employee positions. We have recently acquired two positions for approximately twenty hours per week. This not only allows us to support more research projects but also gives us a chance to train additional undergraduates in 3D scanning and expose them to a wide variety of use cases. The goal is to get them comfortable enough with the equipment and the process to help others as well as resolve issues that may come up during the scanning process. Along with their capture notes, we ask them to write down anything that doesn't quite make sense or anything that stands out as really helpful so we can continue to refine our instruction. Hiring and training students has been a great way of spreading the knowledge through peer-to-peer instruction, long-term scanning projects, and assisting in the more complicated collaborations. The ability to work in the lab gives them one more skill set to potentially use in their own fields and on their resumes.

The research demand for 3D scanning has also allowed us to expand our equipment offerings and skill sets. We recently acquired macro lenses to create models of very small objects. We also have a sliding macro rail, which allows us to do focus stacking which is the layering and combining of multiple photographs taken from different focus distances. This is useful for small objects as well as objects with incisions or etching as the lenses necessary for capturing tiny objects have a shallower depth of field and rely on stacking to achieve a complete, in-focus photograph. In addition to equipment, we have been investing time in expanding our skill sets and the support we can offer to researchers. We have explored born-digital modeling via open-source resources like Blender, which allow us to not only create any object imaginable but add engagement features such as animation, shadow, and sound. We are currently applying for grants to acquire several handheld laser scanners. These laser scanners can capture small objects with complex geometry better than photogrammetry and can also create models of objects with smooth and/or reflective surfaces which is not possible using photogrammetry. Additionally, they can generate 3D models much more rapidly than the current photogrammetric process used in the Lab.

CONCLUSION

The increase in growth and usage of the Bizzell 3D scanning lab in the past two years has demonstratively illustrated the role the library can play in campus research. Curating the intellectual expertise alongside the equipment allows the library to participate in all parts of the research lifecycle and become a key part in the research design process. A robust community of professional researchers and entrepreneurs will not grow out of our student body if there is no scaffolding upon which to grow. Investing in research technologies in the libraries provides a non-siloed pipeline for research ideas. This is integral to ensure that all OU researchers can have a large impact via their research and creative activity. However, this success requires not just an investment in its creation, but the development and ongoing assessment of a sustainability plan. To this end we have continuously monitored and collected data on the lab's usage including equipment, space, and personnel. This data collection has helped us define employment opportunities for students in the lab, measure equipment usage and wear, and build a timeline of future equipment service and costs going forward. We also maintain an active log of projects that we cannot accommodate in order to determine where the lab can and should grow. Our goal is to work with library administrators and our campus research partners to define a sustainable development plan that determines the future vision and growth of the 3D scanning lab at OU Libraries.

NOTES

1. Matt Cook and Zack Lischer-Katz, "Integrating 3D and Virtual Reality into Research and Pedagogy in Higher Education," in *Beyond Reality: Augmented, Virtual, and Mixed Reality in the Library*, ed. Kenneth Varnum (Chicago: ALA Editions, 2019), 69–85; Zack Lischer-Katz, Matt Cook, and Kristal Boulden, "Evaluating the Impact of a Virtual Reality Workstation," *The Association for Information Science and Technology* 55, no. 1 (November 2019):

300–308; Elizabeth Pober and Matt Cook, "Thinking in Virtual Spaces: Impacts of Virtual Reality on the Undergraduate Interior Design Process," *International Journal of Virtual and Augmented Reality* 3, no. 2 (July 2019): 23–40; Matt Cook and John Grime, "Motivations, Design, and Preliminary Testing for a 360° Vision Simulator," *Virtual Reality* 25 (March 2021): 247–55, https://doi.org/10.1007/s10055-020-00433-x.

2. Neelam Bharti, Sara Gonzalez, and Amy Buhler, "3D Technology in Libraries: Applications for Teaching and Research," *2015 Fourth International Symposium on Emerging Trends and Technologies in Libraries and Information Services* (2015): 161–66. doi: 10.1109/ETTLIS.2015.7048191.

3. Michael Groenendyk and Riehl Gallant, "3D Printing and Scanning at the Dalhousie University Libraries: A Pilot Project," *Library Hi Tech* 31, no. 1 (March 2013), https://doi.org/10.1108/07378831311303912.

4. Tara Radniecki, "Supporting 3D Modeling in the Academic Library," *Library Hi Tech* 35, no. 2 (June 2017), https://doi.org/10.1108/LHT-11-2016-0121.

5. Jason A. Reuscher, "Three-Dimensional (3-D) Scanning within Academic Libraries: Exploring and Considering a New Public Service," *Pennsylvania Libraries: Research and Practice* 2, no. 1 (Spring 2014), https://doi.org/10.5195/palrap.2014.56.

6. "4-Day Photogrammetry Training," Cultural Heritage Imaging, accessed May 12, 2021, http://culturalheritageimaging.org/What_We_Offer/Training/photogram_training/.

7. "Smithsonian 3D Metadata Model," Smithsonian Digitization Program Office, accessed May 12, 2021, https://dpo.si.edu/blog/Smithsonian-3d-metadata-model; "Community Standards for 3D Data Preservation," CS3DP, accessed May 12, 2021, cs3dp.org; Matt Cook et al., "Challenges and Strategies for Educational Virtual Reality: Results of an Expert-led Forum on 3D/VR Technologies across Academic Institutions," *Information Technology and Libraries (Online)* 38, no. 4 (December 2019): 25–48; "Welcome to GLAM 3D," GLAM 3D, accessed May 12, 2021, glam3d.org.

8. "WebGL Overview," Khronos Group, accessed August 9, 2021, https://www.khronos.org/webgl/; "Model-Viewer," Google, accessed August 9, 2021, https://modelviewer.dev/; "Model-Viewer," Google, accessed August 9, 2021, https://github.com/google/model-viewer; "Voyager," Smithsonian, accessed August 9, 2021, https://smithsonian.github.io/dpo-voyager/explorer/overview/; "DPO-Voyager," Smithsonian, accessed August 9, 2021, https://github.com/Smithsonian/dpo-voyager; "Sketchfab's 3D Viewer," Sketchfab, accessed August 9, 2021, https://sketchfab.com/3d-viewer.

9. "Three.js," Javascript, accessed August 9, 2021, https://threejs.org/; "babylon.js," Microsoft, accessed August 9, 2021, https://www.babylonjs.com/.

10. Thomas A. Mauet, *Trial Techniques and Trials*, tenth edition (New York: Wolters Kluwer, 2017), 316.

11. Mark D. Wilkinson et al. "The Guiding Principles for Scientific Data Management and Stewardship," *Scientific Data* 3, 160018 (2016), https://doi.org/10.1038/sdata.2016.18.

BIBLIOGRAPHY

Bharti, Neelam, Sara Gonzalez, and Amy Buhler. "3D Technology in Libraries: Applications for Teaching and Research." *2015 Fourth International Symposium on Emerging Trends and Technologies in Libraries and Information Services* (2015): 161–66. doi: 10.1109/ETTLIS.2015.7048191.

Cook, Matt, and John Grime. "Motivations, Design, and Preliminary Testing for a 360° Vision Simulator." *Virtual Reality* 25 (March 2021): 247–55. https://doi.org/10.1007/s10055-020-00433-x.

Cook, Matt, and Zack Lischer-Katz. "Integrating 3D and Virtual Reality into Research and Pedagogy in Higher Education." In *Beyond Reality: Augmented, Virtual, and Mixed Reality in the Library*, edited by Kenneth Varnum, 69–85. Chicago: ALA Editions, 2019.

Cook, Matt, Zack Lischer-Katz, Nathan Hall, Juliet Hardesty, Jennifer Johnson, Robert McDonald, and Tara Carlisle. "Challenges and Strategies for Educational Virtual Reality: Results of an Expert-led Forum on 3D/VR Technologies across Academic Institutions." *Information Technology and Libraries (Online)* 38, no. 4 (December 2019): 25–48.

CS3DP. "Community Standards for 3D Data Preservation." Accessed May 12, 2021. cs3dp.org.

Cultural Heritage Imaging. "4-Day Photogrammetry Training." Accessed May 12, 2021. http://culturalheritageimaging.org/What_We_Offer/Training/photogram_training/.

GLAM 3D. "Welcome to GLAM 3D." Accessed May 12, 2021. glam3d.org.

Google. "Model-Viewer." Accessed August 9, 2021. https://github.com/google/model-viewer.

———. "Model-Viewer." Accessed August 9, 2021. https://modelviewer.dev/.

Groenendyk, Michael, and Riel Gallant. "3D Printing and Scanning at the Dalhousie University Libraries: A Pilot Project." *Library Hi Tech* 31, no. 1 (March 2013): 34–41. https://doi.org/10.1108/0737883131130391.

Javascript. "three.js." Accessed August 9, 2021. https://threejs.org/.

Khronos Group. "WebGL Overview." Accessed August 9, 2021. https://www.khronos.org/webgl/.

Lischer-Katz, Zack, Matt Cook, and Kristal Boulden. "Evaluating the Impact of a Virtual Reality Workstation." *The Association for Information Science and Technology* 55, no. 1 (November 2019): 300–308.

Mauet, Thomas A. *Trial Techniques and Trials*. Tenth edition. New York: Wolters Kluwer, 2017.

Microsoft. "babylon.js." Accessed August 9, 2021. https://www.babylonjs.com/.

Pober, Elizabeth, and Matt Cook. "Thinking in Virtual Spaces: Impacts of Virtual Reality on the Undergraduate Interior Design Process." *International Journal of Virtual and Augmented Reality* 3, no. 2 (July 2019): 23–40.

Radniecki, Tara. "Supporting 3D Modeling in the Academic Library." *Library Hi Tech* 35, no. 2 (June 2017): 240–50. https://doi.org/10.1108/LHT-11-2016-0121.

Reuscher, Jason A. "Three-Dimensional (3D) Scanning Within Academic Libraries: Exploring and Considering a New Public Service." *Pennsylvania Libraries: Research & Practice* 2, no. 1 (Spring 2014). https://doi.org/10.5195/palrap.2014.56

Sketchfab. "Sketchfab's 3D Viewer." Accessed August, 9, 2021. https://sketchfab.com/3d-viewer.

Smithsonian. "DPO-Voyager." Accessed August 9, 2021. https://github.com/Smithsonian/dpo-voyager.

———. "Voyager." Accessed August 9, 2021. https://smithsonian.github.io/dpo-voyager/explorer/overview/.

Smithsonian Digitization Program Office. "Smithsonian 3D Metadata Model." Accessed May 12, 2021. https://dpo.si.edu/blog/Smithsonian-3d-metadata-model.

Wilkinson, Mark D., Michel Dumontier, IJsbrand Jan Aalbersberg, Gabrielle Appleton, Myles Axton, Arie Baak, Niklaus Blomberg, et al. "The FAIR Guiding Principles for Scientific Data Management and Stewardship." *Scientific Data* 3 (March 2016). https://doi.org/10.1038/sdata.2016.18.

8

Collaborative Implementation of a Semi-Automated 3D Printing Service

Amy Van Epps, Matt Cook, and Susan Berstler

This is the story of starting a 3D printing service at Harvard Library. A range of use cases, benefits, and applications inspired the initiative, which we saw as a means to facilitate the *physical* reproduction of scholarly source materials that a range of Harvard scholars are actively producing. This chapter details a 3D printing service pilot—conducted at Cabot Science Library in collaboration with Rob Hart of the Harvard Physical Science Education Group, who leads the physics department fabrication laboratory located in the Science Center. At the core of the pilot was a web application, which allowed students, faculty, and staff at Harvard University an end-to-end 3D printing system to remotely submit and produce physical reproductions of scholarly materials and pickup at Cabot Science Library, thus removing the staffing overhead many 3D printing operations invite. MakerFleet, the software in question, has since ceased operations (which provides a valuable lesson with regards to vendor source). While they were in business, our partnership with their (alumni-led) team represents a modest investment back into the local entrepreneurial ecosystem.

Once implemented, the new service saw steady uptake through the 2019–2020 academic year. Indeed, the 2-month pilot at Cabot from mid-October to mid-December 2019 saw one hundred and ten people signed up for the service and more than one thousand hours of printer operation, all with little promotion. The recurring costs for maintaining this service indefinitely are reasonable, especially when compared with manually maintained print services in other locations. One-time costs to establish the ongoing service in Cabot were less than approximately $10k, while expected annual recurring costs for both the control software and a supply of filament are just under $4k a year. A cost recovery model would further offset these annual recurring costs, making our modest implementation eminently reproducible.

The increasingly common (3D) data type that defines this production method is pervasive across disciplines and institutions, while associated production and associated visualization capabilities already exist within Harvard Library, making 3D printing a natural extension of existing services and expertise. This chapter presents the linkages, as well as the general motivations for the pilot service, (current and potential) use cases, and feedback/usage statistics we've compiled about the program thus far. In conjunction with related, existing services (e.g., Virtual Reality and 3D scanning), the post-COVID maturation of this pilot service stands to further impact the teaching, learning, and research for myriad Harvard Library stakeholders, including a range of local practitioners who have already demonstrated the scholarly use of 3D data.

BACKGROUND

Given the increasing size and complexity of research data, and the advancement of various scanning and visualization methods (e.g., photogrammetry and virtual reality), 3D data is emerging as the discrete scholarly asset *of record* across multiple academic disciplines.[1] This data type exists along an interrelated set of tools and services, and *holistic* support structures—implemented for students and scholars to engage with 3D scholarly material—that accounts for scanning, visualization, and multiplatform publishing (i.e., 3D printing, web-based publication, etc.). Harvard Library has made progress in deploying tools and services along the 3D data pipeline (see figure 8.1) that support both the creation and visualization of 3D content, although the publication and dissemination of that same data is oftentimes left in the hands of practitioners who may be unaware that their scholarly data is *physically*, as well as digitally, portable. The 3D printing pilot service aims to fully support this final output stage and thereby strengthen the 3D publishing capabilities of users across disciplines and schools.

Why is 3D content important for scholarship? Per Buckland, "primary sources of information [are] not the literature . . . but observation of the relevant natural phenomena."[2] Basically, 3D data and associated technologies represent an attempt to provide physical access to *primary* source material—that is, objects-of-study themselves—rather than observations of interpretations that comprise traditional scholarly material, like monographs and journal articles. Academic fields of study that engage regularly with artifacts, specimens, anatomical structures, and any scholarly source material that is spatially extended (i.e., part of the physical world), are impacted by the advent of 3D, and the means to reproduce this scholarly source material—especially in the face of a historic "culture of 'data holding'" that define archival practices—is one benefit, as is the ability to repeatedly invoke and analyze a true-to-life reproduction.[3] Indeed, surrogates that more closely approximate spatially extended source material, "facilitate a number of innovative analyses that were not possible before."[4] *Printed* models further empower end users by virtue of their tactile nature, their real-world dimensionality, and increasing surface texture detail.

Local researchers and instructors have begun producing these hyper-portable 3D assets, at scale, for the benefit of Harvard stakeholders and the visiting public. Through the ongoing "Digital Giza" project, faculty in the Semitic Museum have produced a range of 3D content, including, quite recently, a digitized set of full-sized sarcophagi.[5] Outside of the realm of material history and cultural heritage, the Museum of Comparative Zoology recently embarked upon a MicroCT-based scanning project in conjunction with a number of partner institutions to found the openVertebrate (oVert) project.[6] In contrast to the photogrammetric or structured light capture methods relied upon by most cultural heritage institutions engaged in 3D scanning, the use of tomographic methods, like MicroCT—while expensive and requiring special (radiological) controls—affords *volumetric* outputs that reveal object interiors without damaging specimens.[7]

Finally, faculty teaching undergraduate classes are beginning to integrate complex 3D objects into their curriculum, as demonstrated in two courses; Staging Shakespeare and Organic Chemistry.[8] In these courses, virtual simulations allowed students to experience the dimensions of—and relationships between—the stage, pit, and balconies of the Globe Theatre, and molecular structures, respectively. Critically, this content was already part of the regular curriculum, but visually inaccessible or otherwise difficult to physically access. With the Shakespeare class, the in-class experience can be further supplemented with a 3D print, a take-home replica of the in-class VR experience students can use as a reference object as they continue to develop their understanding of theatre history.

Beyond Harvard, large-scale repositories have been developed to accommodate access to—and preservation of—printable 3D assets originating from both in and outside of the academy. Perhaps the largest, Sketchfab, hosts millions of models, including a variety of educationally valuable content, much of which is free to download and print. Unfortunately, the Sketchfab platform is not designed for the long-term preservation of research data, which places further requirements on hosting platforms that include varying permissions levels, robust metadata, and so on. Fortunately, some disciplinary platforms have sought to fill these gaps in rigor.[9] Morphosource, for example, includes accession data about each uploaded scan, linking physical and digital archives in a way that provides a useful chain-of-evidence.[10] Coupled with flexible hosting platforms like Open Science Framework and Zenodo, 3D content on Sketchfab and/or Morphosource is citable as peer-reviewed source material in the research literature, and subsequent analyses (performed upon a 3D print of a scan, perhaps) represents rigorous inquiry.

USE CASES

Perhaps the most practical use of 3D printing is the ability to produce repairs for common scientific equipment and—in some cases—to produce low-cost iterations of the equipment itself. The NIH 3D Print Exchange's "Labware and Devices" category is a good example of how one might leverage 3D printing in this way.[11] There we can see an iPhone microscope adaptor with a public domain license; a mechanical modification that allows for the 3D printing of biogels from a standard 3D printer; and assorted tube racks, microscopic slide holders, and much more. Given the availability of a 3D printing service like ours, students, postdoctoral researchers (and indeed anyone with or without laboratory affiliation) can maintain and upgrade their own equipment at minimal cost. Thingiverse, a ubiquitous model hosting platform, is likewise replete with mounts, housings, and mods for common electronics, which extend the usefulness of this "Open Hardware" application beyond the laboratory setting to various microelectronics projects.[12] These open hardware initiatives have especially timely benefits in the time of COVID-19, and institutions have deployed plans for crowdsourced personal protective equipment.[13]

Disciplinary practitioners are also regular users of 3D printing technology. Clinicians have begun using true-to-scale 3D visualization of physiological structures to aid diagnosis, reporting, and preoperative treatment planning.[14] 3D prints have also proven to be valuable teaching tools in medical fields, especially where issues related to anatomical variation across patients is concerned. Given 3D visualization, including physical visualization achieved via 3D printing, the inherently spatial nature of the complex learning objects means that "instances of individual variations, anomalies, and pathologies are easily preserved."[15] Importantly, these anatomically correct learning objects represent a much more affordable alternative to replicas or cadavers, which historically feature centrally in medical education but are typically inaccessible outside of the laboratory.

Finally, there are accessibility implications to providing ready access to 3D printers. The tactile nature of the outputs means that visually impaired learners can benefit from the variety of physical visualizations available on some of the open-access 3D asset repositories described above. Take NASA's "Touchable Universe in a Box," for example.[16] As per Arcand et al., 3D prints enable "Blind persons . . . to gain an understanding of information that is very similar to that of sighted people in regards to phenomena that are normally experienced in a purely visual way, regardless of their different mechanisms of internally representing these concepts."[17] Such benefits apply to the microscopic (i.e., 3D printed protein molecules) and the human scale as well.

DESCRIPTION OF THE SERVICE

In recent years, the hardware and the software needed to produce and host 3D content has increased in accessibility and decreased in cost. Digital modeling can be done at zero cost, on the web, using open CAD software like TinkerCAD, while (somewhat more sophisticated) open-source photogrammetry software, like AliceVision,[18] allow for the digital recreation of real-world objects. For hosting, Thingiverse represents a robust community of 3D printable content, and Sketchfab.com now supports a community of more than five million members, whose 3D content is viewable online and often downloadable for 3D printing.[19] Finally, graphics processing hardware capable of rendering these objects has become commonplace, and if end users are unable to produce these objects on their personal machines, several on-campus facilities are equipped to support production. After modeling, scanning, or downloading existing 3D assets, content is sent by the end user to the 3D print queue for pickup at Cabot Science Library. Figure 8.1 shows the printers in the enclosure holding them, and the monitor to show the printer status and information about ongoing print jobs.

Figure 8.1. Custom enclosure with printers in the library.
Image by Matthew Cook.

For the pilot, we used MakerFleet software, developed by Harvard Alumni Harnek Gulati as part of the Harvard University iLab "Venture Teams."[20] A web-based 3D printer management system, MakerFleet had two key features: (1) The ability to orient, slice, and remotely submit models for 3D printing on a "fleet" or set of printers; and (2) onsite administrative functionality that empowers the end user to reset the printer at the time of model pickup, thereby providing for semi-automatic print queue maintenance with minimal staffing. Value-added functionality included the ability to track your print, in real time, through printer-mounted webcams and an automatic email-based notification system, which alerts users when their print has finished (or if it fails). The software even included a handful of built-in "model maker" tools, to make keychains or cookie cutters, which provides an approachable first print opportunity for the new user.

To initiate a 3D print, the user first logged into the MakerFleet website, with their Harvard credentials, and uploaded a 3D model file. Models had to be in the standard STL file type, and were converted using one of the many free conversion tools available for files in another format. The STL file was scaled and oriented in the browser, on the MakerFleet "models" page, before "slicing" (a layer-by-layer breakdown necessary to guide the print nozzle) at the "prints" page. After orienting and slicing a digital 3D model, the user received an estimated print time and selected a 3D printer profile, which can include specialized characteristics ranging from filament color, to material type, to layer height (i.e., resolution). Support structure can also be enabled at the "prints" stage. Finally, prints—to come, ongoing, and completed (or failed)—were monitored and archived on the "print jobs" page. It is there, at "print jobs" that the user is provided with a webcam stream of a print-in-progress and can view a history of previously submitted print jobs.

Unfortunately, MakerFleet will not be the printer management software for Harvard Library moving forward. Due in part to a drop-off in core clientele (universities) during COVID, Harnek was forced to shut down the service in early 2021. Yet, while MakerFleet will not be available for future use, a number of established vendors are available who might support all or some of the abovementioned functionality. Proprietary vendors in the 3D printer fleet management arena include the 3DPrinterOS, Astroprint, and BuildBee.[21] Alternatively, a set of open-source tools can be deployed in tandem to support the abovementioned functionality (e.g., remote submission, model prep, printer monitoring, etc.) if third-party subscription costs prove to be prohibitive, the organization has access to local technical support and maintenance resources.[22]

SURVEY DATA

As mentioned above, users need to register at the MakerFleet website to send print jobs to the printers in the Cabot Science Library. As a result, a list of everyone who participated in the pilot project was readily available and became the sample population for a survey that was distributed to determine how people used the service, if they had access to 3D printing elsewhere on campus, and the advantages of having a service in Cabot Science Library, among other topics. A full copy of the survey is presented below in table 8.1.

Table 8.1. Survey for 3D Printing at Cabot Library

Thank you for participating in our 3D printing service pilot. The following survey is designed to help us determine the long-term feasibility of 3D printing at Cabot Science Library.

1.	On a scale from 0–10, how likely are you to recommend 3D printing at Cabot Science Library to a friend or colleague?

Not Likely   Extremely Likely

0   1   2   3   4   5   6   7   8   9   10

2.	How would you feel if the 3D printing pilot were not continued?

Disappointed   Happy

0   1   2   3   4   5   6   7   8   9   10

3.	Tell us about your 3D printing experience at Cabot Library.

[Open text box]

4.	Tell us about your purpose for using 3D printing? (e.g., class work, prototyping, personal/fun, etc.)

[Open text box]

5.	Do you have access to 3D printing elsewhere? If yes, where?

No   Maybe   Yes (and Where?) [Open text box]

6.	Please tell us why you chose to print in Cabot.

[Open text box]

7.	If we continue providing 3D printers, how often do you anticipate using the 3D printers at Cabot Science Library?

Daily   Weekly   Monthly   Yearly   Never

8.	Do you have any recommendations on how/where we should advertise our new service?

[Open text box]

9.	What training or events would you like to see offered in support of 3D printing?

[Open text box]

10.	Which Harvard school are you affiliated with?

Harvard College / FAS	GSAS / FAS
Engineering and Applied Science	Design
Division of Continuing Education	Divinity
Education	Business School
Kennedy School	Law School
Medical School/Public Health/Dental	Radcliffe

Created by Amy Van Epps, Matthew Cook, and Susan Berstler.

One hundred and ten people signed up to use the MakerFleet program and were sent the survey and given a week to complete it. During that time, forty-six surveys were submitted through Qualtrics for an overall return rate of 41 percent. The majority of the users for our pilot are affiliated with the Faculty of Arts and Sciences, thirty-seven undergraduate and five graduate students. Of the remaining responses, one was from the medical campus, and we received no response about affiliation from the remaining three. This distribution is expected, given the location of the pilot in Cabot Science Library and the primary user group in the Science Center, which are undergraduate science majors.

Of the survey respondents, more than 85 percent of them would be very likely (8 out of 10 or higher) to recommend using the 3D printing service at Cabot Library, and all of them would be disappointed if the service were discontinued. It is good to hear that users would recommend the service and not surprising to know they would be disappointed to see it discontinued. When asked to describe their experience with printing via MakerFleet in Cabot, the respondents took time to explain what they liked or what did not work. The top responses included feedback that users "loved it," it was a great resource, a good location, and easy to use. There were some responses that noted challenges that included needing better support and having all the printers busy. During the pilot, about 60 percent of the printing was for fun or personal reasons. The remaining 40 percent was split between prototyping, class-related, learning a new skill, and research. A certain amount of personal and fun use will always exist on 3D printers, even if there is a charge to print, but class-related use would be expected to grow over time.

We also asked the users if they had access to 3D printing anywhere else, and about 25 percent percent (12 out of 44) of them do have other options; in most cases the other option was the School of Engineering and Applied Sciences Active Learning Labs. A variety of other locations were available to individuals, but no locations with broad or common accessibility among the users of the Cabot printing pilot. We asked why they chose to print in Cabot. The majority chose Cabot due to its convenient location, even when they had other printing access. In descending order of frequency, the next two responses about why Cabot was selected as the location of choice were equally popular, the remote access and the simplicity to use, both of which are a strong vote in favor of the MakerFleet software to interface with the printers. The other responses included capacity (in reference to having six printers available), that it was free, and that the prints are high quality. The users were also asked what other services or training they would like that are associated with a 3D printing service. The most popular option is software training, and there were three specific programs called out: AutoCAD, SolidWorks, and Fusion360. This information is helpful for considering what a full printing service and associated programming might include.

SERVICE USAGE

The MakerFleet platform included basic analytics tracking. The graphs generated by the software that are included in this section represent use from the pilot rollout on

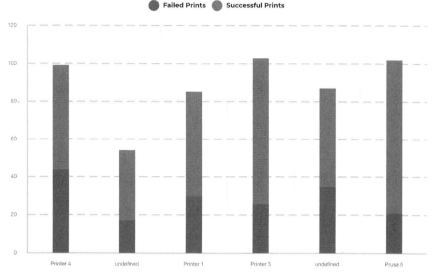

Figure 8.2. Graph of successful and failed 3D prints.
Image reproduced from Harnek Gulati, MakerFleet founder.

October 22, 2019 through December 20, 2019, when Cabot closed for the semester break. Figure 8.2 highlights a number of interesting statistics including a successful print rate of 67 percent. This is considered high in comparison to other use cases described by MakerFleet. The majority of the failed prints were caused by breaks in communication; a situation that has been fixed by switching from using Wi-Fi to wired Ethernet to connect to the Raspberry PIs.

The pilot project was advertised only on-site in the library and through word of mouth and gathered one hundred and ten users in two months. Printing was free throughout the pilot. The MakerFleet software can interface with Harvard IT's installation of the PaperCut system for implementation of a pay for printing model. All six printers were also available throughout the entire pilot, three printers were borrowed back by the Physics Fabrication Lab, which owns them, toward the end of the semester to support class projects.

The Fab Lab also supported the maintenance efforts, and will continue to do so moving forward, which is a singular benefit given the expertise of the staff and the lab's proximity to Cabot Science Library.

Anecdotal data gathered through conversations and email with users of the pilot project showed a wide variety of types of 3D prints from practical to playful to visionary. More than one undergraduate remarked that they had access to 3D printing at their high school and were disappointed to find that it was not widely available at Harvard. A number of exceptions were made to accommodate print jobs that were longer than our fifteen-hour limit. A couple of examples of prints completed in Cabot include a large box-like object that forms the top portion of an enclosure for electronics used in a lab and a prototype of an ergonomic keyboard.

NEXT STEPS

As a result of this pilot, we are now determined to implement a 3D printing regular service within the library; develop and expand training opportunities and collaborations that support and highlight the scholarly uses for the printers; and prepare and implement a cost model to ensure the long-term viability of the service. Expanding on the issue of cost, it is important to consider what it would cost to offer this service as a regular part of the larger Harvard Library services in support of teaching, learning, and research at the university. Installation of six printers as a regular service in the Cabot Science Library would have a number of costs associated with it, both up-front, one-time expenses and other ongoing costs. The one-time expenses include purchasing three printers, fully assembled, rather than purchasing kits to assemble ourselves. The printers used for the pilot were loaned from the Physics Fabrication Lab, they are willing to loan us three for long-term use, but the library would need to purchase another three for a full-fleet equivalent to the pilot. For the printers to talk with the MakerFleet program and coordinate the camera feed of the print jobs, each printer needs to be connected to a small piece of hardware called a Raspberry Pi, costing $200 apiece. For printers used and actively printing in a common, public space, each one needs to be included in an enclosure with filtering that passes Environmental Health and Safety (EH&S) review for removing particulates and gasses from the air. The custom-built enclosure shown in figure 8.1 does not meet EH&S guidelines for particulate removal.

In addition to the quantifiable costs, there are invisible costs of staff time to support the printers and ensure maximum ability to print. This includes removing completed jobs from the printer if the users do not arrive in a timely fashion, clearing any filament clogs and resulting failed prints, and other maintenance required from regular use. While over time we may be able to develop a group of students who would be interested in helping with this work, particularly those who have taken maker classes or worked in the Fabrication Lab, initially the support and training for ongoing support will fall on the staff of Cabot Science Library. A cost recovery model could be developed to help support the ongoing cost of filament and the ultimate replacement/upgrade of the printers over time. Current practice uses either a cost per hour of printing time, or a cost per gram of filament used for the print job. The cost recovery model currently in place at the Harvard iLab, located across the river in Allston, is one dollar per hour, so there is a precedent on campus for a pricing structure that is below the costs of commercial access to 3D printers and would generate ongoing revenue to support the program.

Programming/Workshop Goals

Local practitioners are prepared to offer 3D printing-oriented programming on-site, at Cabot Science Library, to encourage use of the service and inspire new use cases across disciplines. Dave Weimer, who—with partners at Northeastern University—developed the "Touch this Page" project, is ready to present on the historical context and impetus for these physical production services, especially as it relates to accessible pedagogy, while we have seen strong attendance numbers for our hands-on "Immersive Design: Concept-to-3D Print Workflows Using Virtual Reality" workshop. In the case of the latter, specific curricular integration of 3D printing workflows within Introduction to Digital Fabrication, has impacted undergraduate teaching and learning.[23] Importantly, tool-oriented training opportunities—which have been specifically requested by pilot service users—do not require the use of high-end interfaces like virtual reality. Entry-level, web-based modeling software, like Autodesk's TinkerCAD, have made CAD design amazingly accessible.[24] This assortment of training opportunities, ranging from the historical to the practical, will feature heavily in the development of the 3D printing service model at Cabot Library and extension of the existing Media& series of learning opportunities.[25]

Marketing/Archiving

The Cabot pilot was unique in many ways. Created in partnership with the director of the Physics Fabrication Lab and the founder of MakerFleet, the pilot was launched to test demand and use of 3D printers placed in a centrally located library open almost 24/7. It was a soft launch with minimal promotion to test the interest in and durability of the MakerFleet software, the Prusa printers, and even the Harvard Wi-Fi network. Users signed up after seeing the printers in the library or hearing about the printers via word of mouth. Very little promotion was done outside of Cabot Science Library itself.

Should 3D printing become a permanent library service, a full-fledged promotional campaign would be developed in coordination with Harvard Library Communications as well as library liaisons. As with all of the innovative technology Cabot makes available to the Harvard community, growing a robust cross-disciplinary user group is our goal. Due to existing campus partnerships, Cabot is well-situated to support both new and expert users. Social media, the Harvard Library's website and digital signage, and a large variety of campus e-newsletters can be used to promote this service to students, faculty, and staff. Following the example of the Cabot Media Studios, we would work with our colleagues to find a way to share and archive projects.[26] One fun way of encouraging sharing would be to ask users to post an image of their project on Instagram with the hashtag #Cabot3D.

CONCLUSION

University stakeholders become empowered innovators when they are provided with access to 3D printing, and the library—as the discipline-agnostic heart of the university—is well positioned to support research, teaching, and learning by providing the service. At Harvard, this centrality was not merely conceptual. Cabot's location, in the Science Center adjacent to Harvard Yard, and almost 24/7 open hours, make it accessible to more members of Harvard's community than any other 3D printer location. Three-dimensional printing-as-a-service is also a valuable upskilling opportunity, and, through the pilot, Cabot staff have learned the best ways to promote, train, and support the use of this innovative technology in the Harvard community through its collaboration with Lamont Library staff as part of the Media& series.

Beyond the benefits related to the centrality of the service and associated staff training opportunities, it is important to remember the role the library plays in democratizing access to the non-traditional scholarly resources that support data manipulation activities like audio and video production, immersion through virtual reality, and, finally, prototyping in 3D. Given that academic librarianship has evolved in recent years to encapsulate services that support knowledge creation, analysis, and dissemination in *all forms*, and the legitimacy of 3D data as a rigorous scholarly source material, the addition of 3D printing represents a powerful, defensible addition to most any academic library suite of services. A Harvard Library-supported 3D printing service allows students, faculty, and staff ready access to rapid prototyping and ideation tools. When 3D printing is coupled with feedback and feedforward use cases that rely on media production at other Harvard libraries, and crossover applications from outside the engineering fields, we anticipate heavy usage for the service moving forward. So, 3D printing services in academic libraries centralize and democratize new forms of information production and access while fostering training and collaboration. This set of interrelated benefits should of course define any sustainable academic library service offering, but the 3D printing pilot team was able to witness all of these high-level benefits firsthand, and, despite an extended hiatus resulting from the pandemic as well as the loss of a service-critical vendor, we feel that the timing could not be better for a dedicated, library-based 3D printing service at Harvard. Software, like Makerfleet, significantly decreases the operational overhead associated with maintaining this service with nearby partners (e.g., the physics fabrication lab and the Lamont Media Lab) means that servicing these machines will not require costly intervention from outside vendors. We have programming lined up and the costs are quite reasonable, especially given the range of scholarly applications and academic beneficiaries. Ultimately, we foresee the imminent reawakening, and then the expansion, of this valuable service.

NOTES

1. Jennifer Grayburn et al., eds., *3D/VR in the Academic Library: Emerging Practices and Trends* (Arlington, VA: CLIR, 2019).

2. Michael K. Buckland, "Information as Thing," *Journal of the American Society for Information Science* 42, no. 5 (June 1991): 2–3, doi:10.1002/(SICI)1097-4571(199106)42:5<351::AID -ASI5>3.0.CO;2-3.

3. Doug Boyer, "Virtual Fossils Revolutionise the Study of Human Evolution," eds. Corey S Powell, *aeon* (blog), February 25, 2016, https://aeon.co/ideas/virtual-fossils-revolutionise-the-study-of-human-evolution.

4. Fred Limp et al., "Developing a 3D Digital Heritage Ecosystem: From Object to Representation and the Role of a Virtual Museum in the 21st Century," *Internet Archaeology* 30 (2011): 14, doi:10.11141/ia.30.1.

5. Peter Der Manuelian, "Three Ancient Egyptian Coffins at Harvard University," *Cultural Heritage* (blog), *Sketchfab*, March 25, 2020, https://sketchfab.com/blogs/community/three-ancient-egyptian-coffins-at-harvard-university/.

6. Rushabh Haria, "oVert to Scan Over 20,000 Vertebrates for Free Download and 3D Printing," *3D Printing Industry*, December 15, 2017, https://3dprintingindustry.com/news/overt-vertebrates-download-3d-print-free-126189/.

7. Analytical Methods Committee AMCTB No 98, "X-ray Micro Computed Tomography in Cultural Heritage," *Analytical Methods* 12, no. 36 (2020): 4496–500, doi:10.1039/d0ay90112a.

8. Matthew Cook and Zack Lischer-Katz, "Practical Steps to an Effective Virtual Reality Course Integration," *College and Undergraduate Libraries* (forthcoming). Special Issue.

9. "About Sketchfab," Sketchfab, accessed May 14, 2021, http://sketchfab.com.

10. "MorphoSource BETA," MorphoSource, accessed May 14, 2021, https://www.morphosource.org/.

11. "Discovery 3D Models," NIH 3D Print Exchange, accessed May 14, 2021, https://3dprint.nih.gov/discover?terms=&field_model_category_tag_tid%5B%5D=93&uid=&field_model_license_nid=All&sort_by=created&sort_order=DESC.

12. "Raspberry Pi," (search results) Thingiverse on MakerBot, accessed on May 14, 2021. https://www.thingiverse.com/search?q=raspberry+pi&dwh=105e5d24562597b.

13. "Studio Librarians Provide Guide and Design for 3D-Printable Face Shields," Columbia University Libraries Studio, March 21, 2020, https://studio.cul.columbia.edu/2020/03/21/studio-librarians-face-shields/?fbclid=IwAR18nOj-Xkro-Qd0PQqGxpJcVOOBP9BcCpU3QiTmQeiMv0C73ZvEWrvjI30.

14. Ramin Javan, Douglas Herrin, and Ardalan Tangestanipoor, "Understanding Spatially Complex Segmental and Branch Anatomy Using 3D Printing: Liver, Lung, Prostate, Coronary Arteries, and Circle of Willis," *Academic Radiology* 23, no. 9 (2016): 1183–89, doi:10.1016/j.acra.2016.04.010.; Ming-Chih Hsieh et al., "Role of Three-Dimensional Rotational Venography in Evaluation of the Left Iliac Vein in Patients with Chronic Lower Limb Edema," *The International Journal of Cardiovascular Imaging* 27, no. 7 (2011): 923–29, doi:10.1007/s10554-010-9745-6.; Figen Govsa et al., "Development of Life-Size Patient-Specific 3D-Printed Dural Venous Models for Preoperative Planning," *World Neurosurgery* 110 (2018): e141–49. doi:10.1016/j.wneu.2017.10.119.

15. Robert B. Trelease and Antoine Rosset, "Transforming Clinical Imaging Data for Virtual Reality Learning Objects," *Anatomical Sciences Education* 1 (2008): 5, doi:10.1002/ase.13.

16. "Touchable Universe in a Box," NASA's Universe of Learning, accessed on May 14, 2021, https://chandra.harvard.edu/tactile/touchable.html.

17. Kimberly Arcand et al., "Touching the Stars: Improving NASA 3D Printed Data Sets with Blind and Visually Impaired Audiences," *arXiv* 2 (2019), https://arxiv.org/abs/1906.06457.

18. "About AliceVision," AliceVision, accessed on May 14, 2021, https://alicevision .org/#about.

19. Alban Denoyel, "Sketchfab Reaches 5 Million Members!," *Sketchfab* (blog), March 26, 2021, https://sketchfab.com/blogs/community/sketchfab-reaches-5m-members-on-its-9 -year-anniversary.

20. "Venture Teams: MakerFleet," Harvard Innovation Labs, accessed on May 14, 2021, last modified Summer, 2019, https://innovationlabs.harvard.edu/current-team/makerfleet/.

21. 3DPrinterOS website, accessed August 15, 2021, https://www.3dprinteros.com/; As-troPrint website, accessed August 15, 2021, https://www.astroprint.com/; BuildBee website, accessed August 15, 2021, https://buildbee.com/.

22. OctoPrint website, accessed August 15, 2021, https://octoprint.org/; Slic3r: Open-Source 3D Printing Toolbox, accessed August 15, 2021, https://slic3r.org/.

23. Nathan Melenbrink, "Introduction to Digital Fabrication," Harvard Physical Sciences, accessed May 14, 2021, https://nathanmelenbrink.github.io/ps70/index.html.

24. AutoDesk TinkerCAD (webpage), accessed May 14, 2021, https://www.tinkercad.com/.

25. "Media& Workshop Series," Harvard University Libraries, accessed May 14, 2021, https://library.harvard.edu/events/media-workshop-series.

26. "Cabot Media Studios," Harvard University Libraries, accessed on May 14, 2021. https://library.harvard.edu/services-tools/cabot-media-studios.

BIBLIOGRAPHY

Analytical Methods Committee AMCTB No 98, "X-ray Micro Computed Tomography in Cultural Heritage." *Analytical Methods* 12, no. 36 (2020): 4496–500, doi: 10.1039 /d0ay90112a.

Arcand, Kimberly K., April Jubett, Megan Watzke, Sara Price, Kelly T. S. Williamson, and Peter Edmonds. "Touching the Stars: Improving NASA 3D Printed Data Sets with Blind and Visually Impaired Audiences." *arXiv*. Published electronically June 15, 2019. https:// arxiv.org/abs/1906.06457.

AutoDesk, TinkerCAD. Accessed May 14, 2021. https://www.tinkercad.com/.

Boyer, Doug. "Virtual Fossils Revolutionise the Study of Human Evolution," edited by Corey S. Powell. *aeon* (blog). February 25, 2016. https://aeon.co/ideas/virtual-fossils-revolu tionise-the-study-of-human-evolution.

Buckland, Michael K. "Information as Thing." *Journal of the American Society for Information Science* 42, no. 5 (June 1991): 351–60. https://doi.org/10.1002/(SICI)1097 -4571(199106)42:5<351::AID-ASI5>3.0.CO;2-3.

Cook, Matthew, and Zack Lischer-Katz. "Practical Steps to an Effective Virtual Reality Course Integration." *College and Undergraduate Libraries* (forthcoming).

Denoyel, Alban. "Sketchfab Reaches 5 Million Members!" *Sketchfab* (blog). March 26, 2021. https://sketchfab.com/blogs/community/sketchfab-reaches-5m-members-on-its-9-year -anniversary.

Der Manuelian, Peter. "Three Ancient Egyptian Coffins at Harvard University." *Cultural Heritage* (blog). *Sketchfab*. March 25, 2020. https://sketchfab.com/blogs/community/three -ancient-egyptian-coffins-at-harvard-university/.

"Discovery 3D Models." *NIH 3D Print Exchange.* Accessed May 14, 2021. https://3dprint
.nih.gov/discover?terms=&field_model_category_tag_tid%5B%5D=93&uid=&field
_model_license_nid=All&sort_by=created&sort_order=DESC.

Govsa, Figen, Asli Beril Karakas, Mehmet Asim Ozer, and Cenk Eraslan. "Development of
Life-Size Patient-Specific 3D-Printed Dural Venous Models for Preoperative Planning."
World Neurosurgery 110 (2018): e141–49. doi: 10.1016/j.wneu.2017.10.119.

Grayburn, Jennifer, Zack Lischer-Katz, Kristina Golubiewski-David, and Veronica Ikeshoji-
Orlati, eds. *3D/VR in the Academic Library: Emerging Practices and Trends.* Arlington, VA:
CLIR, 2019. https://www.clir.org/wp-content/uploads/sites/6/2019/02/Pub-176.pdf.

Harvard Innovation Labs. "Venture Teams: MakerFleet." Harvard University. Last modified
Summer 2019. Accessed on May 14, 2021. https://innovationlabs.harvard.edu/current
-team/makerfleet/.

Harvard University Libraries. "Cabot Media Studios." Accessed on May 14, 2021. https://
library.harvard.edu/services-tools/cabot-media-studios.

———. "Media& Workshop Series." Accessed May 14, 2021. https://library.harvard.edu
/events/media-workshop-series.

Hsieh, Ming-Chih, Po-Yen Chang, Wen-Hsien Hsu, Shih-Hung Yang, and Wing P. Chan.
"Role of Three-Dimensional Rotational Venography in Evaluation of the Left Iliac Vein
in Patients with Chronic Lower Limb Edema." *The International Journal of Cardiovascular
Imaging* 27, no. 7 (2011): 923–29, doi: 10.1007/s10554-010-9745-6.

Javan, Ramin, Douglas Herrin, and Ardalan Tangestanipoor. "Understanding Spatially
Complex Segmental and Branch Anatomy Using 3D Printing: Liver, Lung, Prostate, Coronary Arteries, and Circle of Willis." *Academic Radiology* 23, no. 9 (2016): 1183–89, doi:
10.1016/j.acra.2016.04.010.

Limp, Fred, Angie Payne, Katie Simon, Snow Winters, and Jack Cothren. "Developing a 3D
Digital Heritage Ecosystem: From Object to Representation and the Role of a Virtual Museum in the 21st Century." *Internet Archaeology*, no. 30 (2011): 14, doi: 10.11141/ia.30.1.

Melenbrink, Nathan. "Introduction to Digital Fabrication." Harvard Physical Sciences. Accessed May 14, 2021. https://nathanmelenbrink.github.io/ps70/index.html.

MorphoSource. "MorphoSource BETA." Accessed May 14, 2021. https://www.morpho
source.org/.

Sketchfab. "About Sketchfab." Accessed May 14, 2021. http://sketchfab.com.

Trelease, Robert B., and Antoine Rosset. "Transforming Clinical Imaging Data for Virtual
Reality Learning Objects." *Anatomical Sciences Education* 1 (2008): 50–55. https://doi
.org/10.1002/ase.13.

9

Making Space for Non-Traditional Makers

Annalise Phillips and Jennifer Brown

This chapter will explore UC Berkeley's efforts to create an open-access barrier-free library makerspace, in collaboration with student organizations, by looking at the three stages in our service design process. The beginning will describe the makerspace as it existed previously (b.Makerspace), examining the advantages and limitations of an entirely student driven service. The second section will focus on the space as it is now: a no-barrier beginner makerspace for students, faculty, and staff. This section will also describe our transition into a remote environment, exploring the pros and cons of making in an entirely virtual space, and our goals for transitioning back to campus in a post-COVID environment. The final section will explore our future and goals for innovation and leadership in open-access making. Berkeley is undertaking an ambitious library redesign project by creating the Center for Connected Learning (CCL), a "collider space" where students will flow between multimedia classrooms, collaborative project spaces, and hands-on learning studios—all within the same building.

LITERATURE REVIEW

Makerspaces are often linked with ideas of democratized access to technology and STEM education. However STEM fields continue to be white male dominated, which means that "persistent stereotypes remain, and are not easy to dismantle."[1] As such, women and marginalized groups often fail to see themselves represented in the design or offerings of a makerspace.[2] Often, makerspaces give influence and control to those who can spend the most time and space in them, a luxury only available to those in positions of privilege.[3] Several resources note Dr. Leah Beuchley's keynote address from the 2013 FabLearn conference; there she pointed out that in *Make* magazine's nine-year publication history, 85 percent of the people on the cover were male, 15 percent were female and 0 percent were people of color.[4] Make Media Inc. often positions itself as the leader of the maker movement, and as Beuchley points out, it is therefore responsible for promoting equity, diversity, and representation. While the maker movement is meant to break down barriers to access and increase the availability of STEM education for previously marginalized groups, it can sometimes perpetuate that divide by focusing primarily on computational, robotic, and electronic making, at the expense of craft, repair, and more traditional arts. There is quite a bit of academic discussion around what "counts" as making and "the forms of ingenuity present in communities that are not benefiting from dominant economic structures—such as material repair and trade, hacking, making as social or artistic practice, and economic survival—are deemphasized."[5] Makerspaces in schools and libraries are often seeking to distance themselves from these stereotypes, striving to create spaces that welcome diversity and inclusion. However, surveys of these spaces often find that while the diversity of student populations is shifting, positions of power in these spaces remain the same. As Kye points out, "teachers continue to be mostly middle-class and White."[6] STEM is increasingly pointed to as the pathway to creative innovation and economic success, and makerspaces are often positioned as the place where diverse audiences can gain access to the knowledge and skill in those fields. According to Britton, "If technical tinkering, STEM, and digital fabrication are the economic forces that will empower makers, and women and people of color are not participating in these activities in a visible way, that power will remain unequally distributed."[7] Academic and community makerspaces are faced with the challenge of diversifying these spaces, creating welcoming environments that represent a broad set of users and their needs.

Maker culture at UC Berkeley has historically been for those who already see themselves as makers. Prior to the establishment of the Moffitt Library Makerspace, all UC Berkeley makerspaces required special training and a fee for use. While fees can be waived for students in need of financial assistance, these programs still have a membership cap designed to keep access to equipment equitable, but this cap can sometimes be perceived as a barrier. Berkeley has a rich and expansive student organization culture that sought to democratize access to making and established a maker club that would eventually evolve into the library-run makerspace we have today. Now, as we embark on a project to reimagine Moffitt Library as the Center for Connected Learning, we are seeking to establish a space cocreated between staff and students, one that brings together student desires, designs, and ideas alongside trained specialists in a university-supported space.

Makerspaces traditionally have focused on metal working, woodworking, electronics, robotics, and computer engineering, and have been historically white, male, and affluent-dominated spaces. These practices typically have a high cost and time barrier to entry that many lower-income and Black, Indigenous, and other communities of color (BIPOC) cannot overcome to access. While democratizing access by removing or lowering fees and providing training helps, it does not immediately create a more equitable and diverse maker environment. Britton explains that, "as it stands now, the maker identity and technical DIY activities are not for everyone; in many ways it actually reinforces an ingrained culture of white masculinity in the design and deployment of technology while rhetorically claiming universality."[8] Makerspaces have been so traditionally held as white male spaces that it is often difficult for other groups to see themselves as makers; members outside of these communities will often assume the makerspace is not for them, particularly on university campuses where makerspaces are often seen solely as the realm of engineering and design students. The Moffitt Makerspace seeks to shift that definition of "maker" to create a community and a culture where every person feels welcome, included, and able. The authors of this chapter believe that the value of the tools and practices available in a space extends to the cultural tools and practices that are brought in by diverse users. Makerspaces are meant to be collider spaces, where users work collaboratively, building off of ideas and resources created by others. While the breadth of tools and materials can be exciting and inspiring, they can also become intimidating and challenging if a user does not have experience with either the tools or the culture of making. Our makerspace seeks to create an environment that is as rich in cultural tools as it is in physical ones.

MAKING AT THE UNIVERSITY OF CALIFORNIA, BERKELEY: A RETROSPECTIVE

Berkeley is an immensely diverse campus and libraries are meant to be spaces of equitable open access. As such, the Moffitt Library Makerspace has sought to actively create a more equitable and diverse maker environment, reaching beyond a no-fee model to include more craft offerings, low-barrier software training (such as Tinkercad and Silhouette Studio), create an open and welcoming physical environment, and actively reach out to diverse student groups and organizations. The Moffitt Makerspace began in 2014 as a student organization located in the Bridges Engineering Lounge, an open space located in the foyer of the Engineering Library. While the space was open and available to all, its location naturally targeted and attracted engineering students. In 2015, the Jacobs Institute for Design and Innovation opened in Jacobs Hall, one of the primary engineering buildings on campus. Intended to attract makers from across campus, Jacobs offers comprehensive online shop training and several small-group hands-on training sessions for each tool each semester. The Jacobs Institute and the Citris Invention Lab (another campus design studio and makerspace located in the engineering building) both operate under the "Makerpass" model, where students pay a semester fee, take an online training course, and are allowed to book machine time in the labs. Both labs are well staffed and offer in-depth training for tools and necessary software. Initially, these spaces drew traffic away from the Bridges Makerspace (later to become b.Makerspace), drawing the largely engineering crowd into higher tech and better equipped spaces. Unlike b.Makerspace, which primarily housed 3D printers, Jacobs and Citris boast an impressive tool library ranging from standard woodshop tools to a large bank of 3D printers, laser and plasma cutters, and a range of electronics equipment. However, the complexity of their tools, fee structures, and required training can be daunting to novice users, particularly those that do not see themselves as repeat users of the space. As such, b.Makerspace filled a void for beginner users, but still only truly existed as a 3D printing lab rather than a comprehensive makerspace.

UC Berkeley is a unique campus in that it has more than fourteen hundred student-led organizations. As part of that student organization culture, b.Makerspace built partnerships with other clubs to develop a service model that could meet users' needs while providing free access to tools and materials. b.Makerspace relied on the manpower these student groups provided to staff the space and run the space and workshops. These connections came from natural crossover in student members. Students who were a part of the b.Makerspace Club were often members of the 3D Modeling Club, the Virtual Reality Club, and similar organizations. Together, these members would promote the makerspace as a place where clubs could exchange time for space and storage.

As we return to campus in a post-pandemic environment, the makerspace plans to continue forging new partnerships with student organizations and other campus groups. Before campus closed, the makerspace was in conversation with the Berkeley Art Studio, a campus-run art space in the Associated Students of University of California building. We hope to continue to build that partnership and engage in their Crafterdark events, while encouraging students, faculty, and staff to build their work between studios. As the makerspace continues to evolve we hope more partnerships are formed and that many groups and organizations feel they are a part of what makes the makerspace run. The next phase in this evolution will rely heavily on the Undergraduate Library Fellowship students to develop a plan for identifying and marketing to new prospective users.

In addition to this robust club atmosphere, many student organizations offer DeCals, student-led single-unit courses that club members and students alike can enroll in to broaden their skills and networks. In an effort to expand the available services, b.Makerspace partnered with several of these student groups including the 3D Modeling Club, Enable Tech (an assistive technology group), Robotics at Berkeley, and Virtual Reality at Berkeley (now XR@Berkeley). These partnerships allowed the group to provide additional technology to users and to expand their hours and availability. b.Makerspace also began to offer a popular and successful 3D modeling DeCal for beginners. In 2017, b.Makerspace and the Moffitt Library's paths collided. While the library was looking to add makerspace services as part of its planned renovation into the new Center for Connected Learning, b.Makerspace was asked to vacate their location in the Bridges Lounge. During this transition, b.Makerspace partnered with the campus' Education Technology Services (ETS) and a library liaison. Through these partnerships, they secured a substantial grant through the Student Technology Fund, a student-led voting body that allocates money from student tuition and fees to purchase and implement technologies.

Through this same fund, b.Makerspace was able to pay its student staff and continued on in this way from 2017 to 2018.

As part of the newly-formed partnership between the library liaison and ETS, several makerspace-affiliated staff attended maker and tinkering trainings at various institutions around the Bay Area. These efforts were part of an attempt to broaden the makerspace's offerings and create a more novice-centered space, but the b.Makerspace was still a primarily student-run space, and, while it sought to provide more variety and attract new users, it often struggled to do so. Despite their best efforts, the b.Makerspace ran into a lot of difficulty. The student organization suffered from a lack of consistent leadership, and membership periodically waned as students graduated. It also lacked leveraging power to secure permanent, dedicated space, endured a difficult transition period as it moved locations and began new partnerships with the library and ETS, and struggled to attract novice users outside of their student club partnerships. b.Makerspace introduced recreational virtual reality to remedy this, and though it bolstered student attendance in their 3D modeling DeCal, those students often had prior modeling experience, or engineering/design-related fields of study. In addition, the b.Makerspace maintained a heavy digital technology focus, and did not have any resources for crafting, textile work or hand tool usage.

While b.Makerspace faced many challenges, they also experienced successes that carried over into the current makerspace. Partnering with student clubs allowed them to expand their staffing model without needing additional funding. Club members staffed tools and equipment in exchange for tool storage and meeting space, an arrangement that continued in the library's partnership. Partnering with student clubs also allowed b.Makerspace to broaden their offerings, expanding from a primarily 3D printing space to include virtual reality, robotics, electronics, and wearable technology. The current makerspace fosters additional club partnerships in an attempt to broaden our user base, but b.Makerspace's working model still drives those relationships. In late 2018, the first floor of Moffitt Library flooded during a heavy rainstorm, causing extensive damage to the makerspace, its equipment, and other first-floor library resources and classrooms. Following the flood, b.Makerspace disbanded and the library reestablished the makerspace as a vision-driven library service, paving the way for an entirely new maker studio and workshop design, as part of Moffitt Library's transformation into the Center for Connected Learning.

CHANGE AND REINVENTION: THE MOFFITT MAKERSPACE

In early 2019, following flood renovations and repairs, the library hired a full-time maker education service lead, one of the authors of this chapter, to oversee the instruction and operations of the space. To set itself apart from the other makerspaces on campus, the Moffitt Makerspace was redesigned with an open floor plan, free of barriers and access codes, with equipment visible and available to all who were interested. The lead re-envisioned the space to be collaborative and inviting, where all students, faculty, staff, and the larger UC Berkeley community are invited to learn, create, and make together. There are no financial or knowledge barriers to entry; the space is filled with QR codes and signage directing visitors to make appointments for training, attend workshops, or schedule machine time. While the makerspace is open to all, the specific aim of the space is to attract novice users and those not typically represented in makerspaces.

As one of the only libraries on campus that is open seven days a week and nearly twenty-four hours a day, Moffitt was and continues to be a hub for student learning and connection. Now, as it transforms into the Center for Connected Learning, it will take a new shape with a design to match its intentions. The Moffitt Makerspace is in the prototyping phase of that design. As the library transitions, it is experimenting with new makerspace layouts and service models while soliciting feedback from current and future users. One such partnership came through the university's Invention Corps—"an interdisciplinary group of students driven to create meaningful global impact through human-centered design. Invention Corps students partner with people and organizations with the objective of creating tangible solutions in the realms of society, health, poverty, and the environment."[9] In late 2019, the makerspace education service lead partnered with a group of Invention Corps students to create solutions around reaching a broader user base, identifying possible users, and advertising explicitly to underrepresented groups. The Invention Corps team created a user engagement survey, new wayfinding materials, and a print/digital advertising campaign to help the space identify and draw in new users.

STUDENT PARTNERSHIPS AS SERVICE MODEL

In addition to working with Invention Corps, the makerspace participates in the Undergraduate Library Fellowship. The Undergraduate Library Fellowship is a "cohort driven program that promotes peer-to-peer learning and mentorship opportunities with the shared goal of improving Berkeley Library services and spaces. Fellows receive training in different aspects of librarianship, from user experience and design thinking to research and instruction. Using this knowledge, fellows are expected to foster connections between the library's ecosystem and undergraduate communities by prototyping peer-to-peer services developed in teams."[10] For the past two academic years, the Maker Education Service lead has worked with the library fellows to increase student awareness of the makerspace, provide basic online training, and create a diverse and inclusive space. In the 2019–2020 school year, the fellow working with the makerspace created a web guide, training users to operate equipment before they entered the space. These training modules are free and available to anyone, helping democratize access while encouraging novice users to come and create. The drive behind these guides was that novices could familiarize themselves with a tool and its operation before entering the space, allowing them to preview its use and functions prior to workshops, project work, or one-on-one training sessions.

The subsequent fellow's cohort focused their efforts on identifying deficiencies in diversity and inclusion in relation to library resources. They designed and conducted surveys on student and staff experiences with diversity, equity, and inclusion (DEI) across library services. This further informed the makerspace's growth, along with other library services. In addition, the library is always seeking to improve its offerings; thus, our Communications Department conducts its own surveys to determine whether students are aware of or accessing resources and what barriers they experience while doing so.

These student partnerships and library surveys, coupled with the maker service lead's ten plus years of makerspace experience, led to our current floor plan and equipment layout. Familiar tools and materials—like sewing machines, textile arts, and button makers—are front and center in the new, open floor plan. Placing these familiar tools up front helps students form a connection. Even if they've never been in a makerspace, they likely know what a sewing machine is and possibly grew up with one in their home. Other entry-level tools, like our button makers, are laid out with sample projects nearby. Students are encouraged to grab pre-made buttons, or to create their own. A stack of pronoun buttons and Berkeley Pride buttons were designed and created by a student to leave near the button machines, helping to encourage interest but also to provide small reminders for tolerance, representation, and understanding. A lack of walls presented an inviting environment that encouraged students to explore the space, even when it was closed. A large, adhesive vinyl collaborative coloring mural highlighted a sense of community while drawing attention to the vinyl cutter, located nearby. Three-dimensional printers were also front and center in this new space design, but were surrounded by QR codes leading to information and resources, including training videos and an appointment tool for one-on-one support. Similar QR code signage is located around all of our other tools, displayed on the floor. In addition, the space was arranged with several large collaborative tables and plenty of power outlets. All of these design choices were made to make the space feel open, inviting, and encouraging. Presenting users with familiar tools up front, and the resources to learn more about areas of interest, create a welcoming environment that draws users in and encourages engagement. In its first semester open, the makerspace welcomed 675 students, faculty and staff for workshops, drop-in projects, and previously scheduled appointments.

In addition to working with the Invention Corps and the Undergraduate Library Fellows program, the makerspace also partnered (pre-pandemic) with several student organizations to increase the user base, offer additional resources for training, and broaden access to materials. Student partnerships that carried over from b.Makerspace included the Robotics at Berkeley and 3D Modeling Clubs. As the new Moffitt Makerspace established itself, we developed partnerships with Berkeley's Engineering Student Council; their support enables us to double our 3D printing machines and offer additional training, while better supporting and maintaining devices. Through its first full semester of operation, Moffitt Makerspace made additional partnerships linked to specific workshops and events.

While student partnerships broaden our reach and resources, hosting workshops and providing resources for student clubs has deeply impacted our ability to champion diversity and inclusion. To connect with underrepresented and novice groups, the makerspace lead created a series of introductory workshops for makerspace tools and software. Workshop topics vary widely, but are designed with those targeted groups in mind. For example, a sewing workshop, titled "Power Pockets," teaches basic machine and hand sewing, while adding pockets to almost anything, addressing the lack of adequate storage in female-targeted clothing. "Clothing Repair and Redesign" uses similar tools and principles, but encourages students to repair rather than throw away damaged clothing; it also teaches how to use or design sewing patterns for creating new pieces. By regularly rotating such workshops, the makerspace attracts users who might only think of makerspaces as places for 3D printing and laser cutting. Once they enter the space and have successful experiences, they are more likely to return and try something new.

It was through the "Clothing Repair" workshop that the Moffitt Makerspace formed a partnership with ReUse at Berkeley. This student organization runs a thrift store and repair clinic for clothing on campus. Prior to the pandemic, ReUse planned to implement a sewing machine training workshop, alongside makerspace staff, using our sewing machines. These widely advertised workshops are often the best source of new users, drawing in individuals who then reach out to other campus organizations. The makerspace partnered with Berkeley's Queer Art and Fashion Show through similar means; that student organization planned to run a "Thrift and Fix" workshop as part of their programming. Participants were going to hack, redesign, and create their own unique pieces using thrifted, damaged, and donated items. While the pandemic unfortunately stymied these plans, UC Berkeley is in the midst of transitioning back to in-person, post-COVID operations. When it does, the makerspace will resume partnerships like the ones described, evolving our space design and service offerings, and further establishing the Moffitt Makerspace as a place for all users.

CULTURES OF COMMUNITY: WORKSHOPS AND ACCESS

The makerspace service model is specifically designed to encourage novice users. While familiar technology is the first thing you see in the space, all equipment is accompanied by signage with QR codes that lead to additional learning resources. During makerspace open hours, staff are always available and visible, wearing aprons and name tags that encourage users to approach or ask questions. In addition, all workshops are held in an open drop-in format, so anyone passing by can both see what is happening and drop in and join. Workshop topics cover use of all equipment: 3D printing, soldering, sewing, knitting, vinyl cutting, button making, book binding, and wood working but also software and general design thinking. They are free to attend and held on regular, rotating schedules to capture wider swaths of student availability. This drop-in model removes fee barriers while encouraging students who may just be studying nearby to drop in and learn. While workshops are advertised online and through the library's LibCal site (an appointment scheduling system we use for booking consultations and library events), there is no attendance cap. These working sessions create a sense of welcome and community. Tables for workshops are arranged in a circle so all users can see one another, and staff move through the group as they instruct. Users are encouraged to support one another, and as the makerspace grew its user base, repeat workshop attendees would often become unofficial instructors, helping their peers design stickers or run their first 3D prints. In the first semester of operations, workshops averaged an attendance of five users at a time, with the most popular topics begin vinyl decal design and introductory knitting.

In addition to workshops on specific topics, users are encouraged to make training appointments using the Library's LibCal appointments tool. In that form, users can select any tool or topic the makerspace provides and receive individual, hour-long training with the Maker Education Service lead, anytime between 9 a.m. to 4 p.m. These appointments are designed to capture users who perhaps learn best outside of group workshops, and sessions move at the user's pace, allowing them to deepen their understanding without constraints. To sign up, users select appointments through LibCal, filling in their areas of interest, project(s) they areworking on (if any), and accommodations they might need. These sessions alleviate some anxieties novice users feel when learning new technologies, allowing them to build comfort and familiarity before joining a group. The appointment service is well utilized, with fifty-four appointments made and held in the first semester of operation. In addition to workshops and appointments, the Makerspace LibGuide hosts video tutorials and links to software training and a regularly rotating selection of projects to inspire users at all levels. These remote offerings support those who can't fit workshops into their schedule, or who require visual and written instruction, and support continued movement at one's own pace. Users can stop and rewind to develop comfort and familiarity before visiting the space.

THE CURRENT CHALLENGE: POST-PANDEMIC OPERATIONS

Six months into operation, while the Moffitt Makerspace was just beginning to gather steam and develop a steady user base, the COVID-19 pandemic hit and disrupted operations. Like all library services, the makerspace had to pivot to a remote-only environment, balancing limited resources and a challenging environment with its student-focused mission. As spring 2020 transitioned into online learning, students finishing design projects continued to reach out to the makerspace through online appointments and drop-in "ask me anything" style Zoom workshops. Through these digital avenues, users could get help with specific projects, ask general questions, and seek resources for existing projects. Early on, some users were even able to access makerspaces in their home regions; they used these online sessions to consult around finding local makerspaces near them or connect with other users with nearby access to tools. As the pandemic progressed, and it became increasingly clear that in-person instruction would not resume for some time, a more robust remote learning model was implemented.

Over the course of summer 2020, the makerspace established a series of weekly rotating projects and tutorials featured on the LibGuide.[11] Virtual training sessions were still held to instruct users on design software such as Fusion360, Adobe Illustrator, and Silhouette Studio. Even though students would not have access to the tools, they could continue to expand their knowledge of software, and equip themselves for a reopening the entire campus community hoped was imminent. In fall of 2020, the Jacobs Makerspace and Citris Invention Lab opened access to remote academic 3D printing for all users. Through the use of an online form, all members of the Berkeley student community could access their 3D printers, submit a model, and have it printed. Models could then be picked up at designated locations during specific time windows. Through various modeling workshops and research appointments, users of the Moffitt Makerspace were made aware of this resource, and some who lived locally were able to apply the skills they had learned in virtual workshops to produce tangible models and prototypes.

As the pandemic wore on, more virtual workshops were added to the LibGuide, this time with a focus on accessible, affordable tools and materials. Workshops initially focused on specific skills such as sewing or knitting, teaching just the basics of each skill with no particular project in mind. Through testing and surveying workshop participants, it became clear that users wanted a specific project; the workshop model shifted to provide specific skills through project development. In order to keep materials costs low, topics focused on textiles and paper work, and all users were encouraged to participate even if they lacked access to materials. In several of these workshops, "ingredients substitutions" sessions would be held in the first ten minutes, in which users could get advice on substituting materials they had for the required materials of a project. Through these substitutions, users were still able to learn a skill, even if they were knitting with two pencils and shoelaces rather than knitting needles and yarn. At the time of this chapter's authoring, an archive of these tutorials is being created, which will be hosted on the LibGuide.

Virtual consultations also became a regular part of the makerspace's COVID offerings. Through our LibGuide and workshops, users were encouraged to make appointments for help with specific design challenges, to acquire certain skills, or build software knowledge. These consultations often informed the selection of videos and tutorials posted on the LibGuide. For example, if several students seemed to be troubleshooting in Adobe Illustrator, a workshop series on Illustrator would be posted, or a link to a preexisting tutorial video on that topic would be provided.

Before the pandemic, the makerspace discussed incorporating programs and services more officially into several UC Berkeley courses. As campus transitions back to an in-person teaching model we will continue to pursue those curricular integration opportunities for the spring of 2022. The LibGuide encourages faculty to bring students to the makerspace for a thirty-minute tour and to reach out for consultation on how to include making and design thinking into their curriculum. Faculty are encouraged to use the space themselves, and it is promoted to students in undergraduate and graduate library classes.

The makerspace budget is tied to the budget for the Instruction Services Division with partial funding coming from ETS. As previously mentioned, in the past, funds for tools and materials were also voted on and provided by the Student Technology Fund, a student-run organization that determined how to allocate university funds based on student desires. As the makerspace continues to grow and evolve with the Center for Connected Learning, it will remain a no-fee space.

As the pandemic winds down and the Moffitt Library Makerspace plans its transition back to campus, the rich virtual workspace that was developed will continue to exist. In order to keep users and staff safe, a hybrid model of instruction is planned for the fall of 2021. Part of these new safety considerations has been to move the makerspace behind walls. While this will remove the immediate visibility of the makerspace, it will help library and makerspace staff properly sanitize tools and materials, while regulating the flow of users throughout the space. Access, training, and materials will still be provided without a fee, use of tools will still be available to everyone regardless of previous experience, and our mission will remain focused on creating space for those not typically represented in makerspaces. Currently, the Moffitt Library Makerspace is staffed solely by the Makerspace Education Service lead. All training and workshops are developed and run by that staff member. As campus resumes in-person operations, workshops and subject-specific training will be held by additional members of the library's Instruction Services Division. As the space continues to grow and evolve into the Center for Connected Learning, we envision a more robust staff model that includes regular student workers, along with possible staff and student volunteers.

Through continued partnerships with the Undergraduate Library Fellowship, the makerspace seeks to expand its reach, as Fellows in the 2022 cohort will tackle issues of access and outreach, designing solutions to help the makerspace reach its target audience. Additionally, existing partnerships with student organizations are already restarting, with plans for club-sponsored workshops, training sessions, and events already underway.

LOOKING FORWARD: MAKING AT THE CENTER FOR CONNECTED LEARNING

Beyond the makerspace, UC Berkeley Libraries had long-held visions of creating an innovative hub to support undergraduate learning. This meant reimagining the existing confines of Moffitt Library in its entirety, across four existing floors already brimming with critical service points and shared classrooms. This work began years ago, well before the Moffitt Makerspace existed; now, it encompasses new visions and spatial designs for Moffitt Makerspace, with the intention of further establishing the space's identity.

Since its inception, the Center for Connected Learning was meant to serve as a "collider space" that moves beyond "housing a department or function," toward "serv[ing] an idea: a transformational vision of the purpose and potential of the library as a place of gathering, instruction, access to resources, and self-enhancement."[12] It encompasses remodeling the entire undergraduate library, transforming Moffitt Library into a space fueled by peer-learning spaces expertly supported by existing library staff. With redesign plans spanning four floors, the Center for Connected Learning is expected to build-out a series of learning studios (including a Grand Learning Studio, with additional capacity for large-scale public events), new general-assignment classrooms, course-in-residence suites, and specialized computing studios to support media and design, making, digital scholarship, and augmented and virtual reality projects. The construction plans also lay out discrete areas for the circulation of library materials, copious study spaces, and staff offices. Altogether, it's meant to function as a living building that hums with energy, where UC Berkeley community members engage with interdisciplinary, multimodal learning. Going forward, Moffitt Makerspace's growth and re-envisioning are bound to the Center for Connected Learning's ongoing

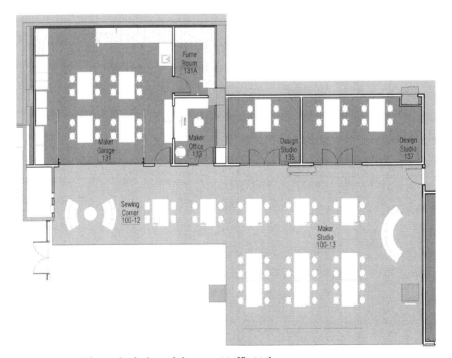

Figure 9.1.   Schematic design of the new Moffit Makerspace.
Created by BNIM Architects.

development. Quite literally, the makerspace—along with other existing services—will be redesigned from the ground-up as a large-scale Maker Studio and Workshop.

The new Maker Studio remains in its first-floor location (shown in figure 9.1) but is now redesigned in the spirit of connected learning. With that in mind, the studio will support an open area, shown in the lighter orange shade, outside a series of semi-closed workspaces. The "Maker Studio" portion (labeled "120") features expected accompaniments: tables and chairs; a "soft materials" section where sewing and other textile artistry can be done. However, this new design presents an exciting opportunity to blend the concept of an open makerspace with closed studios for focused work. In this way, users might be invited in by the openness. We anticipate workshops will still occur in the Maker Studio, which—by nature of its open connection with other first-floor seating areas—will continue to invite and inspire passing users. Openness is a critical design intervention, replicated across many of the new CCL spaces.

Of course, the new Maker Studio must continue to hold space for critical one-on-one training, focused learning, and deep study. In the "Maker Enclosed (120A)" spaces, and the adjacent "Design Studios (102C–120D)," we have designed an enclosed garage area beside spacious study rooms. This is where users can take associated makerspace equipment, work (either individually or in small groups) on targeted projects, and have dedicated space for making. Though not as visible, the "Enclosed" space features a garage door functionality that—even when closed—provides users with a glimpse of the tools and materials inside. This area provides lockable storage, offering critical upgrades to the makerspace's existing storage infrastructure. In this new design, that garage can be locked after hours, allowing makerspace staff flexibility and freedom to arrange materials more efficiently.

Perhaps the most critical design intervention, while small, is the inclusion of the "Maker Office (120B)." Generally, other makerspaces that the authors have toured or worked in de-prioritize staff office space, in favor of increased square footage for public programs. However, the Maker Education Service lead—and any associated student staff—*are* the heart of our maker studio; without adequate landing spots for administrative staff, we endure copious challenges. Right now, the Maker Education Service lead occupies an office that's located outside of the makerspace, which requires inconvenient amounts of travel. Staff space, in any building design, is critical, as programs and services only function because of staff who lead them.

In the spirit of connected learning, the maker studio and workshop will also house an adjacent location for extended learning. Across the first floor, there will also be a "Maker Learning Studio," as shown in figure 9.2. Each learning studio serves a different purpose—some are focused on media, while others trend toward emerging technologies. The Maker Learning Studio will directly support the digital and hands-on learning activities our Maker Education Service lead provides. Designed as a flexible space, chairs and tables can be moved, collapsed, or grouped to support a variety of learning methods. When not in use, we expect this room to remain locked for safety. The idea is to encourage a flow between the various rooms, not to imagine

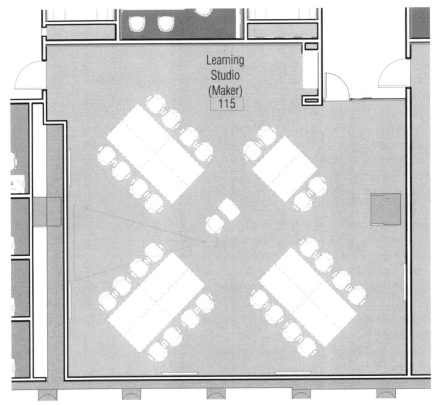

Figure 9.2. Schematic design of the new Maker Learning Studio.
Created by BNIM Architects.

each room as separate entities. In fact, we see synergistic opportunities between the primary Maker Studio, the adjacent Maker Learning Studio, and other learning studios inside the building—after all, users may move from using specialized software in the digital scholarship space to designing a physical prototype inside the makerspace. The reverse could also be true, and the possibility for endless connections make us confident in the CCL's ongoing designs.

Now, the process for transforming the existing Moffitt Library is a years-long one; it predates either author's employment at the university and has been guided by many hands and visions over the years. As of 2020, visions for this building coalesced into a firmer reality. One author was hired on as the Undergraduate Learning and Research librarian in January 2020; part of her new role includes serving on a steering committee for the Center for Connected Learning. In March of 2020, this committee met with project architects at BNIM[13] to kick off a new phase of the design process: schematic design. At this point, long-standing discussions about the building transitioned into a schematic design phase. BNIM rendered drawings, while steering committee members discussed critical building elements, such as fire codes and necessary design elements across all floors. The steering committee also solicited feedback from key library staff and stakeholders, including: circulation supervisors and access services staff; library instructors; and campus stakeholders. Throughout a series of ideation sessions, which encouraged staff to re-imagine and re-think schematics drawn up by BNIM Architects, the steering committee moved the project into more concrete territory. Of course, certain spaces—like the Moffitt Makerspace—required focused meetings. We solicited feedback from existing staff but held several design meetings with the maker education service lead to discuss furnishings, equipment, and technical design specifications.

CONCLUSION

This work, at times, has been challenging. The new Maker Studio and Workshop design is critical to the CCL's visions, but the Center for Connected Learning also contains a number of other learning spaces. We're still melding visions across many floors into cohesive plans, while minding how the building, in its entirety, must function. The transition work in this area is ongoing. We wrapped the schematic design in March of 2021 and expect the makerspace's vision to continue morphing as the building nears construction. A critical part of that morphing, though, not only involves the space–it involves the programs, too. Student partnerships were critical to the Moffitt Makerspace's success early on. In the new Center for Connected Learning, we imagine this becomes even more true. Each learning space, including the new Maker Studio and Workshop, will benefit from close collaboration with student groups and peer-to-peer learning models. Partnership opportunities seem endless here, but, in particular, we're hoping to continue to connect to student groups rooted in anti-oppression, anti-racism, and equity. To support the makerspace remaining an inclusive, encouraging place for learners at every level, student partnerships with organizations like ReUse at Berkeley, Queer Art and Fashion, Enable Tech, and our Undergraduate Library Fellows must continue.

The makerspace is in a continual state of growth and change, embodying the principles of inclusive design thinking, iteration, and prototyping that it teaches. While the COVID-19 pandemic presented unexpected challenges in the very early stages of the space's development, the community of staff, individual students, and student organizations that define the space had the flexibility and perseverance to overcome these and any future barriers they might face. As the university transforms the Moffitt Library into the Center for Connected Learning and the Moffitt Makerspace subsequently becomes the Maker Studio and Workshop, the physical space and resources will begin to align more visibly with its mission and goals. The drive behind the Maker Studio's design, staffing, and offerings will always be to foster a rich making community, empowered by its diversity and strengthened by its inclusivity.

NOTES

1. Jennifer Eckhardt et. al., "Gender in the Making: An Empirical Approach to Understand Gender Relations in the Maker Movement," *International Journal of Human-Computer Studies* 145 (2021), doi:10.1016/j.ijhcs.2020.102548.

2. Ibid., 3.

3. Christian Voigt, Elisabeth Unterfrauner, and Roland Stelzer, "Diversity in FabLabs: Culture, Role Models, and the Gendering of Making | SpringerLink," *INSCI 2017: Internet Science* (2017): 52–68.

4. Leah Buechley, "FabLearn Keynote," presented at the 2013 FabLearn Conference, October 27, 2013, http://leahbuechley.com/?p=60.

5. Shirin Vossoughi, Paula K. Hooper, and Meg Escude, "Making through the Lens of Culture and Power: Toward Transformative Visions for Educational Equity," *Harvard Educational Review* 86, no. 2 (2016): 206–32.

6. Hannah Kye, "Who Is Welcome Here? A Culturally Responsive Content Analysis of Makerspace Websites," *Journal of Pre-College Engineering Education Research* 10, no. 2 (2020), doi:10.7771/2157-9288.1190.

7. Lauren Britton, "Power, Access, Status: The Discourse of Race, Gender, and Class in the Maker Movement," Technology and Social Change Group blog, March 18, 2015.

8. Ibid.

9. "About Us," Invention Corps, accessed May 27, 2021, https://inventioncorps.org/index.html#landing.

10. "Undergraduate Library Fellows," UC Berkeley Library, last modified July, 2021 https://www.lib.berkeley.edu/level-up/resources/fellowships.

11. "Moffitt Library Makerspace LibGuide," UC Berkeley Library, last modified August 2021, https://guides.lib.berkeley.edu/make.

12. "Center for Connected Learning," Berkeley Library Giving, *UC Berkeley Library* (online), https://give.lib.berkeley.edu/initiative/center-connected-learning.

13. "BNIM," BNIM Architects, https://www.bnim.com/.

BIBLIOGRAPHY

"BNIM." *BNIM*. Accessed August 14, 2021. https://www.bnim.com/.

Britton, Lauren. "Power, Access, Status: The Discourse of Race, Gender, and Class in the Maker Movement," Technology and Social Change Group blog. March 18, 2015. https://tascha.uw.edu/2015/03/power-access-status-the-discourse-of-race-gender-and-class-in-the-maker-movement/.

Buechley, Leah. "FabLearn Keynote." Presented at the 2013 FabLearn Conference, October 27, 2013. http://leahbuechley.com/?p=60.

"Center for Connected Learning | UC Berkeley Library Giving." Accessed August 14, 2021. https://give.lib.berkeley.edu/initiative/center-connected-learning.

Eckhardt, Jennifer, Christoph Kaletka, Bastian Pelka, Elisabeth Unterfrauner, Christian Voigt, and Marthe Zirngiebl. "Gender in the Making: An Empirical Approach to Understand Gender Relations in the Maker Movement." *International Journal of Human-Computer Studies* 145 (2021). doi:10.1016/j.ijhcs.2020.102548.

"Invention Corps." Accessed August 14, 2021. https://inventioncorps.org/index.html#landing.

Kye, Hannah. "Who Is Welcome Here? A Culturally Responsive Content Analysis of Makerspace Websites." *Journal of Pre-College Engineering Education Research* 10, no. 2 (2020). doi:10.7771/2157-9288.1190.

"Undergraduate Library Fellows." *University of California, Berkeley Library: Level Up*. Accessed August 14, 2021. https://www.lib.berkeley.edu/level-up/resources/fellowships.

Voigt, Christian, Elisabeth Unterfrauner, and Roland Stelzer. "Diversity in FabLabs: Culture, Role Models and the Gendering of Making | SpringerLink." *INSCI 2017: Internet Science* (2017): doi:https://doi-org.libproxy.berkeley.edu/10.1007/978-3-319-70284-1_5.

Vossoughi, Shirin, Paula K. Hooper, and Meg Escude. "Making through the Lens of Culture and Power: Toward Transformative Visions for Educational Equity." *Harvard Educational Review* 86, no. 2 (2016): 206–32. doi:10.17763/0017-8055.86.2.206.

Section 3

FUTURE LITERACY DEVELOPMENTS

10

Maker Literacy, Metaliteracy, and the ACRL Framework

Sarah Nagle

Throughout the last decade, makerspaces and other experiential learning labs have grown in popularity in academic libraries, following trends set by community makerspaces, public libraries, and K–12 schools. Academic libraries have been established as ideal spaces on college campuses for makerspace technology and the experiential learning that it enables. The central, open nature of the campus library meshes well with the collaborative and interdisciplinary character of makerspaces. But trends move quickly in the realm of emerging technologies, and librarians must demonstrate the sustainability and enduring benefits of makerspaces in order to garner the continued support of administrators. The huge potential that makerspaces hold for student engagement and learning may be the key to ensuring that makerspaces remain relevant in the future. Most academic library instruction focuses on information literacy competencies as defined by the ACRL (Association of College and Research Libraries) Framework for Information Literacy. This chapter will use two of the foundational concepts of the ACRL Framework—metaliteracy and liminality—to demonstrate how maker-centered learning can help librarians further their institutions' information literacy goals.

MAKER-CENTERED LEARNING

As makerspaces have become more popular in all levels of education, some important projects have arisen to study the benefits and outcomes of maker-centered learning. Agency by Design (AbD) is a multi-year research project that has studied maker-centered learning in K–12 environments.[1] Clapp et al. explain that, in contrast to some of the popular narratives, the benefits of maker-centered learning are seen most on a personal, character-building level. The culminating outcome of the research project, the AbD Framework for Maker-Centered Learning (AbD Framework), revolves around maker empowerment and design sensitivity. The project found that through maker-centered learning, students develop design sensitivity, defined as "being attuned to the designed dimension of objects and systems, with an understanding that the designed world is malleable."[2] The empowerment that students gain from maker-centered learning is the result of a sense of agency, described as "seeing oneself as an agent of change within the designed environs of one's world."[3] With these goals in mind, the AbD Framework contains thinking routines and activities that educators can use in their classrooms. Although the project focused mainly on K–12 education, many of the findings can apply to maker-centered learning for any age level. Later in this chapter, I will describe how I have successfully used an AbD thinking routine with college-age students.

One of the most prominent and well-developed frameworks for maker-centered learning in higher education is the Maker Literacies Project,[4] an initiative started at the University of Texas, Arlington. The project has developed a list of maker competencies for higher education, in addition to providing a wide range of examples of makerspace course integrations. The project, funded by a $50,000 grant by the Institute of Museum and Library Services (IMLS) and bringing in four partner institutions (University of Nevada, Reno; University of Massachusetts Amherst; Boise State University; and University of North Carolina Chapel Hill), was based on faculty partnerships to incorporate maker projects into courses. The resulting list of fifteen maker competencies listed on the Maker Literacies Project website cover a range of outcomes for maker learning, including identifying needs that can be fulfilled through making, working in teams, and understanding the cultural and social issues that making entails.[5] What is not included in the list of maker competencies are specific tools or technology skills. The competencies, like the AbD Framework, instead focus on enduring, transferable skills that students gain through maker-centered learning.

Other scholarship has studied the ways that academic makerspaces can further support learning at the university level, without explicitly arguing for either maker literacies or connections to the ACRL Framework. Nichols, Melo, and Dewland demonstrate that through the collaborative, transdisciplinary nature of the academic makerspace, "scholars find dynamic relationships that support multiple points of inquiry, expertise across design, programming, a marriage of science and arts, and a nexus of innovative and scholarly production."[6] Referencing the iSpace at the University of Arizona, Tucson, the authors highlight partnerships with student organizations as well as digital humanities curriculum integrations through the College of Humanities. Mathuews and Harper also point out the importance of collaborative learning to the future sustainability of academic makerspaces, arguing that the true value of library makerspaces can be found in cross-disciplinary knowledge sharing practices.[7] Other scholarship on academic makerspaces has advocated for incorporating maker technology into curricula. Lippincott, Vedantham, and Duckett, in a 2014 article, when makerspaces were very new additions to university libraries, argue for the integration of emerging technology into coursework, as a way to increase student engagement, allow students to explore new technologies and create more innovative work, and allow for more individualized work from students.[8] Wilczynski et al. studied how makerspaces can not only create "an intentional collision of random ideas" when open to all disciplines on campus, but can also be useful for discipline-specific accreditation, specifically ABET standards for engineering education.[9]

While the above literature reflects varying outcomes of maker-centered learning, whether creating campus collaborations, improving student engagement, or obtaining disciplinary accreditation, many academic makerspace practitioners place emphasis on enduring, transferable skills rather than discrete acquisition of technical knowledge. A common thread for maker-centered learning frameworks is the development of a maker mindset, which includes personal empowerment, failure positivity, and critical thinking. In other words, even though students are learning specific tools, technologies, and software, the enduring value that they receive from maker-centered learning experiences is primarily related to mindset development.

CONNECTING MAKER LITERACY
TO INFORMATION LITERACY

The question of how maker-centered learning connects to information literacy instruction remains largely unanswered. The literature on maker-centered learning in higher education often does not approach the concepts in the context of the ACRL Framework but, rather, examines maker literacy as a separate set of competencies. However, Milne-Lane and Vecchione from the Boise State University MakerLab created a "Maker Instruction Toolkit," which provides a roadmap for implementing maker instruction in an academic library setting through the lens of the ACRL Framework.[10] The Toolkit includes practical tools such as lesson planning templates, as well as a literature review on academic library makerspaces and an argument for experiential learning in academic libraries. The section, "Matching the MakerLab with ACRL Framework," provides examples from the Boise State University MakerLab that highlight the ways that maker learning connects to each ACRL Framework frame.

Attempting to map maker literacies to the ACRL Framework can be a difficult task on the surface; there are many similarities, but there are also many outcomes of maker-centered learning that may not fit perfectly with the ACRL Framework. However, Milne-Lane and Vecchione's work helped me to begin making connections and prompted me to view the ACRL Framework as it was designed to be viewed— not as a set of skills to master, but as the fostering of enduring, lifelong dispositions. From there, I delved into two of the underlying concepts of the ACRL Framework, metaliteracy and liminality, where I found strong and deep connections to maker literacy. The concepts of metaliteracy and liminality emphasize students as active creators, contributors, and independent agents in the world of information—goals which line up nicely with the practices and outcomes of maker-centered learning.

Maker Literacy and Metaliteracy

Metaliteracy puts emphasis on students as active "consumers and creators of information who can participate successfully in collaborative spaces."[11] Metaliteracy was first proposed by Mackey and Jacobson in a 2011 paper, but the concept has since grown and been interpreted by a variety of librarians and scholars. Rather than presenting literacy as a set of skills to master, metaliteracy represents a more student-centered idea of information literacy in which students are functioning participants and creators in the information economy. "In proposing metaliteracy as overarching and related to many literacy frameworks, we suggest changes to the way information literacy is perceived as a primarily skills-based approach to learning."[12] Mackey and Jacobson explain that through metaliteracy, students can use their knowledge of technology topics to build a real-world resume or portfolio. They propose that in addition to metaliteracy broadening the scope of information literacy, it can be used at a larger scale as a model to bring together a variety of similarly technology-focused literacies.[13] Maker literacy is an emerging literacy, alongside digital literacy, media literacy, visual literacy, and can be seen as a new subset of metaliteracy. Metaliteracy broadens the scope of library instruction and makes room for new and innovative literacies, such as maker literacy. Some of the important mindset elements that connect maker literacy and metaliteracy include student empowerment, the shift from consumer to creator, civic mindedness, and metacognition. As mentioned earlier, important frameworks for maker-centered learning, such as the AbD Framework and the Maker Literacies Project, as well as a wide range of literature on maker-centered learning, place emphasis on similar mindset development.

Many instructors have found metaliteracy useful in helping students develop a similar critical and creative mindset. Borrowing from feminist pedagogy, Wallis and Battista designed a one-credit course, The Politics of Information, which had the overarching goal of empowering students to not only question traditional power structures in academic information creation but also to develop their own identities as creators of information.[14] Setting the tone for the course, no traditional textbook was used, but instead, Wallis and Battista created a free zine, called *Authorize This!*, in which the authors showcased, in their own drawings and handwriting, childhood experiences that related to questioning authoritative information sources. Students also developed five creations throughout the semester, which were delivered in non-traditional formats—a Buzzfeed article, a Wikipedia edit, engaging in a blogosphere, creating a "Bizarro research paper," and, finally, creating a way to spread the message of said paper. The author/instructors concluded that "metaliteracy teaching helps students develop as critical creators and users of both digital and traditional forms of information."[15]

Irene McGarrity similarly incorporated metaliterate learning practices into an undergraduate course, Digital Identity and Participatory Culture.[16] The librarian-taught course used the flipped classroom model and asked students to create the assignments rather than the instructors. Placing their practice upon a strong foundation of decades of research on student-centered learning, including Jean Piaget's constructivist philosophy, Paulo Friere's *Pedagogy of the Oppressed*, Lev Vygotsky's social constructivism, as well as the more recent work of George Siemens on connectivism. McGarrity designed the four-credit course to emphasize student agency and empowerment, she acknowledged that metaliteracy has been an important instigator in the shift toward the incorporation of active, student-centered learning in information literacy instruction. McGarrity underlined the importance of students' active role in their learning, stating, "Agency is about empowerment, but it's also about responsibility. For those students who are trained as passive recipients of knowledge and learning, the prospect of making decisions about their learning can be paralyzing."[17] McGarrity and her co-instructor helped students to move beyond these fears and undergo the mindset shift to take control of their own learning. Although these examples of metaliterate teaching and learning do not connect directly to maker-centered learning, they employ many of the same tactics and have similar outcomes. Incorporating maker projects into course content is a tool for instructors to foster active, experiential, and student-centered learning in the classroom. Next, we will look more closely at four elements of the maker mindset that are encompassed by the overarching framework of metaliteracy.

From Consumer to Creator

The "2018 Metaliteracy Goals and Learning Objectives" represent years of work in developing and refining the main tenets of metalierate learning, and include overarching goals, each of which consist of several learning objectives.[18] The document explains that multiliterate learning falls into four domains: behavioral, cognitive, affective, and metaliterate. Each objective is assigned one or more of these categories. Goal 3 of the "2018 Metaliteracy Goals and Learning Objectives" includes students' ability to view themselves as producers of information, along with the ability to ethically share and evaluate information in collaborative environments. This lines up with some of the important outcomes of maker-centered learning, including the student's shift in mindset from consumer to creator, as well as a student's ability to understand the cultural and societal significance of the things that they create. Rooted in the ideals of the maker movement, the shift from consumer to creator fundamentally changes students' outlook and connects closely with the theme of empowerment. Students are no longer blindly consuming information and things, but rather looking critically at all aspects of the designed world around them, with a confidence that they can analyze, tinker with, and design new objects.

Student Empowerment

In Jacobson, Mackey, and O'Brien's "Metaliterate Learner Roles," the concept of empowerment is directly linked to students' ability to step into the various scholarly roles that are represented.[19] Empowerment is important to metaliteracy learning practices, as evidenced by the classroom examples outlined previously in this chapter. Empowerment is also a key outcome of maker-centered learning, both in the predominant maker learning frameworks and in the literature on maker-centered learning. As described previously, the ultimate outcome of the AbD Framework for maker-centered learning is maker empowerment. Clapp et al. state, "Maker empowerment is a sensitivity to the designed dimension of objects and systems, along with the inclination and capacity to shape one's world through building, tinkering, re/designing, or hacking."[20] Maker-centered learning culminates in students' ability to critically evaluate the world around them, to understand how things work, and to become confident in their ability to tinker, fix, improve upon, and create things from scratch.

Civic Mindedness

One of Mackey and Jacobson's "Metaliterate Learner Characteristics"[21] is the tendency to be civic-minded, a mindset where students use what they have learned to better their communities or the larger society. This proclivity toward civic-mindedness is also a natural outgrowth of the maker mindset. As I explained in a 2020 blog post for Metaliteracy.org, "when students experience empowerment through maker-centered learning, this empowerment begins to extend beyond themselves, often resulting in students' commitment to use their newfound agency to make a difference in the world at large."[22] Within the maker movement, there is a definite trend of makers using their skills and experience to give back to their communities and to the world at large. Many nonprofits and other organizations have emerged from maker projects because tinkering and making resulted in technology that could benefit humanity in some way. One example is Enabling the Future, a project that provides open-source schematics for prosthetic hands.[23] The project started in 2011 when a maker named Ivan Owen created a moveable metal hand for a steampunk cosplay. As it turned out, the technology that made the cosplay hand moveable was also revolutionary for the prosthetics community. It led to the e-Nable project, which now exists under the title of Project Enable. The organization not only provides plans and resources for the creation of low-cost, easily replicable prosthetics, but also acts as a connector between interested makers and those who need prosthetics. Project Enable is just one example of maker projects that have become worldwide humanitarian efforts.

Another recent example of the civic-mindedness of the maker community is the response to personal protective equipment (PPE) shortages resulting from the COVID-19 pandemic. Early on in the pandemic, the worldwide medical community was overwhelmed by the sudden need for PPE, hygienic supplies, and medical devices. The maker community's response to this crisis was immediate and huge. Individual makers and large organizations launched a monumental effort to design and manufacture PPE, such as face masks and shields, as well as parts for medical devices, particularly ventilators.[24] A guide that I created in April 2020, lists many of these efforts, which include commercial companies and organizations such as Matterhackers and America Makes helping to match makers and hospitals in need, as well as challenges for the design of PPE and devices with large prizes.[25] According to AbD, community making is an important benefit of maker-centered learning, defining it as, "Finding opportunities to make things that are meaningful to one's community and taking ownership of that process of making, either independently or with others."[26]

Metacognition

Metacognition is an integral component of metaliteracy, and is one of the four domains of metaliterate learning. In the "2018 Metaliteracy Goals and Learning Objectives," the metacognitive domain is defined as "what learners think about their own thinking—a reflective understanding of how and why they learn, what they do and do not know, their preconceptions, and how to continue to learn."[27] To my knowledge, the current literature on maker literacy learning does not address metacognition as an outcome of maker-centered learning. I would argue that metacognition is integral to the maker learning process. Although metacognition is not specifically addressed, many practitioners place emphasis on introspection, reflection, and critically evaluating one's own core beliefs and principals. Wallace et al. explain that the incorporation of self-reflective components into maker projects, such as journaling, led to observable growth in students.[28]

I have found this to be true in my own practice as a makerspace librarian and educator. I start my instruction sessions by introducing students to the maker mindset, which gives students the opportunity to understand and evaluate their own shift in thinking as they develop themselves as makers. A favorite activity to kick off my maker learning sessions is, "Memorable Making Experience," an activity from AbD that I have modified.[29] In this activity, students are asked to think of a time they made something and to think about why it was memorable. It sounds extremely simple, but the great thing about this activity is that it helps students to expand their idea of what "making" is. I make sure to emphasize at the beginning that by "making," I don't just mean 3D printing, sewing, or something that might have initially come to their minds. I explain that making can be anything where they are using their hands to create something, digital or physical; it could be baking a cake, or fixing a car, or drawing a picture. After students have shared their making experience, I finish the activity with these words from the original AbD activity:

- We do this activity to make the point that everyone is a maker in some way—we have all had memorable making experiences: making is what makes us human!
- We do this activity to show the range of activities that may be considered making—it's not just about robots, drones, or the latest technology.
- We do this activity to show that making is not discipline specific—it's not just about increasing proficiency in the STEM subjects.
- We do this activity to demystify making and maker—it's not an esoteric practice practiced by few, but something we all do/are.[30]

By doing this activity at the very beginning of the maker learning experience, just as students are being introduced to the idea of maker literacy and the maker mindset, we not only encourage metacognition throughout the learning process, but we immediately make students feel more included and capable of working in the makerspace environment. This small metacognitive activity spurs creativity and helps students get past any potential hesitancy they may have about whether they are makers. Another important thing to note is that this activity was developed for K–12 learners (AbD's focus area), but, in my experience, it works equally well for college-age students. This illustrates that frameworks like AbD can be beneficial tools for students of all ages.

Maker Literacy and Liminality

The concept of liminality originated in the field of anthropology, coined in 1908 by Arnold van Gennep and further developed in the 1960s by Victor Turner.[31] In anthropology, liminality represents "the transition from one social identity to another, such as from child to adult, from citizen to king, or from living body to dead corpse."[32] Individuals enter a state of liminality when they are in between who they used to be and who they are becoming. Liminality has evolved beyond its anthropological origins to find its way into many disciplines, including performance studies, religious studies, literature, and popular culture. The concept is interpreted differently based on the area of study, but generally represents the in-between—of identities, understandings, states of being, or of space. Meyer and Land apply liminality to higher education learning theory, in the context of threshold concepts. Threshold concepts, conceived by Meyer and Land in 2003, are irreversible and transformative learning events that are integral to students' understanding of a particular subject. In the process of students' navigation through threshold concepts, they pass through a liminal space, in which there may be uncertainty or anxiety, or feel that they are "stuck."[33] While threshold concepts may be structured by the instructor and more or less predetermined, liminality "offers less predictability, and appears to be a more 'liquid' space, simultaneously transforming and being transformed by the learner as he or she moves through it."[34]

In a 2015 paper presented at the LILAC conference, Fister discussed the concept of liminality, while reflecting on the newly-created "ACRL Framework for Information Literacy." Fister began by pointing out that information literacy, especially as represented in the ACRL Framework, is much more than just learning to find information. Instead, she explained that information literacy is the active process of acquiring "experiences, skills, and dispositions" that empower students to become creators and effective users of information.[35] Speaking about threshold concepts, Fister discussed the idea of liminality. She describes liminality as "the place where we are between understandings. It's the borderland we're passing through as we move from a familiar place to an unknown place. It's where we are unsettled, where we might turn back because it's just too uncomfortable—or where we might feel exhilarated by the challenge."[36] She explains that when students learn to navigate this area of uncertainty, they develop enduring, transferable skills that go beyond their major of study and benefit them in the workplace of the future.

I argue that maker-centered learning exists in this liminal state. The mechanisms of maker learning depend upon pushing students just beyond their comfort zone, while also supporting them and making them feel empowered and capable. In my makerspace classes and workshops, I have found that the best way to encourage creativity and push students toward developing a maker mindset is to allow for some uncertainty, improvisation, and even failure in the making process. If students are told exactly what to do, exactly what to make, they will not learn as much as they would if allowed to tinker and iterate. In *The Art of Tinkering*, Wilkinson and Petrich describe the benefits of this type of learning. They explain that tinkering is "whimsical, enjoyable, fraught with dead ends, frustrating, and ultimately about inquiry."[37] But the sometimes-frustrating process of tinkering is well worth the effort, because it is when we enter this state of uncertainty, when we struggle and overcome obstacles, that we create amazing things, learn enduring skills and dispositions, and develop a maker mindset.

Another interesting connection between maker learning and liminality comes to light when we imagine the role of makerspaces on college campuses. Miller et al. make the observation that makerspaces on college campuses exist in a "liminal space," because they are informal learning spaces that fall outside of the structured university curriculum.[38] Using the example of the Curtin Library Makerspace in Australia, they argue that makerspaces have great creative potential because of their location at the outskirts of the traditional university. Makerspaces often work alongside and in collaboration with faculty teaching semester-long courses, but offer students a place in which to explore, tinker, and play that falls outside of their normal courses. In this way, the university makerspace not only facilitates learning opportunities for students that push them into the area of liminality, and foster deep, inquiry-based learning, but the makerspace *itself* lives in an area of liminality that allows for flexibility and creativity potentially not available in students' daily university life.

Maker Literacy in Action

As I have taken the underlying concepts of maker-centered learning and translated them into practice, I have witnessed how these theoretical frameworks affect real-life students, both in formal classroom settings and informal interactions in the makerspace at Miami University Libraries. In 2019, I worked with Kristan Kanorr, an instructor for one of Miami's University Studies (UNV 101) courses to develop an assignment that prompted students to explore their identity. Students used several tools in the makerspace for two projects, "Who I Am Not," at the beginning of the semester, and then "Who I Am," near the end of the semester.[39] For "Who I Am Not," students created a wood block on the Carvey CNC machine of the Miami "M" logo, and then cut three words out of vinyl on the Silhouette Cameo craft cutter that represent stereotypes that others may hold about them. For "Who I am," after a semester of experience and personal growth, students designed a personal logo in Inkscape that contained three to five words that represent who they truly are. They then cut out their logos as stickers on the Silhouette machine.

The students in these sections UNV 101 are first-year undecided students, and part of the goal of the course is not only to help students adjust to university life but also to better understand their own goals and dreams in order to situate them for success during and after their college life. This project provides a way for students to explore their various identities through making. The project incorporates metaliteracy in several ways, by helping students develop skills as creators of information and things, by empowering students to embrace their true selves, and through metacognition, as students must introspectively explore their growth throughout their first semester at university. Additionally, I incorporate liminality by allowing students creative freedom in designing their "Who I Am" logos. I give the students the basic concepts of vector design and a quick tutorial of Inkscape but stop short of any prescriptive instructions on how to create their logos. The students must overcome the initial uncertainty of how to make a logo from scratch, which pushes them into the area of liminality and allows for creative thinking to blossom. This project is one of many that I have facilitated within existing courses; I have worked with faculty in a wide variety of disciplines (English, History, Public Speaking, Chemistry, Italian Renaissance, Spanish/Portuguese, Fashion Design, etc.) in the past three years. By situating maker-centered learning within academic library information literacy practices, the possibilities of engaging students in maker-centered learning are virtually limitless.

CONCLUSION

In order for academic library makerspaces to maintain relevance in the ever-changing realm of innovation in academia, makerspace organizers must continually demonstrate that these spaces align with library and university priorities, and provide enduring benefits for learning. We can do this by connecting makerspaces to the information literacy goals of academic libraries, as represented by the ACRL Framework. And as Milne-Lane and Vecchione attest, "The ACRL Framework is the embodiment of the maker spirit, cementing the home of the makerspace on a college campus to belong squarely within the responsibilities of the academic library."[40] Viewing maker literacy through the lens of metaliteracy and liminality further connects maker learning to information literacy and the ACRL Framework, imbuing maker literacy with legitimacy and ensuring the long-term survival of maker services in academic libraries. The future of academic library makerspaces lies in the enormous potential of maker-centered learning to transform student engagement and learning, allowing students to develop lifelong, transferable skill sets, such as critical thinking, creativity, empowerment, and many more. Maker-centered learning can have long-lasting positive effects on students that they can carry with them into their future lives and careers.

NOTES

1. Edward P. Clapp et al., *Maker-Centered Learning: Empowering Young People to Shape Their Worlds* (San Francisco: Josey-Bass, 2017).

2. Clapp et al., *Maker-Centered Learning*, 117.

3. Ibid., 19.

4. Wallace et al., "Maker Competencies and the Undergraduate Curriculum" (Paper presented at the 2018 International Symposium on Academic Makerspaces, Stanford, CA, August 3–5, 2018), http://hdl.handle.net/10106/27518.

5. "Maker Competencies," Maker Literacies Project, accessed May 4, 2021, https://library.uta.edu/makerliteracies/competencies.

6. Jennifer Nichols, Marijel (Maggie) Melo, and Jason Dewland, "Unifying Space and Service for Makers, Entrepreneurs, and Digital Scholars," *portal: Libraries and the Academy* 17, no. 2 (April 2015): 366, https://doi.org/10.1353/pla.2017.0022.

7. Katy Mathuews and Daniel Harper, "One Size Does Not Fit All: Maintaining Relevancy in the Modern Makerspace Movement," *College & Research Libraries News* 79, no. 7 (2018): 358, https://doi.org/10.5860/crln.79.7.358.

8. Joan Lippincott, Anu Vedantham, and Kim Duckett, "Libraries as Enablers of Pedagogical and Curricular Change," *Educause Review*, October 27, 2014, https://er.educause.edu/articles/2014/10/libraries-as-enablers-of-pedagogical-and-curricular-change.

9. Wilczynski et al., "The Value of Higher Education Academic Makerspaces for Accreditation and Beyond," *Planning for Higher Education* 46, no. 1 (October 2017): 32–40.

10. Stephanie Milne-Lane and Amy Vecchione, "Maker Instruction Toolkit," accessed May 20, 2021, https://www.boisestate.edu/library-makerlab/makerlab-instruction/maker-instruction-toolkit/.

11. "Framework for Information Literacy for Higher Education," American Library Association, February 9, 2015, http://www.ala.org/acrl/standards/ilframework, accessed April 16, 2021.

12. Tom Mackey and Trudi Jacobson, "Reframing Information Literacy as a Metaliteracy," *College & Research Libraries*, 72, no. 1 (January 2011): 70.

13. Tom Mackey and Trudi Jacobson, *Metaliteracy: Reinventing Information Literacy to Empower Learners* (Chicago: ALA Nealp-Schuman, 2016), 15.

14. Lauren Wallis and Andrew Battista, "The Politics of Information: Students as Creators in a Metaliteracy Context," in *Metaliteracy in Practice* eds. Trudi Jacobson and Thomas Mackey (Chicago: ALA/Neal-Schuman Publishers, Inc., 2016), 23–46.

15. Ibid., 39.

16. Irene McGarrity, "Developing Agency in Metaliterate Learners: Empowerment through Digital Identity and Participation," in *Metaliteracy in Practice*, eds. Trudi Jacobson and Thomas Mackey (Chicago: ALA/Neal-Schuman Publishers Inc., 2016), 159–82.

17. McGarrity, "Developing Agency," 167.

18. Jacobson et al. "2018 Metaliteracy Goals and Learning Objectives," *Metaliteracy*, 2018, https://metaliteracy.org/learning-objectives/2018-metaliteracy-goals-and-learning-objectives/.

19. Trudi Jacobson, Tom Mackey, and Kelsey O'Brien, "Metaliterate Learner Roles," 2018, https://metaliteracy.org/ml-in-practice/metaliterate-learner-roles/.

20. Clapp et al., *Maker-Centered Learning*, 103.

21. Tom Mackey, "Empowering Metaliterate Learners for the Post-Truth World," in *Metaliterate Learning for the Post Truth World*, eds. Tom Mackey and Trudi Jacobson (New York: ALA/Neal-Schuman Publishers, Inc., 2019), 1–32.

22. Sarah Nagle, "Metaliteracy and Maker Literacy," *Metaliteracy*, July 21, 2020, https://metaliteracy.org/2020/07/21/metaliteracy-and-maker-literacy/.

23. "About Us," Enabling the Future website,, accessed May 20, 2021, http://enablingthefuture.org/about/.

24. Lucia Corsini, Valeria Dammicco, Lin Bowker-Lonnecker, and Robbie Blythe, "The Maker Movement and its Impact in the Fight against COVID-19" (working paper, Centre for Technology Management working paper series, 2020), https://aspace.repository.cam.ac.uk/handle/1810/313163.

25. Sarah Nagle, "Making from Home Resources: COVID-19: Make a Difference from Home," Miami University Libraries, April, 2020, https://libguides.lib.miamioh.edu/make-from-home/COVID19.

26. Clapp et al., *Maker-Centered Learning*, 41.

27. Jacobson et al. "2018 Metaliteracy Goals and Learning Objectives," para. 2.

28. Wallace et al., "Maker Competencies," 5.

29. Agency by Design, "Memorable Making Activity," Project Zero, http://agencybydesign.org/sites/default/files/AbD%20Memorable%20Making%20Experience%20.pdf.

30. Agency by Design, "Memorable Making Activity," para. 4.

31. Kim Skjoldager-Nielsen and Joshua Edelman, "Liminality," *Ecumenica* 7, nos. 1–2 (2014): 33–40.

32. Ibid, 33.

33. Jan H. F. Meyer and Ray Land, "Threshold Concepts and Troublesome Knowledge (2): Epistemological Considerations and a Conceptual Framework for Teaching and Learning," *Higher Education* 49, no. 3 (April 2005): 377.

34. Ibid., 379–80.

35. Barbara Fister, "The Liminal Library: Making Our Libraries Sites of Transformative Learning" (Paper presented at the LILAC Conference, April 13, 2015), 4, https://barbarafister.com/LiminalLibrary.pdf.

36. Fister, "The Liminal Library," 6.

37. Karen Wilkinson and Mike Petrich, *The Art of Tinkering* (San Francisco: Weldon Owen, 2013), 13.

38. Miller et al., "The Role of Responsive Library Makerspaces in Supporting Informal Learning in the Digital Humanities," in *Digital Humanities, Libraries, and Partnerships*, eds. R. Kear and K. Joranson (Cambridge: Chandos Publishing, 2018), 91–105.

39. Mark Dahlquist, Stefanie Hilles, and Sarah Nagle, "Information Inspiration: Creativity Across Disciplines in Academic Libraries," *LOEX Quarterly* 46, no. 4 (2020): 13–16.

40. Milne-Lane and Vecchione, "Matching the MakerLab with ACRL Framework," para. 1.

BIBLIOGRAPHY

"About Us." Enabling the Future website. Accessed May 20, 2021. http://enablingthefuture.org/about/.

Agency by Design. "Memorable Making Activity." Agency by Design. Project Zero. http://agencybydesign.org/sites/default/files/AbD%20Memorable%20Making%20Experience%20.pdf.

American Library Association. "Framework for Information Literacy for Higher Education." February 9, 2015. Accessed April 16, 2021. http://www.ala.org/acrl/standards/ilframework.

Clapp, Edward P., Jessica Ross, Jennifer O. Ryan, and Shari Tishman. *Maker-Centered Learning: Empowering Young People to Shape Their Worlds.* San Francisco: Jossey-Bass, 2017.

Corsini, Lucia, Valeria Dammicco, Lin Bowker-Lonnecker, and Robbie Blythe. "The Maker Movement and its Impact in the Fight against COVID-19." Working paper, Centre for Technology Management working paper series, 2020. https://aspace.repository.cam.ac.uk/handle/1810/313163.

Dahlquist, Mark, Stefanie Hilles, and Sarah Nagle. "Information Inspiration: Creativity Across Disciplines in Academic Libraries." *LOEX Quarterly* 46, no. 4 (2020): 13–16. https://commons.emich.edu/loexquarterly/vol46/iss4/6/.

Fister, Barbara. "The Liminal Library: Making Our Libraries Sites of Transformative Learning." Paper presented at the LILAC Conference, April 13, 2015. https://barbarafister.com/LiminalLibrary.pdf.

Jacobson, Trudi, Tom Mackey, Kelsey O'Brien, Michele Forte, and Emer O'Keeffe. "2018 Metaliteracy Goals and Learning Objectives." 2018. https://metaliteracy.org/learning-objectives/2018-metaliteracy-goals-and-learning-objectives/.

Lippincott, Joan, Anu Vedantham, and Kim Duckett. "Libraries as Enablers of Pedagogical and Curricular Change." *Educause Review*, October 27, 2014. https://er.educause.edu/articles/2014/10/libraries-as-enablers-of-pedagogical-and-curricular-change.

Mackey, Tom. "Empowering Metaliterate Learners for the Post-Truth World." In *Metaliterate Learning for the Post Truth World*, edited by Tom Mackey and Trudi Jacobson, 1–32. New York: American Library Association (ALA)/Neal-Schuman Publishers, Inc. 2019.

Mackey, Tom, and Trudi Jacobson. *Metaliteracy: Reinventing Information Literacy to Empower Learners.* Chicago: American Library Association (ALA)/Neal-Schuman Publishers, Inc., 2016.

———. "Reframing Information Literacy as a Metaliteracy." *College & Research Libraries* 72, no. 1 (January 2011): 62–78.

Mathuews, Katy, and Daniel Harper. "One Size Does Not Fit All: Maintaining Relevancy in the Modern Makerspace Movement." *College & Research Libraries* 79, no. 7 (July 2018): 358–59. https://doi.org/10.5860/crln.79.7.358.

McGarrity, Irene. "Developing Agency in Metaliterate Learners: Empowerment through Digital Identity and Participation." In *Metaliteracy in Practice*, edited by Trudi Jacobson and Thomas Mackey, 23–46. Chicago: American Library Association (ALA)/Neal-Schuman Publishers, Inc., 2016.

Meyer, Jan H. F., and Ray Land. "Threshold Concepts and Troublesome Knowledge (2): Epistemological Considerations and a Conceptual Framework for Teaching and Learning." *Higher Education* 49, no. 3 (April 2005): 373–388.

Miller, Karen, Erik Champion, Lise Summers, Artur Lugmayr, and Marie Clarke. "The Role of Responsive Library Makerspaces in Supporting Informal Learning in the Digital Humanities." In *Digital Humanities, Libraries, and Partnerships*, edited by R. Kear and K. Joranson, 91–105. Cambridge: Chandos Publishing, 2018.

Milne-Lane, Stephanie, and Amy Vecchione. "Maker Instruction Toolkit." Accessed May 20, 2021. https://www.boisestate.edu/library-makerlab/makerlab-instruction/maker-instruction-toolkit/.

Nagle, Sarah. "Making from Home Resources: COVID-19: Make a Difference from Home." Miami University Libraries. April 2020. https://libguides.lib.miamioh.edu/make-from-home/COVID19.

———. "Metaliteracy and Maker Literacy." *Metaliteracy* (blog), July 21, 2020. https://meta
literacy.org/2020/07/21/metaliteracy-and-maker-literacy/.

Nichols, Jennifer, Marijel (Maggie) Melo, and Jason Dewland. "Unifying Space and Service
for Makers, Entrepreneurs, and Digital Scholars." *portal: Libraries and the Academy* 17,
no. 2 (April 2015): 363–74. https://doi.org/10.1353/pla.2017.0022.

Skjoldager-Nielsen, Kim and Joshua Edelman. "Liminality." *Ecumenica* 7, nos. 1–2 (2014):
33–40.

Wallace, Martin K., Gretchen Trkay, Katie Musick Peery, Morgan Chivers, and Tara Radniecki. "Maker Competencies and the Undergraduate Curriculum." Paper presented at
the 2018 International Symposium on Academic Makerspaces, Stanford, CA, August 3–5,
2018. http://hdl.handle.net/10106/27518.

Wallis, Lauren, and Andrew Battista. "The Politics of Information: Students as Creators in a
Metaliteracy Context." In *Metaliteracy in Practice*, edited by Trudi Jacobson and Thomas
Mackey, 23–46. Chicago: American Library Association (ALA)/Neal-Schuman Publishers
Inc., 2016.

Wilczynski, Vincent, Aubrey Wigner, Micah Lande, and Shawn Jordan. "The Value of Higher
Education Academic Makerspaces for Accreditation and Beyond." *Planning for Higher Education* 46, no. 1 (October 2017): 32–40. https://search-ebscohost-com.proxy.lib.miamioh
.edu/login.aspx?direct=true&db=eft&AN=128004643&site=eds-live&scope=site.

Wilkinson, Karen, and Mike Petrich. *The Art of Tinkering*. San Francisco: Weldon Owen, 2013.

11

Off the Cutting Edge

Lessons Learned from Centering People in Creative Technology Spaces

Kelsey Sheaffer, Oscar K. Keyes, Eric Johnson, Jason Evans Groth, Vanessa Rodriguez, and Emily Thompson

In the last two decades, libraries have expanded their literacy efforts to incorporate digital and media literacies, often through the use of creative technologies. Many university libraries have seen the rise of technology loan programs to augment traditional print collections, create multimedia studios and makerspaces, and hire nontraditional librarians to support these new initiatives. Additionally, the concept of digital literacy has been adopted by university administration advocating for career preparedness and multimodal communication. Over time, digital literacy has become an accepted component of many library initiatives and is no longer the cutting edge. However, this movement can serve as a robust model for libraries developing innovation in new cutting-edge initiatives such as immersive environments, data literacy, and artificial intelligence.

At many institutions, digital literacy support is channeled through creative technology spaces that are loosely oriented around multimedia, makerspace and/or digital scholarship programs, and are broadly composed of three kinds of resources: (1) space, (2) technology, and (3) people. In contemporary library budget contexts, it is common to emphasize space and technological resources at the onset of a new center, with the mantra: "if you build it, they will come." Many libraries are responding to either institutional directives or national trends when building new innovative services, and securing technology and/or space can appear to satisfy the interest. However, we can document through the trajectory of many creative technology spaces over the last decade that the most institutionally-integrated and sustainable centers are those that prioritize people as the essential component. Making technology available is not enough; new movements must train, support, and integrate people who teach and promote the technology.

Here we will examine creative technology centers at five academic libraries. Each library has developed its unique vision for integrating new technologies into the institution, continually emphasizing the importance of people. We will expand on our shared philosophies; hiring and training; sustainability and innovation through supporting staff and budgets; equity, access, and inclusion; and the various successes and challenges associated with an initially emerging and now more established creative library resource. Envisioning future literacies is to imagine the future itself, and our experience compels us to advocate for sustainable frameworks in order for this creative work to continue. While industrial processes often focus on the product, our instructional practices focus on people. We see this as an opportunity to shift the conversation for the next generation of makers in libraries. By focusing on people, we can approach future literacy movements that embed the values of sustainability, connection, and equity into their code.

THE HISTORY OF CREATIVE TECHNOLOGY SPACES

The modern university multimedia center is braided from a number of historical developments within libraries and media technologies. The first of these in the history of libraries is the establishment of non-textual media collections; these early collections were largely consumption-oriented. As new media formats developed through the nineteenth and into the early twentieth centuries, modern libraries worked to keep up with them, giving patrons access to knowledge captured in these new ways. In 1818, Harvard University received the first map collection given to a university library,[1] then the Library of Congress established a map collection in the 1860s.[2] Between 1880 and 1910, there was a rapid succession of new media recording formats in library collections: slides, circulating image collections, Library of Congress motion picture deposits, and phonorecords. The American Library Association introduced audiovisual librarianship as a specialty in 1924. In the 1940s and 1950s, universities and school systems established audiovisual libraries, including film collections and 35mm slides.[3] Starting in the 1970s, the pace of technological change increased, with an accompanying impact on library collections and the technology needed to access them: audiocassettes succeeded reel-to-reel; CDs replaced cassettes and vinyl; digital downloads and streaming succeeded CDs; U-matic, Betamax, and VHS videocassettes replaced film, and in turn they were followed by DVD, digital downloads, and streaming services.

The second strand of development came in the middle of the twentieth century, when libraries started formally supporting content creation. No longer was it enough to merely consume media produced by others; patrons wanted the ability to create. In 1945, the Drew University Library supplied "radio-phonographs" to its students who used them to record the college band, a play, speeches, and songs to send home to their parents.[4] In the late 1970s and early 1980s, public libraries began lending cameras, most notably from a program created by Polaroid, which donated twenty thousand cameras to public libraries throughout the United States.[5]

This same period saw the creation of early versions of library media centers whose modern descendants are examined in this chapter: in 1973, the Hennepin County (MN) Library system opened a "neighborhood workshop for the community"—with equipment for processing film, videotapes, and slides.[6] The Brooklyn Public Library opened one with equipment to edit Super 8 film, 1/2- and 3/4-inch video tape, and audio tape. By the late 1970s, they were offering workshops for the public. During this same period, primary and secondary school library media centers discussed supporting media creation as well as consumption.[7] The 1980s saw a seismic technological shift with the introduction of microcomputers; libraries built on past practices of sharing limited resources by creating "computer resource centers" that offered hardware and software and instruction to patrons.[8] Makerspaces emerged in the twenty-first century as a related kind of space whose grounding in creativity, community-building, and technology is shared and overlaps with that of creative technology centers. The first library-based makerspace opened in 2011 at the Fayetteville Free Library in New York state.[9]

The third strand feeding into the history of centers like ours is the further refinement of digital technologies and the development of the internet, and the affordances they allow. The friction caused by limited availability to specialized equipment has been greatly reduced with the widespread access to computers and mobile devices that can serve as media creation and editing platforms. The relative cost of media creation hardware—cameras, video cameras, audio recorders—has come down, not least because mobile devices usually have them built in. In addition, software has made possible some of the work that used to involve specialty hardware (e.g., audio and video editing, photo correction, graphic design). It is easier than ever to create with this technology: beginner-level software exists, software-based and online tutorials are widely available, and communities of practice are more easily found than ever. Perhaps the biggest difference from what came before, though, is the existence of the internet as a community-building, publishing, and distribution platform; never has it been so possible to share one's creation with the world.

All of this means barriers to participation are lowered and motivation for creativity is heightened: because of the ubiquity and relative ease of this technology and the new ways of communication that it permits, students, faculty, and staff are finding that creative technology gives them a new way to share their voices. This means there is high demand for these services, but we are not quite at the point when just anybody feels like they can pick up any creative technology; access and approachability remain barriers and people are often unsure how to start or how to solve problems. The multimedia center fills this need.

FIVE CREATIVE TECHNOLOGY SPACES

Creative technology spaces within libraries are now somewhat common, especially within mid-to-large academic libraries. Our collective experience has been shaped by running, and in some cases, starting, five unique creative technology spaces located in university libraries in the southeastern United States. These spaces are the Adobe Digital Studio and Cooper Makerspace at Clemson University, Digital Media Lab at North Carolina State University (NCSU), Creative Studio at University of Miami (UM), University of Tennessee at Chattanooga Library Studio (UTC), and The Workshop at Virginia Commonwealth University (VCU). The directors of the spaces began an informal community of practice at the start of the COVID-19 pandemic to share experiences and shifting procedures; this was developed into the Southeastern Multimedia Librarians group (SEML).

Clemson University Libraries' main library is home to the Adobe Digital Studio and the Cooper Makerspace. The Adobe Digital Studio was initiated in 2014, out of a partnership with the company Adobe, to create a physical space that would expand digital media resources to the campus community. It contains a video studio, audio studio, and computer workstations in an open-access, collaborative lounge area. The Studio is run by a faculty librarian, who coordinates a team of interns that provide one-on-one expert help with digital media projects and assist with the studios. The Cooper Makerspace is adjacent to the Adobe Digital Studio and was founded in 2019 as a second location for an existing campus makerspace organization. The Studio and Makerspace coordinate with other library and campus creative technology resources, including a second digital media lab in a branch library, technology equipment loan circulating from the main library desk, and a new Digital Scholarship Lab.

D. H. Hill Jr. Library at NCSU is home to the Digital Media Lab (DML). The DML opened in 2001 with a focus on scanning, VHS transfer, graphic design, digital video, and digital photography. This space relocated in 2003 and continued expanding over the following decade to acquire a green screen studio and approximately twenty individual terminals for multimedia transfer and graphics editing. In 2013, the Hunt Library opened on a new innovation campus and further developed the vision of the DML. Eschewing the lab idea, four individual Music Rooms and two individual Media Production Studios were installed, all containing the same basic setups for multimedia production but with additional unique elements in each room. Initially, the DML at D. H. Hill Jr. and the Music Rooms/Media Production Studios were managed by the Digital Media librarian for Learning Spaces and Services, and supported by Ask Us staff and Media Consultant students. Starting in 2015, the DML added four individual Music Booths, replicating the software/hardware at Hunt Library. That same year, the DML Studio upgraded their hardware and software, making all eleven spaces across both libraries possess identical hardware and software.

UM Libraries' Creative Studio is a multimedia lab with service locations in multiple libraries. The studio developed informally prior to 2003 by offering access and training to multimedia software at Otto G. Richter Library, the campus' main library. It was formally established on the first floor of Richter Library by 2012 and has since expanded services to three subject libraries. Creative Studio has computer workstations, poster and 3D printing, loans of audiovisual equipment and VR/AR devices, video games and consoles, and digitization. Audio recording booths are located in the Weeks Music Library location. The studio is led by a faculty librarian overseeing three full-time staff and five student workers who specialize in a field of audiovisual and multimedia creation and are able to assist users with their projects through consultations and class workshops. Additionally, the head and staff of Creative Studio manage a video recording studio and a VR/AR demo space.

The UTC Library Studio opened in January 2015 as part of the new library building. Originally planned to be a small area with a recording studio and a couple of computers, it was expanded to approximately a third of the public area of the third floor by the time the building was finished. It contains a small audio suite, a video/photography suite, a 3D printing suite, and an open lab with twenty-four computers. The Studio is led by a director, with two tenure-track faculty librarians, three full-time staff, and four to six student workers rounding out the team. Known as "the library within the library," the team also circulates a large technology equipment collection.

VCU Libraries' multimedia and makerspace, The Workshop, opened in fall 2015 as part of a library expansion with the mission of helping the VCU community explore and express ideas using creative technologies. The center comprises five spaces: a main room with equipment lending and multimedia workstations, a video studio, an audio studio, a gaming/VR studio, and a makerspace. A team of student employees, totalling between twelve and twenty, with three working at a time, serves as the initial point of contact for most patrons; assisting with circulation, facilitating equipment/studio orientations, and answering questions about departmental hardware and software. Four full-time employees back them up; managing the department and its resources, providing in-depth consultation, and working with faculty and classes. The Workshop works closely with a similar though smaller set of spaces, equipment, and services at the university's Health Sciences Library.

The five centers all support multimedia creation through resources and expertise. They range in organizational structure but all have a director and rely on student employees for some frontline support. Each of them include some form of video and/or audio studio and are directly responsible for or proximate to equipment loan. Most significantly, each space focuses on student engagement and learning; rather than the pure technological resources that are available.

SHARED PHILOSOPHY

The five university libraries represented in this chapter have independently evolved a common philosophy that drives decision making for services, spaces, and resources: people are the most essential aspect of an innovative specialized center, not the technology. A space that is intended to support unique and experiential services can work without the technology, but it cannot work without centering the patrons and employees of the spaces. This shared philosophy, which is aligned to many library missions and will be explored further through this chapter, is deeply ingrained into all aspects of our spaces. The physical design of the centers can serve as a case study for the short- and long-term implications of our shared, people-centered philosophy.

The evolution of several of our spaces has involved interaction with non-library, specialized-technology consultants, from other departments within the university like central IT or consulting firms outside the university, tasked with helping to design the tech-heavy spaces. Using our experiences with specialized-technology consultants, we see that their suggestions typically trend in two directions: (1) The consultants create extremely high-end, high-tech spaces with complicated professional equipment and workflows. They have little experience with spaces designed for teaching or beginners, therefore, the resulting studios require extensive training and upkeep and are often offputting to beginner students. (2) Alternatively, consultants create a studio solution that seeks to remove human-technology interaction—and thus the teaching element—entirely. For example, one-button solutions for video recording and audio digitization that are intended to allow the patron to complete entire processes with ease. This style of technology solution is initially appealing to administrators: it provides patron access to the tech, without training and without staff management (hypothetically, though in practice it tends to need a high level of maintenance). However, these set-ups rarely teach students new technology or skills.

Of course, there are numerous reasons why engaging outside consultants for tech space design would be considered a good practice: outside teams have extensive, specialized knowledge around elaborate studio set-ups; high-end studios expose the campus community to industry-standard technology; the specialized library staff has not been hired yet to run them. However, these outside teams design spaces for hypothetical users: either total beginners or total experts. Librarians must consider a range of people using the spaces. This is not to say that the studios should not involve high-end equipment but, rather, that an ideal studio invites a range of expertise and engagement. Non-librarian university faculty and staff should also be consulted to understand specific community-based needs. This could potentially be the university instructional designers, faculty that teach related subjects, similar labs existing on campus, and student clubs with adjacent interests. Including these stakeholders in the planning process gives insight into what needs the campus has and how the library can help fulfill them. We work to create studios that are exciting to patrons from novices to experts, especially those patrons who do not have access to disciplinary labs. The value of centering people over technology is evident in the design of the spaces, in addition to other themes explored in this chapter, including hiring, sustainability, and accessibility.

HIRING AND CREATING TEAMS

In our experience, the people involved with these innovative library spaces can be sorted into two overlapping groups: patrons who use the space and a team of employees who manage its short- and long-term operations. Creating a motivated, patron-centered, access-focused team is critical for the success of our spaces. Team makeup will vary and there is no single, correct structure for the employee hierarchy. Common roles include a supportive administrator (who may also be the supervisor of the director of the space); a director who is a confident communicator and drives strategic directions; a media-making practitioner comfortable with instruction; and an effective organizer who manages the day-to-day operations with a staff of full-time employees, students, or, often, both.

A supportive administrator who may supervise the space's director is a common theme across our spaces. This is a person who both inspires and is inspired by the potential of the space. This person is also a part of the team, who will work on behalf of both the patrons and employees to ensure resources, space, personnel, and administrative needs are met. It is incumbent upon the director of the space to communicate well with their administrator and/or supervisor, given that this person is often a direct line to the administrative team members that make bigger picture budget decisions affecting the physical needs and human resources that make the space perform at its best.

Directors of these spaces do not necessarily fall squarely in the "media expert" category but, rather, have a litany of skills from domains that all flourish when their practitioners are comfortable making media. In addition to the expected experience in audiovisual fields, graphic design, and web design, the directors share experience in education and instruction at institutions as varied as museums, art schools, and financial literacy in public libraries, IT services, writing, music, theatre, archives, and more "traditional" library skills like reference, tech services, and collections. A director with skills that span multiple disciplines will help them communicate with and share a better understanding with the staff they will hire and whom they will collaborate with. Directors might also be non-traditional librarians without library degrees, who bring advanced credentials in other fields.

When hiring students, customer service and instruction skills are more important (and much more difficult to teach) than technological prowess. The open secret of hiring library student employees is to consider the long-term view and aim to hire good candidates for future librarian positions, who will excel at the reference interview. Creative technology spaces are no different: the job of the employees is to conduct reference interviews centered on media-making technology—that is, their job is to listen to patron questions, help interpret them, and, potentially, get to the bottom of what the patron's question really is so they can be led to appropriate resources. Identifying students that are likely to be good instructors is key, as instruction is key to a good reference interview, a solid workshop, and a welcoming environment.

We also look for students and staff interested in perpetual learning, who have the confidence to admit they do not know everything about any given technology but are more than comfortable using their search skills to figure it out; who are enthusiastic; who are a representative sample of the larger student body; who are good and easy communicators is both challenging and extremely important. These spaces can come with a lot of perceived baggage—that is, the idea of who is welcome in these spaces can sometimes keep prospective patrons from ever walking into them if they do not feel they are "allowed" to be there. Having students with a diversity of backgrounds and skills can be welcoming to patrons, in the same way the director's diversity of skills can make the student workers feel welcome. While some spaces do require previous experience with particular software before hiring, for the most part, we look for an approachable, enthusiastic student who communicates well. Technological training comes with the job, but agreeable personalities are often born, not made.

Staff and faculty hiring practices, while slightly different across our organizations, rely on having a supportive administrator and institution invested in the success of these spaces. Desirable skills include experience in media making, comfort with managing a diverse team of students, comfort with the programming of the spaces (workshops, instructions, etc.), a desire to make spaces and services easy and accessible through better organizational skills, and an understanding of the wide array of work that the whole team must accomplish in order for it to appropriately and effectively serve patrons. While faculty appear to like and feel comforted by the ability to point to particular staff members of these spaces and say "that person is a photography expert," or "this member is a podcast expert," those of us who work in the spaces know that we are perpetual learners with a wide array of skills who need to be very good at knowing how to provide appropriate help on demand. We also need to train our colleagues how to comfortably and confidently provide the same service.

Training is both formal and colloquial in our spaces. Training occurs often in the moment, by a student worker observing someone else doing the media work they need to learn or, in many cases, by the student being asked to help with an unknown skill. In other cases, formal exercises that require the student to interact with all of the equipment in the space are implemented upon hiring, which gives the student or staff member the confidence that they at least have touched the equipment and have a basic knowledge of what it might do. While this training helps students and staff get familiar with possible questions patrons may bring to the space, directors of these spaces have reported that training is also, often, as-needed, and passed down from staff to staff/ student to student. Communication is of the utmost importance in this colloquial way of training, so as not to unintentionally impart incorrect or harmful information/ practices in what might be considered an insidious game of telephone. The directors reported that hiring students and staff with whom interaction is easy is, thus, invaluable, especially in a training situation that is both well-documented and informal. Creating a supportive, approachable team is critical to the success of these people-centered innovative spaces. Through intentional hiring, employee structures, and informal training, we can create teams of employees that support and grow our creative spaces.

DEVELOPING SUSTAINABILITY AND INNOVATION

Experiential learning environments like current creative technology spaces and their successors are built to drive innovation through forming specialized knowledge teams and novel technological resources around project-based initiatives. These centers mimic structures found in industry, especially tech, to expose the university community to new technologies and drive creativity and career preparedness. However, a culture of constant innovation can be immensely draining for personnel and budgets, unless it is bolstered by sustainable methods—including building a supportive internal culture, emphasizing campus ecosystems and outreach, and developing recurring budgets. The academic campus should not model the hyper-competitiveness of the start-up world, instead we can work to create more supportive pathways to development.

Developing a sustainable and innovative center happens through reciprocal processes of building culture. Internally, culture is built through active communication and collaboration between all levels of staffing. The centers represented here range in makeup of personnel—from a single faculty member supervising a group of students, to several faculty members working with several staff members and students—but an essential pattern is that there are multiple people working together. Directors have noted the loneliness of working in this field when there is no additional staff or team. All of our creative centers integrate student employees, generally as frontline responders to patron questions and space access. Students are the best advocates to other students and can provide firsthand information on curricular needs or shifts. Additional staff or faculty brought onto the team can expand the types of services offered or the number of classes served.

One clarity brought on by COVID-19 and the shift to online work is the importance of interaction between team members. If a service is spread between locations, or has a limited size, then there will be fewer personal interactions between teams—making it less of a team and more of a group of disparate people doing the same job. One best practice is to have students and staff working at the same time, especially for newer staff: the more experienced staff will train the newer through exposure and they can form real bonds. At NCSU, prior to the pandemic, the team met weekly but there was limited interaction outside of the meetings because students worked their shifts largely alone. During the pandemic, operations shifted online and the students started spending more time together in virtual drop-in office hours and assigned projects. This initiated a culture of sharing and increased enjoyment and communication.

Another way to support staff and innovation is through ongoing training, either for professional development or to exercise interests in technology. One way of providing training is through certificate programs, appealing to students for their resumes. The initial new-hire training can also be continued throughout an employee's tenure, especially the idea of assigning projects tailored to their interests. Examples from our spaces include student employees creating motion graphic animations, creating bumper stickers for the library, podcasts on recent favorite movies, or a guide to making creative resumes: all of which were developed through conversations between supervisors and the student employees based on their excitement.

The solid structure of the internal community is ideally mirrored by an external community, as specialized library centers are inevitably involved in an existing campus ecosystem of specialized resources. Ideally, connections were made with potential stakeholders on campus at the planning phase of the library center. Creating a community with existing labs on campus can be beneficial to the library and creates a support group for the staff at each of these labs to learn from each other, troubleshoot potential issues, avoid duplication of services, and refer patrons to each other for services or support. These connections are vital to maintaining a balance and partnership among the campus labs, potentially placing the library at the center of innovation due in part to its cross-disciplinary nature as a place without departmental borders. As a truly interdisciplinary resource, university administrative leaders can look to the library to foster innovation where it can reach, impact, and involve everyone on campus, which can also be enticing to corporate partners. For example, when the company Adobe initiated a partnership with Clemson University, part of the deal created the Adobe Digital Studio, which developed into a resource to help support and excite students working with the creative software.

This interdisciplinary mission can make outreach and engagement a delicate balance. Many of us have found deep partnerships and success through saying yes to as many projects, events, and collaborations as possible. When attending events, interacting with individuals is the top priority. Talking one-on-one with students about their individual needs or vision for a project often goes further than a wide-ranging instruction session or event. However, it's also important to understand the center's unique position within campus resources and be wary of saying yes to bringing on new services or resources without sustainable funding or personnel structure. It can be easy to want to do it all: serve all populations, offer all the technology, teach all of the classes. Identifying existing resources on campus and understanding our center's unique offerings can offer clarity on mission and scope.

Growing a team, whether it is an increasing number of student employees or staff or faculty lines, requires an increase in budget, which is not the only type of ballooning cost in a technology center. Libraries are not new to the idea that costs will grow outside of standard inflation rates—just look at the cost of journals and subscriptions—but many spaces are started with a pool of "one-time" money that has to be spent in a relatively short amount of time, with less of a plan for continual addition of resources. However, technology has a life span and will inevitably break or become outdated. An annual recurring technology budget is essential for innovative spaces to maintain their services and remain relevant as new technologies arise and need to be added. Additionally, even with recurring smaller upgrades, most innovative centers will need larger refreshes after five to ten years, including furniture refreshes or even major infrastructure changes.

Additional pitfalls remain even when a center has secured recurring funding or an increased budget. For many of the centers, one of the goals is to ensure that the university community has exposure and access to innovative technology. But this is a tenuous position, as the competitiveness to remain sharp can also make the community feel inadequate if they do not know the technology or how to use it. Additionally, you need robust outreach and people to support, promote, and teach the new purchases. Thus, we try to balance the "cutting edge" by identifying innovative technologies and promoting them while ensuring that the established technologies in the space are still supported, as that will be the key entry point for many in the community and will create new users of the more advanced technologies. In some ways, our service models resemble a pyramid: the base is our basic, introductory equipment such as a fleet of popular digital cameras that can be used for photo and video, and the top is constantly shifting new and innovative tech, in small quantities. Driving constant innovation is unsustainable, but we have found that by committing to sustainable practices including deep support of employees, patrons, and community, it is possible to create space for innovation. Innovation will always require supportive budgets, personnel, and resources to continue, which is often not considered at the start of a project.

ACCESS, INCLUSION, AND INSTRUCTION

"Access" is a common buzzword when discussing issues related to digital equity and inclusion at all levels of education. Often there is a sense that the digital divide can be closed by simply making digital devices available, as mentioned above, "if you build it, they will come." However, availability and accessibility are not the same thing. Through our many conversations, it has become clear that if access is a key part of the work we do with creative technologies in academic libraries, then there is a need to investigate the systemic ways that our tools, services, and spaces are inaccessible to different communities and individuals. What does it mean to make our spaces accessible beyond making tools available?

In order to create a more nuanced understanding of the interconnected issues of inequity, it is important to distinguish between what it means for something to be accessible versus approachable. For a tool, space, or service to be accessible, it must meet the needs of disabled users,[10] while something that is approachable specifically refers to the ease of using said tool, space, or service.[11] This notion of approachability arose while VCU's The Workshop undertook a project to assess and reconfigure its space to be more accessible. It became apparent that even with a framework like Universal Design for Learning as a guiding principle, there were complex use cases to consider. For example, there might be an advanced user who needs a special screen reader script installed to access Pro Tools, while a non-disabled user might be struggling to use a microphone for the first time. While both are related to supporting the use of audio-based tools, the strategies for supporting these users are different.

Within our group discussions, there was an overall consensus that while all our spaces may be ADA-compliant on paper, there is often a gap between what meets the requirements of the law and what meets the needs of disabled users. Heavy doors, high shelving, cramped space between chairs, and even the thick thresholds found around door frames for soundproofing can all create physical barriers to accessing equipment. We recommend collaborating with the accessibility service department(s) available on campus. As these spaces are modified, adapted, and updated to accommodate future literacy initiatives, we believe it is crucial that the needs of disabled users are at the center of these designs. It is our responsibility to consider not only the fastest and most powerful machines, but also prioritize the accessibility features for the software and hardware we choose to support in our spaces. Additionally, we need to consider the various ways that first-time users might be encountering these tools, be it from a place of disability, insecurity, curiosity, or any combination thereof.

Instruction also plays a critical role in reducing barriers to using creative technologies and addressing digital inequities. While we provide support to the academic community in a number of ways, there are three aspects in particular that address the digital divide: (1) access to equipment necessary for completing class assignments; (2) curriculum-integrated support in the form of instructional one-shots, resource creation, and so on; and (3) faculty consultation for equitable and accessible project designs. Often, well-intentioned faculty assume assigning digital/media projects will be a fun and engaging process for their students; however, the implementation without instruction can unknowingly further these digital inequities in their classrooms. As the pandemic has highlighted, many students (and even faculty) lack access to reliable internet connections and functional computers. However, a less obvious barrier relates to instructors' misconceptions about students' technological competencies. By addressing these myths about digital natives,[12] we help faculty incorporate more direct technical instruction and in-class time for working on digital and multimedia projects.[13] An example of this at UTC involves faculty from the Studio working directly with the cohort of thirty plus instructors for the first-year English program, to scaffold projects and provide active instruction on creative topics. Close relationships to specific programs and faculty are beneficial to form a robust and recurring user base. By working closely with faculty across disciplines, we are able to equitably integrate digital, media, and information literacies into the curriculum through projects, instruction, and programming.

However, architecture, equipment, and support are not the only aspects that relate to accessing spaces like ours. Another important consideration lies in creating a welcoming atmosphere. At UM's Creative Studio, artworks by student artists from diverse backgrounds are on display, the staff are from diverse backgrounds, and the space has been designed to feel inviting. This is done with the hope of creating a sense of belonging for visitors, no matter their background. Sometimes technology-focused spaces can be overwhelming for first time visitors, especially if they already sense that these types of spaces and tools are not for them, based on gender, race, and so forth. A human touch in the design can go a long way in welcoming patrons who are curious about the space, concerned with a project, or creating vulnerable work about their lived experiences.

This sense of belonging is an important aspect of any diversity, equity, and inclusion work, as it is the basis through which one can build a sense of community. This spirit of community is part of the history of spaces like ours, as disability activists played a role in developing community-driven makerspaces.[14] When our spaces do not meet the needs of all users, they can dissuade those who might be the most in need of our services. This is one reason developing relationships with students early in their college careers is a key part of our work and might take the form of providing instructional support in first-year writing courses, doing outreach with various student organizations, and focusing on diversity when planning programs and events. It is worth reflecting on who has the most ease of use in our spaces and interrogating why that is the case. Very often our spaces do not reflect the diversity of our own campuses, and why simply making tools available is not a cohesive strategy for addressing issues of digital inequity. A holistic (and humble) approach is required to address these barriers to access in our spaces and should be a critical component of any future literacy initiatives in our field.

CONCLUSION AND VISION

Libraries will continue to expand their services to meet twenty-first-century learner demands, creating new resources and positions to support innovative scholarly pursuits and teaching methods. Our belief is that these new innovative services, especially those that center technology, will become even more wide-ranging and, hopefully, deeply integrated into the library operations. However, the mission should stay true to the core of the library: help people learn and engage with new ways of thinking. Prioritizing people instead of technology can require more labor and resources but, we believe strongly that this effort is worthwhile and ultimately essential in having a technology program and resources with a high beneficial impact on our patrons.

Considering our reflections on our current best practices and in keeping with the people-centered mentality, our vision for future spaces includes more flexible spaces that are better integrated into the whole of the library, continuing to expand access to our patrons, and improved specialization within each individual university setting. As services reach a second phase of existence, when technology is more widely available and understood, these spaces can become even more multipurpose and flexible as they are incorporated into regular library activities. We imagine a possible future when there is no specific, siloed "makerspace" because the whole library is considered to be a "making space." This is especially true for media studios: we carry high-end "studios" in our pockets at all times; in the form of cellphones with incredibly capable software tools. Even then, we have work to do: to teach people how to use their equipment, to create spaces for community and inspiration, to support and encourage.

Additionally, we anticipate even more community-driven specialization within each innovative site. While we have shared our philosophies, it is important to note that each space is designed with individually selected resources and spaces. Each university has unique needs, based on degree programs and community dynamics, and innovative sites need to cater to their own local constituencies. We can, and should, look to other sites for inspiration and examples, but local decisions are different and essential. This is part of the reason that this chapter has detailed philosophies and overlapping developments but does not include a prescriptive list of equipment and spaces essential for this kind of site. Though creative technology spaces have become standard elements of many academic libraries, our role in propelling innovation and supporting student success will continue. As information and digital literacy expand to incorporate ever-evolving skills and proficiencies, libraries must continually adapt to meet those needs. By focusing on the people that are connected to these novel spaces and resources, academic libraries can develop as not just the physical heart of campus, but the heart of community.

NOTES

1. David A. Cobb, "Maps and Scholars," *Library Trends* 25, no. 4 (1977): 819, http://hdl.handle.net/2142/6928.

2. Amy R. Loucks-DiMatteo, "The History of Media Librarianship: A Chronology," in *Media Librarianship*, ed. John W. Ellison (New York: Neal-Schuman, 1985), 75, https://archive.org/details/medialibrariansh0000unse.

3. Loucks-DiMatteo, "The History of Media Librarianship," 75–83.

4. O. Gerald Lawson, "Wired for Sound," *College and Research Libraries* 6, no. 2 (March 1945): 124–25, http://hdl.handle.net/2142/35355.

5. "Polaroid Offers 20,000 Cameras to Libraries through the U.S.," *Library Journal* 108, no. 7 (April 1, 1983): 626–27.

6. "Hennepin County South Area Reference Library, Edina, Minnesota," *Design Quarterly* 90/91 (1974): 69, doi: 10.2307/4090855.

7. Emanuel T. Prostano and Joyce S. Prostano, *The School Library Media Center*, second edition (Littleton, CO: Libraries Unlimited, 1977), 26–30, https://archive.org/details/schoollibrarymed0000pros.

8. Betty Costa and Marie Costa, *A Micro Handbook for Small Libraries and Media Centers* (Littleton, CO: Libraries Unlimited, 1983), 94–105, https://archive.org/details/microhandbookfor0000cost; Danny P. Wallace and Joan Giglierano, "Microcomputers in Libraries," *Library Trends* 37, no. 3 (Winter 1989): 287, http://hdl.handle.net/2142/7613.

9. T. J. McCue, "First Public Library to Create a Maker Space," *Forbes*, November 15, 2011, https://www.forbes.com/sites/tjmccue/2011/11/15/first-public-library-to-create-a-maker-space/.

10. While many style guides advocate for the use of "person-first" language when describing "people with disabilities," we have chosen to use the identity-first description of "disabled users" as it has become the preferred language of many scholars and activists in disability communities. For more on these nuances we recommend: Rosemarie Garland-Thomson, "Becoming Disabled," in *Beginning with Disability: A Primer*, ed. Lennard J. Davis (New York: Routledge, 2018); Rosemarie Garland-Thomson, "Becoming Disabled," *New York Times*, August 19, 2016, https://www.nytimes.com/2016/08/21/opinion/sunday/becoming-disabled.html.

11. Oscar Keyes and Eric Johnson, "Accessibility and the Makerspace," in *Makerspaces in Practice: Successful Models for Implementation*, ed. Ellyssa Kroski (Chicago: ALA Editions, 2021), 67–70.

12. Marc Prensky, "Digital Natives, Digital Immigrants," *On the Horizon* (2001).

13. Emily Thompson and Theo Rhodes, "Difficulties with 'Digital Natives': Bridging the Skills Gap Via One-Shot Library Instruction," *Journal of Creative Library Practice* (December 4, 2017), https://creativelibrarypractice.org/2017/12/04/difficulties-with-digital-natives-bridging-the-skills-gap-via-one-shot-library-instruction/.

14. Aimi Hamriae, "Aimi Hamrie on 'Making Access Critical: Disability, Race, and Gender in Environmental Design,'" YouTube video, 47:21, posted by Othering & Belonging Institute, March 4, 2019, https://www.youtube.com/watch?v=yplo4m1vw7U.

BIBLIOGRAPHY

Cobb, David A. "Maps and Scholars." *Library Trends* 25, no. 4 (1977): 819–31. http://hdl.handle.net/2142/6928.

Costa, Betty, and Marie Costa. *A Micro Handbook for Small Libraries and Media Centers.* Littleton, CO: Libraries Unlimited, 1983. https://archive.org/details/microhandbookfor0000cost.

Garland-Thomson, Rosemarie. "Becoming Disabled." In *Beginning with Disability: A Primer*, edited by Lennard J. Davis, 15–19. New York: Routledge, 2018.

———. "Becoming Disabled." *New York Times*, August 19, 2016. https://www.nytimes.com/2016/08/21/opinion/sunday/becoming-disabled.html.

Hamraie, Aimi. "Aimi Hamraie on 'Making Access Critical: Disability, Race, and Gender in Environmental Design,'" YouTube video, 47:21. Posted by Othering & Belonging Institute, March 4, 2019. https://www.youtube.com/watch?v=yplo4m1vw7U.

"Hennepin County South Area Reference Library, Edina, Minnesota." *Design Quarterly* 90/91 (1974): 68–69. doi: 10.2307/4090855.

Lawson, O. Gerald. "Wired for Sound." *College and Research Libraries* 6, no. 2 (March 1945): 123–26. http://hdl.handle.net/2142/35355.

Loucks-DiMatteo, Amy R. "The History of Media Librarianship: A Chronology." In *Media Librarianship*, edited by John W. Ellison, 72–89. New York: Neal-Schuman, 1985.

Keyes, Oscar, and Eric Johnson. "Accessibility and the Makerspace." In *Makerspaces in Practice: Successful Models for Implementation*, edited by Ellyssa Kroski, 63–85. Chicago: ALA Editions, 2021.

McCue, T. J. "First Public Library to Create a Maker Space." *Forbes* online. November 15, 2011. https://www.forbes.com/sites/tjmccue/2011/11/15/first-public-library-to-create-a-maker-space/.

"Polaroid Offers 20,000 Cameras to Libraries through the U.S." *Library Journal* 108, no. 7 (April 1, 1983): 626–27.

Prensky, Marc. "Digital Natives, Digital Immigrants, Part 1," *On the Horizon* 9, no. 5 (2001): 2–3. doi: 10.1108/10748120110424816.

Prostano, Emanuel T., and Joyce S. Prostano, *The School Library Media Center.* Second edition. Littleton, CO: Libraries Unlimited, 1977. https://archive.org/details/schoollibrarymed0000pros.

Swank, Raynard C. "University of Oregon's Audio-Visual Service." *College and Research Libraries* 9, no. 4 (October 1948): 299–310. http://hdl.handle.net/2142/36103.

Thompson, Emily, and Theo Rhodes. "Difficulties with 'Digital Natives': Bridging the Skills Gap Via One-Shot Library Instruction." *Journal of Creative Library Practice* (December 4, 2017). https://creativelibrarypractice.org/2017/12/04/difficulties-with-digital-natives-bridging-the-skills-gap-via-one-shot-library-instruction/.

Wallace, Danny P., and Joan Giglierano. "Microcomputers in Libraries." *Library Trends* 37, no. 3 (Winter 1989): 282–301. http://hdl.handle.net/2142/7613.

12

Developing an Engati-Based Library Chatbot to Improve Reference Services

Shu Wan

With the development of artificial intelligence (AI) technology in the last decade, the widespread presence of its application has profoundly influenced ordinary people's behavioral models in their everyday lives. For example, drivers may choose to use Siri or other AI chatbot applications on a mobile phone when wanting to know their position on a map. This solution could protect drivers from the danger of mobile phone use while driving. In the meantime, AI chatbots could provide interactive customer services in other significant settings, such as banks and hospitals. Recent publications in 2018 and 2019 have revealed the widespread use of AI chatbots in these two settings.[1] In light of the proliferation of AI chatbots in our everyday lives, we may also anticipate its vast potential in improving library services to patrons. In this chapter, I will start with an overview of the history and impact of chatbot services in the context of academic libraries; then, I will share my experience in developing a chatbot using the Engati platform, and I will conclude with a brief analysis of the possibilities that chatbots can offer for library reference services.

In the setting of higher education, an increasing number of academic institutions began to deliberate on the deployment of chatbots in providing better services to students. It is observed that, "more and more colleges are deploying virtual assistants or chatbots to communicate with students on all aspects of college life, creating a virtual one-stop-shop" for student queries."[2] AI chatbots are expected to provide more individualized and efficient tutoring services to students when encountering specific needs. For example, "one of the popular AI applications in education today, Intelligent Tutoring Systems, provides a personalized learning experience to the students by various techniques such as analyzing responses, observing how they go through the study content, etc." Compared to the traditional form of in-person and person-to-person teaching and tutoring, the deployment of AI technology in the classroom has already gradually transformed the traditional scenario of college teaching and learning.[3] As the AI specialist Robin Singh observes, chatbots "are used to answer the students' queries about the course module, lesson plans, assignments, and deadlines. They can monitor the learning progress of the students. They can provide personalized feedback to the students. They can analyze the students' learning needs and recommend the learning content to them accordingly."[4] It could be expected that the presence of AI chatbots in physical and virtual classrooms will redefine the routine of teaching and learning in US higher education.

Parallel to the widespread use of AI chatbots in improving the quality of customer service and classroom teaching, the traditional reference desk encounters difficulty being accepted by the new generation of patrons born in the Google era. The abundance of online information enables college students, when they have inquiries of library resources, to resort to Google or another search engine instead of reference librarians. According to Joseph E. Weber and Christopher Ross Bowron's current research on the frequency of patrons' use of reference desks in the Austin Peay State University (APSU) Library between 2004 and 2018, "the number of questions declined at various rates during the 14-year period."[5] In light of the fall of the traditional reference desk, it has become imperative to adjust the format to fulfill a new generation of patron needs.

Meanwhile, the traditional reference desk has limits for the improvement of customer service. For instance, in many academic libraries, reference services are only provided during regular business hours, from 9 a.m. to 5 p.m. on weekdays. It is undeniable, with the advance of information technology and its infrastructure in higher education, that an increasing number of college libraries could provide remote reference services through virtual desks beyond the scope of the regular business hours. However, students with urgent needs for professional consultations about library use and information search on weekends, during the night, and other special times, still cannot receive reference services immediately. In particular, those college students born in the new millennium may lack patience for the delayed reply to their inquiries. As Singh notes, "this is a generation of people who never stop. Technology has enabled the students to get everything instantly. Whether it is sending an email, posting a picture, searching a place or even finding online assignment help, everything can be done in just a few clicks."[6] Today, most current library workers in college libraries were born before the ubiquity of the internet and the popularity of Google. Unlike them, the current college students are predominantly cyberspace natives. It could be natural and reasonable for them to expect immediate feedback and answers to their inquiries when they submit their request for reference services. The generation gap may impede the improvement of reference services.

Within the process of writing this chapter, the world encountered the COVID-19 pandemic. Its continuing influence has changed the structure of academic libraries and their reference desks. Almost all colleges across the United States had to transition courses and services to online forms, and library services were no exception. As a result, the temporary suspension of in-person services in most academic libraries further exposed the limits of traditional reference desks. The international crisis cast light on the limits of and the vulnerability of customary in-person services in critical situations. More importantly, it encourages library professionals to imagine an alternative scenario for library services that are no long constrained to the physical space of the library; in other words, both library workers and patrons may communicate with each other anywhere outside library buildings. I propose that library professionals consider the deployment of library chatbots in answering reference questions. This chapter intends to review the progress of library chatbots in the last decade and discuss the practice of developing an AI chatbot and its benefits in providing more efficient and convenient reference services to student patrons in the context of academic libraries.

CHATBOTS IN ACADEMIC LIBRARIES

Despite the convenient searching services provided by Google, college students may still seek reference services when they study for their term papers or class projects during weeknights and weekends. Compared to traditional reference desks that cannot be provided all the time, the prevalence of AI chatbots in everyday life will pave the way for young library patrons' adoption of a new type of interaction between the machine and human beings. Although the boom of AI technology is a recent happening, library scientists began their discussions about its potential in the library space more than a decade ago. In the early 2010s, the affiliates of the University of Nebraska-Lincoln Libraries developed a library chatbot called "Pixel." However, the research team encountered frustrations with this early attempt to deploy an AI chatbot for their library.[7] Parallel to this collaboration on building a chatbot from the ground up, a group of British librarians and computer scientists attempted to develop and deploy an AI chatbot but still encountered failure in creating a chatbot with adequate "intelligence" to answer questions in a human-like manner. Because of the early and limited capability of AI technology before 2010, these two research teams should be appreciated for their pioneering endeavors to explore AI technology prospects in the library space.

In the late 2010s, the chatbot technology developed by Apple, Amazon, and other big tech companies encouraged library professionals worldwide to take an interest in deploying chatbots at their home institutions. The proliferation and prevalence of Alexa, Siri, and similar chatbot products/platforms cast light on the bright future of deploying AI technology in different occasions and contexts. At the same time, an increasing number of library administrators and professionals began to take an interest in potential chatbot services. As a result, the proliferation of scholarly writing on the use of library chatbots and professional reports of their applications demonstrates a shared passion for AI technology in the library profession. As shown in the growth of relevant literature, some large libraries in Canada, Singapore, and Australia began their efforts several years ago. According to Victoria L. Rubin, Yimin Chen, and Lynne Marie Thorimbert's survey, as early as 2009, "the University of Western

Ontario use[d] a text-based artificially intelligent Ask Western Libraries service."[8] Outside North America, the National Library Board of Singapore initiated a large project of deploying AI chatbots in its public libraries because "this enables library users to self-help on simple queries and reduces the manpower required to provide customer service, especially during off-peak or library closure hours."[9] In the meantime, large academic libraries in Australia also initiated their project to explore the practical use and value of a library chatbot in providing better reference services.[10]

Although the librarians in the three developed countries, Canada, Australia, and Singapore, have made significant achievements in deploying chatbots in their libraries, the development of chatbot technology in academic libraries was comparatively slow in the United States. As discussed earlier in this chapter, library professionals were pioneers in exploring the practical value of providing reference services to students. However, Pixel developers' failed attempts might have made other librarians reluctant to pursue AI projects. As a result, with a few exceptions, librarians in the United States certainly lag behind their foreign peers in this subject. In 2013, two librarians, Michele L. McNeal and David Newyear, reviewed the history of AI technology and proposed its potential in the library space: "With the availability of simple and inexpensive options for virtual agent creation, it is easy and cost-effective for libraries to explore this opportunity to expand their information services."[11] In 2017, another librarian, Beth M. Sheppard, reported her experiment on deploying the Amazon AI technology product Alexa in the library.[12] Unlike Canada, Singapore, and Australia, US library professionals' endeavors in exploring the use of chatbots are predominantly individual-driven instead of organized by national and academic institutions.

Reviewing those completed, in-progress, and suspended library chatbot projects so far, it is apparent that most of them are initiated by national and academic libraries such as the National Library Board in Singapore. The development of AI chatbots and their deployments in the library space costs a lot of financial and human resources, including the investment in technological infrastructure for its development and the expense of hiring software developers. The expenses are usually unaffordable for small academic libraries with limited personnel and budgets. In particular, for individual librarians who are curious about testing the applicability of AI chatbots in libraries, it is challenging to complete their tests alone. Without their institutions' financial and technical support, those librarians cannot afford the expense of developing an experimental AI chatbot and testing its efficiency in answering patrons' questions.

ENGATI PLATFORM

Thanks to the increasing number of pre-developed AI chatbot platforms, library professionals with limited knowledge and proficiency in developing software can now deploy chatbots at their institutions.[13] In contrast to Pixel developers' previous attempts to create databases and programs for their experimental library chatbot, contemporary library professionals can utilize these prepared components in developing their chatbots. In other words, this project in the 2020s is not as difficult as the Pixel developers' pioneering work in the dawn of AI technology in the 2010s. With the Engati platform's services, characterized by its reliable maneuverability and compatibility, a small team of librarians are able to create simple-function chatbots according to their institutions' varied needs.

It is noteworthy that, despite the selection of Engati, which I used to develop the chatbot project in this chapter, this product is not the only available solution for library administrators and workers to take into consideration. As mentioned above, Google takes the lead in the development of AI chatbots. Not lagging behind, other hi-tech giants have also engaged in the advancement of AI platforms and their deployment on different occasions. Technology journalist James Maguire's "Top 15 Artificial Intelligence Software 2020" enumerates the most popular AI platforms, including both IT giants' solutions and those small start-ups' products, such as Engati, Wipro Holmes, BigML, and Ayasdi. Among them, "the Engati chatbot platform offers fast and relatively simple AI fabrication (without actual coding) to build your chatbot."[14] Unlike other business chatbot solutions, Engati requires a lower skill set. Taking the comprehensive consideration of the low-expense and low-threshold requirements of Engati in comparison to the other business solutions, I intend to develop my project on this platform to demonstrate the potential chatbot in providing better services in the setting of academic libraries.

THE SEAM-UI EXAMPLE

Mainly designed for individuals and situational users' development and deployment of AI chatbots for different purposes, Engati could ease the coding work on developing a chatbot. As seen in the discussion of those library chatbot solutions in this chapter, their developers predominantly built and developed everything by themselves and did not take assistance from other commercial solutions and platforms. With the assistance of Engati's strength in providing cloud-based calculation for the application, the developer does not need to create a program to process the training data while relying on Engati's cloud services. However, this solution relieves the developers' workloads in designing and coding for the projects and reduces their cost in purchasing commercial solutions to the problem, which are always expensive. This pilot project aims to examine the efficiency of a library chatbot and its prospect in providing better results based on Engati. This chapter does not test the complex functions that have been deployed in other large-scale projects. By contrast, it focuses on a simple function for demonstrating the potential of AI technology in assisting librarians with their everyday workflows, which is displayed in figure 12.1.

The first step of this project is the selection of the "simple function." Working as a graduate student in the Students Engage at Main (SEAM) office of the University of

Figure 12.1. SEAM-UI AI chatbot functions.
Created by Shu Wan.

Iowa (UI) Libraries, I had the goal of assisting reference librarians in answering undergraduate students' questions involving the use of library resources on weeknights. Motivated by the encounters with undergraduate students' questions, I noticed that student patrons stopping by the office were not always asking complex research questions such as, "How do I make an academic bibliography for my research?" but, rather, comparably simple inquiries such as, "I know a book's call number, but could you please help me with locating it on the shelf?" Navigation or directional questions are some of the main student concerns when they come to the UI Library. This observation was substantiated by the records of students' questions and answers available on the website of the UI Libraries. The webpage, "LibAnswers: Frequently Asked Questions," shows four questions: "Where in the main library can I print documents?"; "Where can I scan or photocopy items in the main library?"; "How do I find books on a particular subject?"; and "Where are the classrooms in the main library?"[15] These questions rank in the top ten popular questions raised by student patrons in the last a few years. Apparently, they also constitute the most common inquiries reference librarians in the academic library encounter in their everyday work. Hence, I will train the experimental library chatbot to answer these types of questions.

Following the determination of navigation as the "simple function" for the examination in this research, the next step was selecting a dataset for training the chatbot to know how to answer questions in a human-like manner. Along with those top popular questions, their answers are also available on the same webpage. Those answers provide suitable data for training the chatbot with answering questions in a human-like manner. After processing the training data, the next step I took was to create a chatbot. I created a chatbot function and trained it with the questions and their corresponding answers available on the UI Libraries' website. It was expected that the chatbot could deal with new navigation inquiries in a human-like manner. In reaction to these inquiries, the chatbot was developed and deployed to answer the questions represented in table 12.1

Table 12.1. SEAM-UI AI Chatbot Training Questions

Questions	Answers
1. Where are books about American history in the main library	The third floor
2. Where are books about Chinese history in the main library?	The second floor
3. Where are books about Philosophy in the main library?	The fourth floor
4. Where are books about Chinese politics in the main library?	The second floor
5. Where are books about American politics in the main library?	The third floor

Created by Shu Wan.

As shown in the Q&A chart produced by the experimental AI chatbot, it is proven that the machine succeeded in answering those navigation-related questions in a human-like manner. Despite the limit of the size of the dataset for training examined in the test, the experimental chatbot succeeded in fulfilling my expectation for it. The results demonstrate the potential of AI technology in renewing the traditional reference desks' purpose and reducing human librarians' workloads of answering patrons' simple and navigational types of questions.

DISCUSSIONS

Reviewing the outputs of the experimental AI chatbot, I take the initial findings as follows. With the stance of those pre-developed platforms such as Engati examined in this chapter, individual librarians and small academic libraries could also develop chatbots and provide some level of 24/7 automated reference services to student patrons. Equally importantly, it could deal with student's inquiries immediately. As mentioned above, the new generation of college students are characterized by their requirement for swift feedback to their requests. Although only the simple navigation function was examined for this chapter, there is potential for more complex types of questions that can further support library services. According to target customers' varied needs, developers could use the different data sets in training the chatbot to answer questions for multiple purposes.

Despite the recent growth of chatbot services, many still have concerns about the future of deploying AI chatbots in their workplaces. Undoubtedly, the recent advances in AI technology and its applications in other industries have caused job loss in factories and workplaces. It is expected that, with the further development of AI technology, "as many as 45 percent of the activities individuals are paid to perform could be taken" by machines.[16] Hence, it is reasonable that there are concerns about the implications of chatbots in academic librarians. As shown in Philip Calvert's research, "chatbots have some advantages over human library staff; they do not get tired or need coffee breaks, they are not upset by rude customers, they do not seem threatening to those who feel their question might be too silly to ask of a human, and eventually they might be cheaper."[17] Nonetheless, at this moment, there is no justification for excessive worry about the complete substitution of reference librarians with library chatbots. It is unrealistic to develop a sufficient "intelligent" library chatbot, presently or in the near future, to fulfill human librarians' capabilities. It is noteworthy that the deployment of chatbot in the reference desk could free up time for librarians to help with more advanced research types of questions. In reference librarians' everyday workflows, simple inquiries are common, but complex questions are scarce. Taking my own experience as an example, I felt overwhelmed by "simple" inquiries at the reference desk, which indeed frustrated me. Being awarded with two master's degrees in history—in China and in the United States, respectively—and being enrolled in a graduate program in library school, I had always expected to assist college students with some challenging reference requests before my first day of work in the reference desk. However, as mentioned in the introductory section of this chapter, students mainly asked a few simple inquiries. In a few cases, I felt excited to receive some complex inquiries. For example, a college student stopped by the reference desk and raised questions concerning collecting materials about the history of infanticide in pre-modern China for her term paper. She planned to make a bibliography about this issue. The question was very compelling to me, as someone with expertise in gender and Chinese history. However, in that week, I was occupied with dealing with a multitude of simple inquiries. Consequently, I failed to do my best in providing a "perfect" bibliography to the patron. Although the student might have not expressed her dissatisfaction with the result, it was still frustrating for the me, because I did not have time to produce a more detailed and complete bibliography. In light of the feature of the AI chatbot on answering simple questions mentioned above, I contend that its presence in the setting of academic libraries could assist library workers with dealing with simple inquiries. With the assistance, reference librarians can be liberated from their overwhelmed workloads of answering "simple" questions, such as the navigation examined in the experimental chatbot. Then, they may spend more time dealing with complex reference requests.

Furthermore, the question of whether the Engati-based chatbot could entirely answer human questions in a human-like manner can be answered by a typical Turing Test. Designed by the pioneering British mathematician and computer scientist Alan Turing in the 1950s, this test states that "a computer can be said to possess artificial intelligence if it can mimic human responses under specific conditions."[18] So far, it is acknowledged that no such machine has passed the test. It is seemingly unrealistic to require the experimental chatbot examined in the chapter to succeed in passing Turing's test at the moment. Perhaps Google, Facebook, and other pioneering IT companies in the promising field of AI technology could devise such a "talented" chatbot in the future, but not today. Hence, at least at this moment, there is no need to worry about the consequences of developing AI chatbots and its threat to the indispensable and important role that only human librarians could play in the reference desk.

In addition to the chatbot advantages enumerated above, another benefit brought by chatbots in the reference desk is in its potential in advocating for multilingual reference services, which could particularly match the needs from international students and other patrons whose first languages are not English. As I have mentioned in other publications, my home institution's University of Iowa Libraries have indeed taken all the efforts to promote cultural diversity and racial justice in the library space. Both as a student patron and librarian-in-training there, I felt sufficient support from the large academic libraries.[19] For example, the I was hired as the first non-US citizen library worker in SEAM, in which I was engaged in offering reference services to international students of Chinese origin in their home language. With the concern about the cultural diversity in the reference desk, I produced a bilingual (English and Chinese) LibGuide, which "mainly consists of the following sections: 'Format your citation,' 'Find an article/book,' 'Reference Services,' and 'Interlibrary Loans.' These sections cover the common questions Chinese students raised in my past reference services."[20]

However, as the conventional component of the traditional reference services, the LibGuide may not match the new generation of college students' shared expectation for interactive and timely reference services. For them, as emphasized previously in this chapter, the immediacy of feedback is a prioritized requirement. Nonetheless, the limitations on human resources and institutional budgets may hinder academic libraries from providing non-English reference services on a large scale. After all, hiring a multitude of reference librarians to provide multilingual services is a costly plan. By contrast, chatbots could offer a more cost-effective solution to the dilemma. For example, Engati's feature on the automatic translation could enable institutions to offer multilingual reference services at the basic level. As displayed on its website, "with Engati, you can build a multilingual bot in 50+ international languages. This will not only ensure customer support but will also enable in-depth customer care."[21] Hence, it could be expected that AI chatbots may be deployed in the reference desks to advocate for cultural and racial diversity in the library space.

CONCLUSION

This chapter aimed at exploring to what extent library chatbots could assist reference librarians in dealing with the overwhelming workloads of inquiries and offering interactive services to the new generation of students. Going through the relevant literature regarding the use of chatbots in varied settings and occasions, I contend for the feasibility of popularizing simple functions in the library space. Developing this tentative project on the business platform Engati, I demonstrate the potential of a chatbot, which only could answer simple questions in facilitating the everyday workflow in the reference desk. Moreover, the chatbot could also contribute to the enhancement of cultural diversity in academic libraries. As discussed above, for academic libraries, especially those without adequate personnel and budget to support a diverse team of reference librarians, chatbots could provide an alternative solution to fulfill minority and international student patrons' needs for multilingual services.

After discussing the limits of the technology and applications of AI chatbots and demonstrating their use in the reference desk, this chapter ends with my suggestion to my peers in academic libraries in the United States to consider implementing chatbots at their institutions. As discussed above, some library staff in the US may lag behind in deploying AI technology to offer immediate feedback to patrons' inquiries and interactive services to students. In resonation with the main point of this chapter, the IT industry could provide low-threshold solutions, so AI chatbots are not "rocket science" at present. Hence, it is time to "do it yourself" now.

NOTES

1. Kyungyong Chung and Roy C. Park, "Chatbot-Based Healthcare Service with a Knowledge Base for Cloud Computing," *Cluster Computing* 22, no. S1 (2018): 1925–37; Jay Trivedi,

"Examining the Customer Experience of Using Banking Chatbots and Its Impact on Brand Love: The Moderating Role of Perceived Risk," *Journal of Internet Commerce* 18, no. 1 (February 2019): 91–111; Shannon Bohle, "'Plutchik': Artificial Intelligence Chatbot for Searching NCBI Databases," *Journal of the Medical Library Association* 106, no. 4 (April 2018), 501–3.

2. Engati Team, "Chatbot Applications in Education. Can They Teach Us?," *Drive to Reimagine* (blog), Engati, https://www.engati.com/blog/chatbot-applications-in-education#toc-some-examples-of-the-best-educational-chatbots.

3. Ibid.

4. Robin Singh, "AI and Chatbots in Education: What Does The FutureHold?," *Chatbots Magazine*, May 10, 2021, https://chatbotsmagazine.com/ai-and-chatbots-in-education-what-does-the-futurehold-9772f5c13960.

5. Joseph E. Weber and Christopher Ross Bowron, "The Evolving Reference Desk: If We Scrap It, Then What?" *Tennessee Libraries* 69, no. 2 (2019), https://www.tnla.org/page/69_2_Weber.

6. Singh, "AI and Chatbots in Education"

7. DeeAnn Allison, "Chatbots in the Library: Is It Time?" *Library Hi Tech* 30, no. 1 (February 2012): 95–107.

8. Victoria L. Rubin, Yimin Chen, and Lynne Marie Thorimbert, "Artificially Intelligent Conversational Agents in Libraries," *Library Hi Tech* 28, no. 4 (2010): 499.

9. Yi Chin Liau, "Transforming Library Operation with Robotics," (paper presented at the International Federation of Library Associations World Library and Information Congress, Wildau, Germany, August 21–22, 2019), http://library.ifla.org/2701/1/s08-2019-liau-en.pdf.

10. Indra Ayu Susan Mckie and Bhuva Narayan, "Enhancing the Academic Library Experience with Chatbots: An Exploration of Research and Implications for Practice," *Journal of the Australian Library and Information Association* 68, no. 3 (March 2019): 268–77.

11. Michele L. McNeal and David Newyear, "Chapter 1: Introducing Chatbots in Libraries," *Library Technology Reports*, https://journals.ala.org/index.php/ltr/article/view/4504.

12. Beth Sheppard, "Theological Librarian vs. Machine: Taking on the Amazon Alexa Show (with Some Reflections on the Future of the Profession)," *Theological Librarianship* 10, no. 1 (2017): 8–23.

13. James Maguire, "Top 15 Artificial Intelligence Software 2020," *Datamation*, May 11, 2021, https://www.datamation.com/artificial-intelligence/top-15-artificial-intelligence-software-2020.

14. Ibid.

15. "LibAnswers—Frequently Asked Questions," The University of Iowa Libraries, https://ask.lib.uiowa.edu.

16. Chui Michael, Manyika James, and Miremadi Mehdi, "Where Machines Could Replace Humans—and Where They Can't (Yet)," *McKinsey & Company*, June 8, 2016, https://www.mckinsey.com/business-functions/mckinsey-digital/our-insights/where-machines-could-replace-humans-and-where-they-cant-yet.

17. Philip Calvert, "Robots, the Quiet Workers, Are You Ready to Take Over?" *Public Library Quarterly* 36, no. 2 (2017): 170.

18. Margaret Rouse, "What Is a Turing Test? A Definition from WhatIs.com," Search Enterprise AI, https://searchenterpriseai.techtarget.com/definition/Turing-test.

19. Shu Wan, "An International Student-Librarian's Perspective on Diversity in Library Space," *Intersections: Advocacy, Legislation & Issues* (blog), https://www.ala.org/advocacy/diversity/odlos-blog/international-student-librarians; Shu Wan, "The Use of Libguides in

Struggling Against Pandemic and Racism in Iowa," *Social Responsibilities Round Table (SNRT) Newsletter*, June 2021, 5.

20. Shu Wan, "Preparing Bilingual LibGuides for International Students at the University of Iowa Libraries," *Library Services to Multicultural Populations Section Newsletter*, June 2020, 7.

21. Engati Team, "Building Multilingual Chatbots for Conversations in 50+ Languages," *Drive to Reimagine* (blog), Engati, 2021, https://www.engati.com/blog/multilingual-chatbots.

BIBLIOGRAPHY

"LibAnswers—Frequently Asked Questions." The University of Iowa Libraries website. https://ask.lib.uiowa.edu/.

Allison, DeeAnn. "Chatbots in the Library: Is It Time?" *Library Hi Tech* 30, no. 1 (2012): 95–107. doi:10.1108/07378831211213238.

Bohle, Shannon. "'Plutchik': Artificial Intelligence Chatbot for Searching NCBI Databases." *Journal of the Medical Library Association* 106, no. 4 (2018): 501–3. https://doi.org/10.5195/jmla.2018.500

Calvert, Philip. "Robots, the Quiet Workers, Are You Ready to Take Over?" *Public Library Quarterly* 36, no. 2 (2017): 167–72.

Chung, Kyungyong, and Roy C. Park. "Chatbot-Based Healthcare Service with a Knowledge Base for Cloud Computing." *Cluster Computing* 22, no. S1 (2018): 1925–37. https://doi.org/10.1007/s10586-018-2334-5.

Engati Team. "Building Multilingual Chatbots for Conversations in 50+ Languages." *Drive to Reimagine* (blog). Engati. https://www.engati.com/blog/multilingual-chatbots.

———. "Chatbot Applications in Education. Can They Teach Us?" *Drive to Reimagine* (blog). Engati. https://www.engati.com/blog/chatbot-applications-in-education#toc-some-examples-of-the-best-educational-chatbots.

Liau, Yi Chin. "Transforming Library Operation with Robotics." Paper presented at the International Federation of Library Associations World Library and Information Congress, Wildau, Germany, August 21–22, 2019. http://library.ifla.org/id/eprint/2701/1/s08-2019-liau-en.pdf.

Maguire, James. "Top 15 Artificial Intelligence Software 2020." Datamation, May 11, 2021. https://www.datamation.com/artificial-intelligence/top-15-artificial-intelligence-software-2020.

Mckie, Indra Ayu Susan, and Bhuva Narayan. "Enhancing the Academic Library Experience with Chatbots: An Exploration of Research and Implications for Practice." *Journal of the Australian Library and Information Association* 68, no. 3 (2019): 268–77. https://doi.org/10.1080/24750158.2019.1611694.

McNeal, Michele L., and David Newyear. "Chapter 1: Introducing Chatbots in Libraries." *Library Technology Reports*. https://journals.ala.org/index.php/ltr/article/view/4504/5281.

Michael, Chui, Manyika James, and Miremadi Mehdi. "Where Machines Could Replace Humans—and Where They Can't (Yet)." *McKinsey & Company*, June 8, 2016. https://www.mckinsey.com/business-functions/mckinsey-digital/our-insights/where-machines-could-replace-humans-and-where-they-cant-yet.

Rouse, Margaret. "What Is a Turing Test? A Definition from WhatIs.com." SearchEnterpriseAI, TechTarget. https://searchenterpriseai.techtarget.com/definition/Turing-test.

Rubin, Victoria L., Yimin Chen, and Lynne Marie Thorimbert. "Artificially Intelligent Conversational Agents in Libraries." *Library Hi Tech* 28, no. 4 (2010): 496–522.

Sheppard, Beth. "Theological Librarian vs. Machine: Taking on the Amazon Alexa Show (with Some Reflections on the Future of the Profession)." *Theological Librarianship* 10, no. 1 (2017): 8–23.

Singh, Robin. "AI and Chatbots in Education: What Does the Future Hold?" *Chatbots Magazine*, May 10, 2021. https://chatbotsmagazine.com/ai-and-chatbots-in-education-what-does-the-futurehold-9772f5c13960.

Trivedi, Jay. "Examining the Customer Experience of Using Banking Chatbots and Its Impact on Brand Love: The Moderating Role of Perceived Risk." *Journal of Internet Commerce* 18, no. 1 (2019): 91–111.

Vadapradhan, R., and Hariharan Ravi. "Application of Artificial Intelligence in Investment Banks." *Review of Economic and Business Studies* 11, no. 2 (2018): 131–36.

Wan, Shu. "An International Student-Librarian's Perspective on Diversity in Library Space." *Intersections: Advocacy, Legislation & Issues.* https://www.ala.org/advocacy/diversity/odlos-blog/international-student-librarian.

———. "Preparing Bilingual LibGuides for International Students at the University of Iowa Libraries." *Library Services to Multicultural Populations Section Newsletter*, June 2020, 7.

———. "The Use of Libguides in Struggling Against Pandemic and Racism in Iowa," *Social Responsibilities Round Table (SNRT) Newsletter*, June 2021, 5.

Weber, Joseph E., and Christopher Ross Bowron. "The Evolving Reference Desk: If We Scrap It, Then What?" *Tennessee Libraries* 69, no. 2 (2019). https://www.tnla.org/page/69_2_Weber.

Index

About the Editors and Contributors

EDITORS

Sarah Nagle is creation and innovation services librarian at Miami University in Ohio. She began her library career in public libraries, having served most recently as senior creative services librarian at Pikes Peak Library District in Colorado. Sarah has more than six years of library makerspace experience, and planned and opened a new makerspace at Miami's King Library in 2019. Her work includes supporting maker learning and innovation topics through events, instruction, and outreach. Sarah founded and serves as chair of the Nation of Makers Libraries Working group, and is also a member of the CORE Maker Technology Interest Group. Sarah has a strong research interest in maker-centered learning, both in informal environments and as part of formalized curricula.

Elías Tzoc, originally from Guatemala, is a 2007 graduate of the University of Texas at Austin, School of Information. He is currently the head of the Create and Innovate (C+I) Department at Miami University Libraries, where he works/leads a group of seven creative librarians and technologists working on innovative and entrepreneurial library services that support transdisciplinary and experiential learning. The C+I services include: full-service 3D printing and scanning, open educational resources, maker scholarship, digital scholarship/humanities, multimedia production, and copyright. He has published on topics such as web standards, emerging technologies, digital scholarship, open access, diversity, and technical skills for new librarians. His current research interest is centered around innovation, diversity, and leadership in higher education.

CONTRIBUTORS

Matt Armstrong is the Online Learning and Experiential Studio supervisor at the Brigham Young University Library. He manages a team of students who create a wide variety of learning resources for library instruction. He also supports interdisciplinary efforts in the library's Experiential Studio, an active classroom for students and professors across campus. Prior to his position at the library, Matt worked on the exhibits team for the Thanksgiving Point children's museums in Utah. He studied communications as an undergraduate, earned a master's degree in instructional psychology and technology, and is currently completing a master's in library and information science.

Susan Berstler is technology specialist for libraries in Cabot Science Library at Harvard University. Much of Susan's work is built around the creation and support of media-based classroom and student projects in Cabot, which was renovated and repurposed in 2017 with a focus on innovation and collaboration. She manages Cabot's media studios and has opened an XR studio to introduce faculty, students, and staff to the world of virtual reality. Susan recently served on the Advisory Panel for North Carolina State University's Immersive Scholar Program—a unique opportunity, funded by the Mellon Foundation, for libraries and museums to build a community of practice for those working with immersive technology in learning spaces. Susan holds a BA in humanities from Johns Hopkins University and has done graduate work at the University of Freiburg, Germany, and language classes at the University of Szeged, Hungary. Additionally, she works as a visual artist and arts producer and has exhibited her work broadly. Her main arts interest is in transformative media, especially in the realm of public art.

Jennifer Brown is an undergraduate learning and research librarian at the University of California, Berkeley, where she employs critical pedagogies as part of her reference and instructional approaches. She received her MS in information from the University of Michigan and her BA in media studies from UC Berkeley.

Matt Cook is Digital Scholarship Program manager for Harvard Library. Matt's personal research interests center on 3D data (e.g., photogrammetry, VR, etc.) and embodied cognition. After studying philosophy at the undergraduate and graduate level (at the Universities of Florida and Oklahoma, respectively), he began working full time in libraries and developing new tools and systems to augment research and instruction across disciplines. As a researcher, he also studies the state and trajectory of digital scholarship more generally, as well as what it takes to manage exploratory teams in libraries and the impact of new knowledge services related to physical fabrication and mindfulness. Find out more at mncook.net.

Emily S. Darowski is the psychology librarian at Brigham Young University (BYU), where she teaches information literacy, supports student and faculty research, and develops psychology collections. She also teaches adjunct courses for the BYU Psychology Department, including Writing in Psychology and Cognition. Her research interests include writing instruction, higher order cognitive processes (e.g., working memory), and gender equity. She earned a bachelor's degree in psychology from Idaho State university, followed by a master's and doctorate in cognitive psychology from Michigan State University. After coming to BYU, she earned a master's in library and information science from San Jose State University. She has served on local, state, and national library committees, including five years on the BYU Library steering committee that oversaw the development of the Experiential Studio. She chaired the committee in 2019 during the remodel and transition project.

Amy Van Epps is director of sciences and engineering services in the Faculty of Arts and Sciences Libraries at Harvard University. Prior to moving into management, she developed extensive experience providing instruction for engineering and technology students. Her research interests include investigating different methods to support and promote non-traditional services as part of the mission of the academic library and finding effective methods for integrating information literacy knowledge into the undergraduate engineering curriculum. Ms. Van Epps has a BA in engineering science from Lafayette College, her MSLS from Catholic University of America, and a MEng in industrial engineering from Rensselaer Polytechnic Institute.

Leanna Fry is an instructional design and instruction librarian, teaching information literacy both in person and online. Her research focus is information literacy and English language learners, and she teaches introductory composition classes as well as information literacy classes to first-year and advanced composition students. She has worked as a librarian in Paris and Utah and has taught composition in Arizona, Utah, Idaho, and Turkey. She earned undergraduate and graduate degrees in English, a master's degree in library science, and a doctorate in instructional design with a specialization in second language acquisition.

Dr. Zenobie S. Garrett received her PhD in anthropology from New York University. As postdoctoral fellow in software and research objects curation, she conducts research in digital archiving and software curation for virtual reality and 3D imaging applications. She works closely with staff from the university libraries, as well as faculty and students, to develop and incorporate best practices and standards of digital data curation and preservation in research, teaching, and learning. She also promotes collaborative projects using 3D and VR technology throughout the university and teaches and trains students, staff, and faculty on the significance of software integrity, transparency, and ethics. Her goal is to facilitate the development and use of innovative digital technologies in research and scholarship.

Jason Evans Groth is digital media librarian for the Learning Spaces and Services Department at NC State University Libraries in Raleigh, North Carolina. He helps to support creative making, especially with audio and video in several high-tech creative spaces. He earned his MIS/MLS from the School of Library and Information Science at Indiana University in May of 2013. At IU he worked for the Media Preservation Initiative, at the Indiana University Libraries Film Archive, as a teaching assistant for the classes "The History of Rock and Roll: 70s and 80s," "History of the Beach Boys," and the "Music of Frank Zappa" (among others). Since 2001, he has toured the world as a guitar player and with many bands and artists, including Magnolia Electric Co, Jens Lekman, The Watson Twins, and The Impossible Shapes.

Anne Marie Gruber, MLIS, is associate professor of library services and instruction and liaison librarian serving biology, chemistry and biochemistry, earth and environmental sciences, and physics as well as social work, Tallgrass Prairie Center, Center for Energy and Environmental Education, and the Office of Community Engagement. She is also responsible for advancing open educational resources (OERs) campuswide. Her research interests include the library's role in community-based learning and intersections between library services and student success.

Stefanie Hilles is the arts and humanities librarian at Wertz Art and Architecture Library at Miami University, where she liaisons to the art, architecture and interior design, and theatre departments, manages their collections, and instructs information literacy sessions. Previous to her role at Miami, Stefanie was the library and archives manager at the Akron Art Museum, an associate lecturer in art history at the University of Akron, and part-time faculty in art history at Kent State University. She holds an MA in art history from Case Western Reserve University and an MLIS from Kent State. Stefanie is active in the Art Librarians Society of North America (ARLIS/NA), having served as chapter liaison on the executive board, chair of the Ohio Valley Chapter, and on the membership committee. She has presented at ARLIS/NA, ARLIS/UK & Ireland, IFLA, LOEX, and ALAO and has been published in *Art Libraries Journal* and *Public Services Quarterly*.

Chris Holthe is the experiential learning librarian at the Northern Arizona University Cline Library where he oversees the library's Experiential Learning Unit and associated spaces and services, including the Cline Library MakerLab and Studios. Chris has a background in educational programming design and has managed experiential learning programs and spaces in both public and academic libraries for the past ten years. His research interests include experiential learning, emerging and immersive technologies, extended reality applications for education, 3D printing, research services in libraries, and user experience. Chris received his master's in library and information science from the University of Illinois Urbana-Champaign.

Eric Johnson (he/him/his) is the head of the Innovative Media Department of Virginia Commonwealth University Libraries, where he manages a state-of-the-art, library-based multimedia studio and makerspace called The Workshop that opened under his guidance in late fall 2015. His previous experience includes work as head of outreach & public services in the Scholar's Lab at UVA Library and in librarian and social media positions at Thomas Jefferson's historic home, Monticello. His research interests include creativity in libraries; communicating scholarship through creative technologies; museum and library history; and hospitality theory as applied to libraries and museums. He has an MA in US History from George Mason University and an MSLIS from Florida State University.

Oscar K. Keyes (he/him/his) is the multimedia teaching and learning librarian for Virginia Commonwealth University in Richmond, Virginia. He is currently a PhD student in art education at VCU, where he researches the role of embodied learning in digital-based methods of making. He has taught digital arts in a variety of spaces, including higher education, K–12 schools, summer camps, community-based arts organizations, and detention centers. When he's not busy teaching, Keyes still makes movies with his friends, having worked on award-winning short and feature-length films.

Bohyun Kim is the chief technology officer and professor at the University of Rhode Island Libraries. She is the author of three books: *Moving Forward with Digital Disruption* (2020), *Understanding Gamification* (2015), and *Library Mobile Experience: Practices and User Expectations* (2013) and the former president of the Library and Information Technology Association (LITA). She writes the "Technology & Power" column for *Online Searcher* magazine and is a frequent speaker at library technology conferences.

Annalise Phillips is the maker education service lead at the University of California, Berkeley. Her role there is to develop and run maker programming that seeks to reach the novice user and encourage diversity, equity, and inclusion in making. She is responsible for both the space and its programming and takes pride in creating workshops and lessons that are accessible and inviting.

Vanessa Rodriguez is a librarian associate professor at the University of Miami. As the head of Creative Studio, she provides instruction to the UM community in multimedia software, hardware, copyright, design, and emerging technologies. She is also the librarian liaison for the Interactive Media Department in the School of Communication, manages the library collection in those materials as well as the graphic novel collection, and teaches an Introduction to Visual Design course. She received an MLIS from the University of South Florida in 2006, and her BA in art photography and creative writing, in 2000, from the University of Miami.

Dr. Joshua Sebree received his PhD in chemistry from Purdue University in 2011. After a two-year postdoc at NASA Goddard Spaceflight Center researching the moons of Saturn, he took a faculty position at the University of Northern Iowa in the Department of Chemistry and Biochemistry. Dr. Sebree's research focuses on understanding the formation and transport of organic molecules that are important for life with regards to space exploration and understanding extreme life in underground caves. In his teaching, Dr. Sebree strives to make chemistry relatable to students at all levels with the inclusion of hands-on research projects and guided inquiry problem sets.

Andrew See is the head of user services and experience at the Northern Arizona University Cline Library. He has spent his entire career focusing on creating exceptional experiences for end users in every aspect of systems and services an academic library can provide. With a broad and holistic understanding of library values and operations, Andrew leverages a design thinking approach to making data-driven decisions in creating user centered services. Andrew received his master's in library and information science at the University of Arizona and is a published author and national/regional presenter on such topics as organizational and operational effectiveness, user experience, and data-driven decision making.

Kelsey Sheaffer (she/her/hers) is an artist and educator in rural South Carolina, where she works as the creative technologies librarian at Clemson University. She also directs the Adobe Digital Studio and the Cooper Makerspace at Clemson. She received her BA in art from Davidson College and her MFA in kinetic imaging from Virginia Commonwealth University. Her work investigates contemporary and historical interdisciplinary creative spaces and the pedagogy of line, sound, media, and movement. Kelsey is also a member of Tiger Strikes Asteroid Greenville, which is an artist-run gallery space focused on the southeast.

Emily Thompson is the director of the studio and associate professor at the University of Tennessee at Chattanooga. Originally from Montana, Emily got her BA in theatre from Drake University. After spending several years working as a costume designer and director, she moved to South Korea to teach English. She then moved to Taiwan before heading to the University of Michigan, Ann Arbor, to get her MSI in library and information services. Prior to UTC, Emily was the learning technologies librarian at the State University of New York at Oswego.

Shu Wan recently graduated from the graduate program in the School of Library and Information Science at the University of Iowa. Originally from China, he is deeply concerned about the encounters of non-English-speaking patrons with academic libraries in the United States. In his current research, he intends to explore the potential of technology in providing multilingual services to patrons of diverse backgrounds. His former publications have been present in different online platforms including: the Hack Library School's *Social Responsibilities Round Table (SNRT) Newsletter*; the *Library Services to Multicultural Populations Section Newsletter*, the

ALA's *Intersections: Advocacy, Legislation, and Issues* blog; the *Journal of Electronic Resources Librarianship*, and the ALCTS Metadata Interest Group's *Metadata Blog*.

Kristi Wyatt (BFA, University of Tulsa, 2001; MFA, Ohio State University, 2005) currently serves as an emerging technologies librarian and head of the 3D Scanning Lab in Bizzell Memorial Library at the University of Oklahoma. Her areas of specialization include 3D scanning, photogrammetry, hardware prototyping, and 3D preservation and curation. She led the planning, foundation, and continued development of OU's Scanning Lab, where she collaborates with faculty and students on coursework and research projects. Her recent initiatives also include ArtEdge (a multidisciplinary art and technology experience for school children), VR projects (e.g., exploring Native American archival material and empathy-based experiences on the lives of international students at OU), and various initiatives for accessibility and inclusion. Kristi previously worked for seven years as an exhibition designer and preparator for the Fred Jones Jr. Museum of Art.